Calderdale College Library
Tel: 01422 399350

You may renew this item for a further period by post, telephone
or personal visit, provided it is not required by another reader.
Please quote your ID no. and the seven digit number on the
barcode label.
No more than three renewals are permitted.

NB Overdue books are charged at 5 pence per item per day.

Long Days in Lakeland

First published in 1998 by Grey Stone Books

British Library Cataloguing in Publication Data

A catalogue record of this book is available from the British Library.

ISBN 0-9515996-7-4

Printed by Martins The Printers, Berwick-upon-Tweed
Pre press by Ace Pre Press, Southampton

Long Days in Lakeland

By Ronald Turnbull

Line drawings by John Gillham

Grey Stone Books
Hoddlesden

Also by Ronald Turnbull:
Across Scotland on Foot (Grey Stone)
The Welsh Three Thousand Foot Challenges (with Roy Clayton – Grey Stone)
Coast to Coast (Dalesman)

Forthcoming:
The Lakeland Mountain Challenges (with Roy Clayton – Grey Stone)
Lowthers and Other Hills (Cicerone)

ACKNOWLEDGMENTS

The section 'Borrowdale Rain' has appeared, in a shorter form, in Cumbria
magazine. 'Ice is Nice' and the walk 'Not Great Gable' have appeared, also in
shorter form, in Trail Walker.

The photographs on pages 17, 18, 25, 39, 90, 159 and 170 are by John
Gillham. That on page 126 is by Keith Wilson, and Graham Thompson took
the one on page 158 and the front cover picture.
My thanks to them, and to all companions on the hill: among whom this
book is dedicated to my father Derwent and my children Thomas and Jessie.

CONTENTS

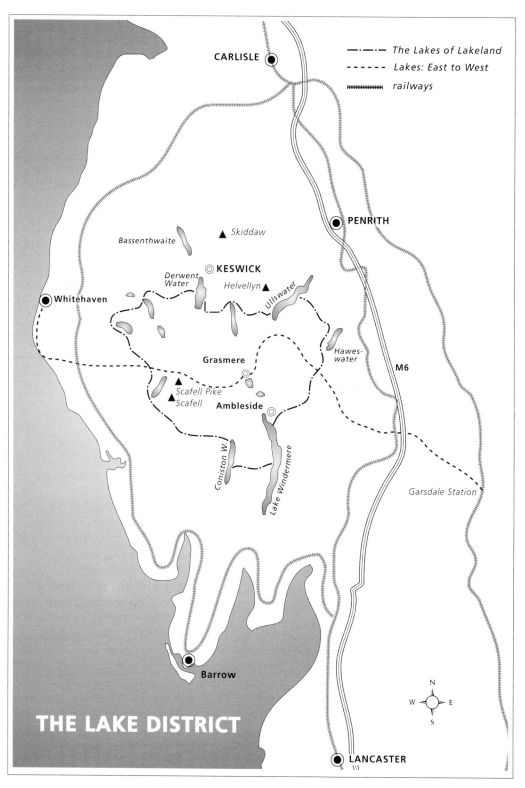

Introduction

Your standard Lakeland day starts in Borrowdale or Langdale; follows some huge stony path by way of Esk Hause to Scafell Pike or else to Great Gable; and then goes back to Langdale or Borrowdale. Why?

One of the worst things in hillwalking is walking up hills. You don't spend your coffee break walking up the fire escape. Helvellyn's a hundred times higher than the fire escape, which makes it a hundred times as much fun, and that still multiplies out to less fun than it could be. The view becomes smaller and further away but otherwise doesn't change. The weather becomes slowly worse until you're in the cloud. And what do you get when you get there but some orange peel and a big pile of stones?

However, there's one thing that's worse than walking up hills: walking back down them. Walking up is tiring but walking down hurts. Walking up, you could console yourself with the hope that eventually you'd turn around and start to walk down. Walking down, there's nothing to look forward to but bed and death.

It beats me how anyone gets started hillwalking. Hillwalking, when you start, consists of walking up some slow unfit and painful hill, stopping for a while to appreciate the orange peel and walking slow unfit and painful back down again. It beats me how I got started, in my school mac and gym shoes, up Gable from Wasdale with an Ancestral Member of the Fell + Rock Climbing Club twenty yards ahead... then fifty yards ahead... then stopping at a cairn until just before I caught up, and striding away again as if Gable was really Great and Wasdale a wonderful place to do it from. As soon as possible I took up rock climbing. On rock you've got the ancestral Fell-and-Rock member tied down with ropes so that he can't get away.

It's only when you've got a bit bigger and fitter that you start having the enjoyable bits between the nasty up at the beginning and the nasty down at the end. The bigger and fitter you get, the more your days consist of ridge. And soon you become an instinctive ridgewalker, your eye naturally following those v-shapes in the contour and your foot following your eye from peak to peak through mist, rain, snow and the occasional Long Hot Summer's Day.

At this point you start to worry. Peak-bagging may resemble stamp collecting – or stamp-collecting with slight added adventure, as it might be if every thousandth stamp hinge were treated with a quick-acting deadly poison. However, there are millions of possible stamps, but only two-hundred and fifteen Lakeland Hills. (Two-hundred and fifteen? Well, I refuse to leave out Pillar Rock.) Will there soon be nothing for it but to buy a deck chair and start studying the works of Wordsworth?

Wordsworth can wait. There's a lot more to the Lake District Hills than just the hills. This book is mostly about bottoms and other bits. First of all, try bagging tarns not tops. Tarns have grassy banks to recline on and romantic crags to overhang them. Also, you never need to carry a waterbottle.

Then there are the valleys, and the natural destination of a valley, which is a high pass. Link them together over several days, throw in a few lakesides, and you have a bad-weather backpack route that's actually better than the fine-weather one over the ridges.

Next there are the sides. The up-and-down path is popular, steep and stony. The path around is narrow and interesting. It has big drops below, and crags above. Thus we have the day of not climbing Great Gable. And thus we have the East-to-West backpack, which strings together such high traverse paths. The East-to-West, as well as not climbing Gable, manages to not climb High Street, Fairfield, Bowfell, Kirkfell, Pillar and even Scafell Pike.

The Lake District isn't the Isle of Skye. The annual rainfall's less, and there aren't nearly enough bogs. Nor is there a Cuillin Main Ridge traverse. To construct an English equivalent of the Skye Ridge, you have to link together 7000ft of scrambling with 30 miles of sides, bottoms, and even – it has to be confessed – the occasional top. Thus we arrive at the Scafell Scramble Circuit which dives round the back of Dale Head, wanders along Buttermere, crosses Pillar Rock and goes up through the crags of Scafell. The Skye Ridge doesn't even have drinking water: the Scafell Scramble Circuit has two large lakes, as well as beer and pub snacks at four different locations.

The pleasures of overindulgence are explored in the walk of the four three-thousands. It's the most satisfying 40 mile day in all England – partly because it's not just those four tops, but also all Borrowdale, the back of Derwentwater, and bang across the middle of the Central Fells. Less arduous is the 42-peak circuit of the famous Bob Graham Round. Less arduous, because – if you've any sense at all – you'll do the whole thing from the comfort of your armchair.

In most of mountain Britain, the best day you can have is to drive as far into the hills as possible: walk up a path to the 600m contour: and stay above that contour until tea-time. Lakeland is better. Combine a fine high summit with a riverside, and a scramble up a gully, and a wood of oaks and boulders. If you must do Scafell Pike, do it from Rydal, or Kendal, or Coniston, or even somewhere in Yorkshire. However, I have peppered the text with one-day walks from car parks. I hope that each of these nine day-walks offers something more than a simple trip to a summit cairn. They are intended as a gentler entry to this world of the worthwhile absurd – of the hill walk without hills, of the ending-up-in-Ambleside, of the path to nowhere.

Then there are days when it simply isn't convenient to walk over, beside or below any Lakeland hill. The weather may be just too dreadful or the boots away being resoled. One may be awkwardly placed in a distant city trying to earn some money to pay for that fully-waterproof, fully-breathable overjacket. (Not worth it. There isn't any fully-waterproof, fully-breathable overjacket.) Recent research has shown that sitting and thinking about it can be just as good...

Mind you, that research involved the training of the little-finger-sideways muscle. It cannot necessarily be applied to the Lakeland-Mountain-sideways muscle. This book is dedicated to the idea that thinking about it afterwards should imperceptibly slide into thinking about it beforehand – and so into going out and doing it. May you enjoy many topping days on the sides and bottoms...

HOW TO USE THIS BOOK

Two hills between Ullswater and the A66 are a different sort of stone. The Mell Fell conglomerate is made of bits gathered from all over the Lake District, held together in a gritty matrix.

The grit that holds this book together is the five excessive expeditions of Chapters 1-5. The sharpest and most immediate intrusions are the ten shorter walks. These you may be looking for in a hurry, on some evening when tomorrow suddenly has a weather forecast that isn't raining. So they're listed on the contents page.

The sitting-and-thinking-about-it sections will be found floating around the book, shaded in the sombre, rain-laden grey of Wordsworth's lonely cloud.

Ronald Turnbull

Ronald Turnbull, Thornhill 1998

Introductory Daywalk

Lakeland has tops, but also valleys. Later I shall give a daywalk over the craggiest top and down into the wildest valley. But here we'll start small. In fact, over the craggiest small top and down into the wildest small valley.

Helm Crag has everything. It has woods with big boulders in. It has crags to look down over the top of. It has a steep slope, and a path across that steep slope, with white-painted farmhouses down below. It has a lake at the bottom and a rock on top.

And Easedale has everything else. Easedale has crags to look up at from below. Easedale has a stream with willows, and a footbridge, and two small waterfalls with a picnic spot. Dorothy Wordsworth didn't mind how often she went up into Easedale, and neither do I.

Distance and climb: 6 miles/2400ft or 10km/700m
START/FINISH: Grasmere, Easedale Road car park GR 334080
Map: OS Outdoor Leisure 6 (SW) or Harveys Western Lakeland

Walk out of Grasmere along Easedale Road, ignoring the right turn at the sign for the youth hostel. After passing the entrance of the Lancrigg Guest House the road crosses an open field. At the end, a sign points right. The road passes a sign 'Unsuitable for Motors' and becomes – well – unsuitable for motors, being greenish slate stones jammed on edge between high walls.

The road bends left through a gate. Here the track for Easedale continues ahead, and this will be the route of return. The track for Helm Crag turns right. It zig-zags up through hollies and under old quarries and older crags, then bends left to slant up the steep side of the hill.

The top rocks of Helm Crag offer several hours worth of pottering around and exploring. If the afternoon should slip away in picnic and scrambling, who cares? Easedale's been there since the Ice Age and will still be there tomorrow. Helm Crag has two summit outcrops. The one at the Grasmere end is overhanging behind, but a simple scramble. The other one, though is higher. That other one is also overhanging behind, and a quite demanding scramble...

It is most easily climbed at the far end of the Easedale face (that is, from the western corner). Go up the crack between a pinnacle and the main rock, then traverse right, onto a slab. Slant up this slab diagonally right, then go easily back left to the top.

Leave Helm Crag on a clear path towards Gibson Knott. After the col, the path runs along the Easedale side. Gibson Knott is a name but not a place, and no single one of its knolls is particularly summital as against any of the others. Those determined to pick off this hill will leave the path to cross them all. Those who just like scrambling about in some slightly rocky places will follow them.

The path turns due west as it climbs up the ridge onto the moors. The going around the head of Easedale is boggy, with the path crossing bare peat. The minor summit of Calf Crag is a few steps left of the path, which then passes a peaty tarn on the right. Now the path is slightly south of west, and drops left to avoid a rocky knoll. It crosses the top of the steep slope of Easedale, and arrives at a col with two iron fence posts and a cairn.

Turn left here, to descend into Easedale. The path isn't clear at first, but descends to join a stream, then turns right to cross it. Here is a small gorge (in the one stream), a

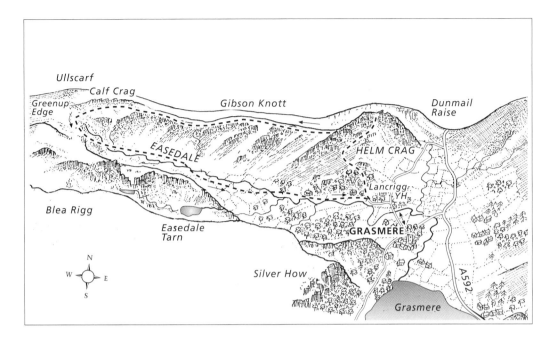

small waterfall (in the other stream), a small lawn (to spread the picnic on) and a view all the way along Easedale. After the picnic spot the path descends quite steeply: on the map it's the grey dotted line, not the bridleway to north of the stream.

After the descent of the valley head, Easedale presents no difficulty. The valley has a slight bend to the right, and unfolds itself a bit at a time. Gradually it becomes gentler, with trees. The path crosses a long footbridge, passes to right of a glacier-smoothed rock knoll, and dives into a little rocky gully. At the bottom it becomes a walled lane, and after another 300yds it rejoins the outward route at the Helm Crag/Easedale signpost.

Keep ahead ('Grasmere') for 100yds and go through the gate. Now steps on the left are marked 'Permissive Path: Grasmere'. This is a nice woodland path, with a left fork after 100yds, and then a small Wordsworth Memorial. Those with a smattering of Latin will translate:

The Lion and the Lamb, Helm Crag

"Here in an eyebrow sat Dorothy Wordsworth while from the mouth of her brother wandering nearby she transcribed songs" – and then check in the library that 'supercilio' is in fact a brow or hummock of the ground as well as of the face. When they lived at Dove Cottage, Dorothy walked either here or around Rydal Water almost every day. In Easedale she pursued her favourite sport of hunting waterfalls.

After the memorial the path drops gently, to go through a gate and along the front of the Lancrigg Hotel. (That's what the path does: the walker may prefer to turn left, into the hotel.) Turn down the hotel's driveway to rejoin the Easedale Road.

The Traverse Path

Suppose you were silly enough to climb the North Face of the Eiger. Above the Difficult Crack and the irreversible Hinterstoisser Traverse, above the First and Second Icefields, the Death Bivouac, the Ramp with its frozen waterfalls – and let's say you survived the snowstorms, the stonefalls, the sudden icing-up of the rocks – you come to a shelf. It's a wide, rubble-strewn ledge, only moderately sloping, that takes you away from the unclimbable rocks of the face's top left corner and into the final icefield and those avalanche-choked couloirs that are the only weakness through the upper cliffs.

Walking along that ledge, you have your left hand on black dripping rocks in slabs and overhangs. On your right, similar rocks fall for four thousand feet. The screes at the bottom appear, from this height, horizontal. Beyond them are green fields, and hotels, and swimming pools. You can hear the two-tone hooting of the post bus, the bells worn by the image-conscious Swiss cows; and you walk along your grey ledge with its little path. Of the feet that made that path, many never reached the summit icefield.

Scary? Yes, that's scary. Let's calm ourselves down with a nice bedtime story.

A little girl called Lucie trots up Catbells, looking for three pocket handkerchiefs and a pinafore. Above her, the grass and bracken rise steep and steeper to the crags of Maiden Moor. Below her you can just see the slate rooves of Little-town - she could drop a pebble down the chimney.

What do Beatrix Potter's 'Tiggywinkle' and the ledge to the White Spider have in common? They are both examples of that delightful moment in hill walking: the discovery of the Traverse Path.

I found one on Wainwright's Coast-to-Coast. Coming off High Street in the rain isn't the most exciting thing in fellwalking, and it's hard to appreciate Angle Tarn when it's just a sploshing sound behind a misty tussock. Angle Tarn's a landmark so you look at the map to see if you're getting anywhere near Patterdale (you aren't). Watching map not feet, you wander onto a path that's rather narrow and not actually official. The cloud sags apart and you see the reason for the narrowness. It's so you can teeter over the edge and roll down four hundred metres of vertical wet grass. Look between the raindrops to cars on the Kirkstone road with their headlamps lit and their sunshine rooves firmly shut.

The best of hillwalking is ridgewalking, and the best of ridgewalking is when you look all the way down both sides at once. There's not a lot of it about. Swirral Edge is good, but short. Striding Edge is better. Sharp Edge is best of all. The crossing from Scoat to Steeple gives a few yards of real ridge, and then there's Scar Crags on Grasmoor. That's it, and it adds up to two miles, which can't be more than three hours out of anyone's lifetime. (Cofa Pike? Hall's Fell Ridge? Birk Fell of Wetherlam? Maybe you should make that three hours twenty minutes.) But if you're content with long steep view down one side only, then what you've got is the Traverse Path. Content you should be; for as well as half a ridge view on the downhill side, you get, on the uphill side, the total crag experience.

Take Moses' Trod. You walk it perhaps for its name, or because you're tired and don't want to do Gable. But from Moses' Trod you gaze up into the northern crags of Gable; crags which those on Gable's top will never see unless they fall over the edge. Moses lurches to avoid a boulder; ingeniously gets round various screes; and stops, just where the view's all the way down Ennerdale, so as to offer you a drink from a spring. Then he swerves round the back of a rocky hollow and manages to make Green Gable into a place that really is as interesting as it looks from down below.

Now Moses' Trod is simply a convenient way of not climbing Great Gable. It offers only: better views than the way over the top; better weather than the way over the top; pleasant horizontal walking; drinking water; and bilberries in season. Moses' Trod is a fairly run-of-the-mill traverse path.

Moses doesn't flirt with crags, or confront you with any sudden gullies. He doesn't drip water on your head, or unexpectedly show you a bit of patterned valley floor from vertically above.

Walking around Napes Needle, Great Gable and near Robinson's Cairn, Pillar – on two of the most spectacular traverse paths

He doesn't at any point offer to drop you into a lake or tarn. He doesn't edge round any vertical corners where the wind blows twice as hard as it does on the summit above that you're managing not to ascend. He doesn't have little lines of ice-axe holes across bands of old snow that ought to have melted two months ago. For these bonus features you have to go round onto the path below the Nape's Needle on Gable... or to Pillar's High-Level Route... or the West Wall on Scafell... or the Climbers' Traverse on Bowfell...

Why go up when you can go sideways?

TEN TOP TRAVERSES

* *

traverse	mountain not climbed	see
High-Level Route	PILLAR	daywalk: Pillar
Climbers' Traverse	GABLE	daywalk: Not Gable
Climbers' Traverse	BOWFELL	daywalk: Langdale
Glencoyne Miners' Track	THE DODDS	daywalk: Ullswater
Tiggywinkle Track	CATBELLS	Mrs Tiggywinkle
Corridor Route	BROAD CRAG	Lakes E to W
Angle Tarn approach	ANGLETARN PIKES	Wainwright's C-to-C
West Wall Traverse	SCAFELL	Scafell Scramble
Climbers' Traverse Buttress	SCAFELL	Lakes 3000s
Jack's Rake	PAVEY ARK	daywalk: Langdale

* *

1: The Lakes East To West

The trouble with the famous Wainwright Coast-to-Coast is this: the Lake District is too good. After Lakeland, all those Yorkshire Dales and Cleveland hillocks seem tame and not even particularly pretty. Wainwright tried to get round this by making the Lakes section as low and unexciting as possible. Trees through Ennerdale, roadside above Honister, out along the reservoir: these are necessary if you're to reach Swaledale and the so-called 'Eskdale' of the North York Moors and not find them totally flat and boring.

However, if we restrict ourselves to just crossing Cumbria, we can go as high and exciting as we like. With only 90 miles to the sea, it'll all be over before we can start to suffer from extreme landscape overload.

This, then, is a high-level backpack route across Cumbria. It's east to west because the sea makes a better destination than an obscure railway station in Yorkshire, and because the best bits are towards the western side. (Also the two gill-scrambles, though not difficult ones, are better taken upstream; and, at Robinson's Cairn, the sudden arrival of Pillar Rock is more dramatic than would be the sudden-not-being-able-to-see-Pillar-Rock-any-more.)

I did this one with Peter Simpson. Peter was the first person to look at Wainwright's Coast-to-Coast and see a running track; he set the first fast time for that route, doing it in just over fifty hours. With such a companion, it's natural to take the Lake District in large chunks, and we did this crossing in two long days and a short one.

Such speed is a form of greed. You don't have to go that long and hard; but if you don't go long and hard, you'll have to go heavy. Hartsop from Cross Keys is 27 miles without shop or accommodation. Langdale to Egremont is shorter, but takes longer.

The eastern half is grassy and peaceful, though the crossing of the Howgills is surprisingly exciting if you don't already know the Howgills, and the path above Borrowdale (no, not that Borrowdale, a different one) has unexpected charm. The two gill scrambles are the easiest available, and serve as a not-very-scary introduction to this absurd way of getting up hills. Gaining height in thousand-foot consignments can be hard on the feet and knees. In gills, you're too busy worrying about loose handholds to feel the pains in the feet. Also, they're a good way to get wet if it should happen not to be raining.

The seven miles from Scafell Pike to Pillar takes a succession of high traverse-paths above Wasdale and Ennerdale. These are slower, tougher, and rockier than the high-ways over the summits. They have better views: only one direction of sideways, it's

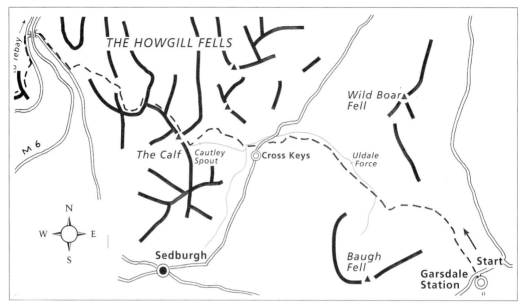

true, but a big bonus downwards.

The runoff from Steeple to the sea gives you Lakeland at its most lawn-like. Finally, we steal a bit of Wainwright's Coast-to-Coast but do it backwards, finishing along the sandstone edges of St Bees Head to Whitehaven. Sneak in along the shoreline, below the smell of the chemical works, to the old stone harbour. Here you can board a pirate ship, sail on westwards, and become the Admiral of the US Navy.

The Route

1: Garsdale Station to Cross Keys
Distance/climb: 8 miles/600ft or 13km/200m

There's always a feeling of abandonment when the train leaves the station. When the station it leaves is Garsdale Head on the Settle-Carlisle line, that feeling is much greater.

You get out of the gay plastic and metal box with its half-read newspapers, its trolley of shrink-wrapped ham rolls, its cuboid of warm air. The gay plastic clatters round the side of the hill and disappears. The humming of the rails dies, like flies in Autumn. Now the only sound is the wind in the yellow grass. Sometimes a car passes on the road along the valley floor, but mostly it doesn't. Several houses can be seen, but nobody's living in any of them at the moment. Or if they are, they don't want to show themselves.

And why should they, on a fading afternoon when clouds hurry across the top of the valley to finish their task of washing away all shape and angle from the saturated hills on the other side? Still, the best way to get warm is to get walking, and never mind the damp night ahead and the 12oz skin of green Goretex to hold between that damp night and you.

Take the road downhill past the red phone box. At the A684 turn right and in a few yards left at a footpath sign and gap stile. The path is narrow and muddy but

Opposite Page: Ennerdale Water in early morning light; overleaf: Pausing for breath on Pillar: view to High Stile

signed at each wall crossing as it rises to look down into the stream; the waterfall 200yds downsteam, like the inhabitants of Garsdale, isn't showing itself. The mud-trail turns north and passes to right of farm buildings with warning 'Beware of the farmer'. Exit to a narrow tarred road at GR 777930 (or use a clever compass-bearing to find an invisible right-of-way that joins the road 400yds further up).

Follow the road uphill as it becomes a track. At the top edge of the enclosed land turn left, north-west, on a grass track (a lower footpath has a 'Private' sign on the gate at its beginning). After about a mile above the field-tops, cross a ladder stile onto open hill.

The path, as it contours round towards the col, becomes very small and loseable. You may be feeling small and loseable yourself, as the dampness creeps through to your feet and you meet your first dead sheep. Don't be disheartened; these moors are a blank green sheet on which all sorts of exciting things are to be written over the coming days.

Uldale Force

Even now, after the second stream crossing, the path (if you're still on it) runs along a line of sink holes. The last of these, at GR752943, is a proper pothole with a stream disappearing into it. Probably unexplored, probably not worth exploring, says Peter, who is a part-time pothole person.

Go through the grassy col and down the left bank of the Rawthey stream. You could join it inside its rocky gorge, if it's not too full, for a bit of silly scrambling – you may have to fall into the water to get underneath the rowan branches.

Every walk should have its bit of limestone country. Limestone country is different: its grass is greener, its slopes are more slippery. Limestone cliffs are blocky and incised, and limestone waterfalls are small but sudden.

Continue on the left bank, contouring up onto the steep left slope above Uldale Force, GR 736957. The contouring path continues at the same level to lose itself among little, blocky, incised cliffs; so, as soon as possible, drop down steep grass to rejoin the stream about 100yds below the sudden but not altogether small falls. Make a way back along the riverbank to inspect them.

Follow the good path along the riverbank under cliffs and thorn trees. Passing a footbridge, the path becomes grass track that slants up left around the slopes of

Bluecaster. After about a mile, it bends left to traverse horizontally above river and road. Stay on it for another mile, then slant down to join the road where it enters the enclosed lands at GR 701970. There's a low place in the fence to step over. Go down the road for 200yds, to a footbridge; the Cross Keys Hotel is 50yds on.

2: Howgills: Cross Keys to M6 Borrowdale Foot
Distance/climb: 7¹/₂ miles/2000ft or 12km/600m

There are on Earth's surface a few rare places where grass climbs into the sky and tries to make mountains. It fails, but peering down the steep green sides of the Ochils, of the Brecon Beacons, or of these Howgills, we're glad it made the attempt.

The green slopes of the Howgills rise and fall like the persuasive cadences of classical oratory. Classical oratory is all very well, but the really interesting bits are where the vulgar heckler leaps up and starts throwing rocks. The rocky interruptions in the Howgills are at Cautley Spout and in the green hole of Carlin Gill.

Cross the footbridge, GR 698969, and take the path towards Cautley Spout. After a mile or so, a little-used path slants right, up the side of Yarlside to the Bowderdale Head col (GR 682980). This is the comfortable ascent, but the discomforts of the steep pull up the side of Cautley Spout are rewarded by views into the waterfall.

Cautley Crags in the Howgills

18

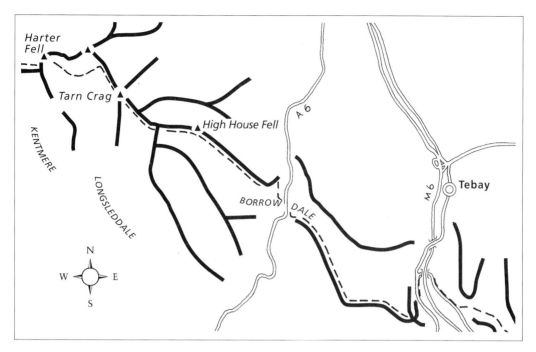

Traverse left, across the top of the falls, on an exciting little path – this is the first of the Traverse Paths that are the recurring theme of this walk. Take the branch-path on the right to enter the little slot of the Red Gill Beck. Where the stream divides take the right fork to reach the col just south of The Calf. A broad path leads right to the trig point.

Now you look down onto various dales of Yorkshire. The dales – Dentdale, Garsdale, a thin wedge of Wensleydale – are an immoderate shade of green, patterned diamond-back with field walls. They creep away like snakes into their holes among the innocent moorland.

Head north-west to White Fell Head, in mist being careful not to be carried off down the well-used path westward. Follow small path and big views northwards over Bush Howe to Breaks Head. A delightful bit of sharp grass ridge leads round to the cairn on Fell Head. The Lake District is now in sight, a crinkly bit at the back right-hand corner of the view.

Descend the western slopes of Ulgill Rigg, keeping well above the stream to avoid side stream gullies. Drop to the stream as it steepens at the end of the upper valley; here a contouring path crosses it. A few yards downstream, everything falls away into the rocky hole of Black Force. A small path contours out to the right.

Follow it for a few yards, and here a rib of loose rock drops into the upper amphitheatre. This is the start of a loose and rather exposed scramble down Black Force (Grade 1 in ascent). But I would just as soon look down into Black Force as fall down into it. Looking down into it is done by continuing right, to descend the steep grass to right of the deep gully. At the bottom cross Carlin Gill Beck to take the jolly little path along the north bank. The beck leads out between high grass walls to a narrow hill road.

Across the valley lies the M6: a band of noise and traffic across our route. Turn right on the hill road for about a mile. Cross the Lune, and bear right at what appears to be a road junction but isn't (the road on the left simply plunges to its death in the motorway embankment). Pass under the high arches of the railway and the M6.

3: Low Borrowbridge to A6 High Barrow Bridge
Distance/climb: 5¹/₂ miles/2000ft or 9km/600m

Compared with the Lakes on one side, the Howgills on the other, these hills are small relations. Small relations are amusing for a short time, until they get overexcited. These hillocks got overexcited at the minor but presumptuous cairn on Combs Hollow. At which point we wiped their muddy fingermarks off our jackets and wandered down across the A6 to join the grown-ups. Note, though, that the route from the A6 onto High House Fell is through two fields with no public right-of-way. A good alternative is to drop from Whinfell Beacon to a ford of the Mint at GR 556993, and follow the Longsleddale bridleway to Sadgill for Kentmere Pike.

Once under the motorway, turn left along the A685 for 600yds to a grey metal gate on the right. Go up grassy slopes onto the ridge of Birk Knott, and follow a wall to its summit (GR 598997). With the first step westwards from the trig point you lose the view back to the Howgills, and also the moaning of the motorway. Moorland plateau leads to the first transmission tower, and a rough road to the second one.

Here the road turns downhill, but head westward along the broad crest, crossing a stile and passing to right of a slender radio pole, to pass the top of another track at GR577004. Beyond a gate, a green track runs north-west along the slopes of Whinfell Beacon. All small boggy hills should have green tracks like this one, with its long dropping view into Borrowdale over the top of an ancestral stone wall. This track is the second of the route's high traverse lines, and lets you omit the thoroughly omissible top of Whinfell Beacon.

It bends round west to cross the ridge. Keep following it until a gate lets you through the wall. Now with a wall on the left you head up to pass to right of the mast on Old High. The rock-sprinkled top on the right is worth visiting, but return to the wall.

The wall turns right, and a ladder stile lets you over onto a path that crosses the broad col before entering a small sparse plantation on the face of Mabbin Crag. A path climbs over bumpy ground to Mabbin Crag's top. The trees down the back have a broad gap running right down through the middle, but instead the path runs just inside the right-hand (eastern) block of trees. It continues over Combs Hollow.

The rocky 454m spot height at the end of the ridge jumps up and down going "look at me with my crags round and my big square cairn! Aren't I a proper grownup Lakeland fell, aren't I?" Well yes, apart from being a thousand foot or so too low. Drop to the A6/track junction, and prepare to enter the real Lakeland.

4: A6 to Hartsop
Distance/climb: 12miles/3800ft or 19km/1150m

If the Howgills were a classical orator, this first moorland ridge off the A6 is a modern politician being interviewed on TV. It won't commit itself to anything in particular; it's

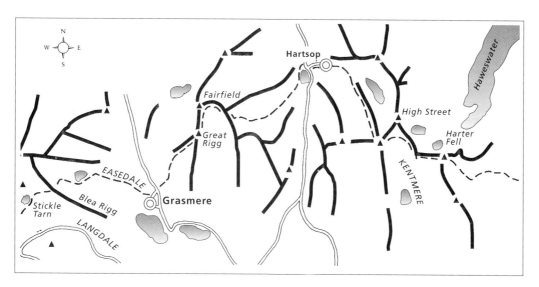

a bit wet; and it goes on far too long. High House Fell is the one that nobody's been on; not one fellwalker in a thousand can even say where it is.

Once at the high square cairn of Tarn Crag, things start to get better; and go on getting better, steadily, for the next two days. By which time they've risen to a very high standard.

Turn right past a lay-by with a phone. Just across the Borrow Beck a track on the left crosses to the old Roman road. Turn right, to go uphill under two lots of power lines to a field gate just beyond the brow of the hill. Through the gate, turn back left – just across the wall from the road you came up – for 300yds, then up the field edge. A gate onto the open hill is on the left, halfway up the field. Go up onto High House Bank.

The left-hand edge of the crest gives grassy walking with drops into Borrowdale and small outcrops below. On the upslope to Robin Hood, a gate through a wall leads onto wheeltracks that take you rapidly across the flat tussocky grassland of High House Fell. The wheeltracks indicate the least messy way through the peat hags beyond. With a fence on the right, ascend onto the ridge just west of Harrop Fell. That summit may be visited for its fine cairn and view to the Shap cement works.

Cross the flat col diagonally to Tarn Crag, with its tall square stone erection and views to real mountains. The land ahead consists largely of craggy hollows, and across the head of Longsleddale, the cone of Yoke is satisfactorily free of peat hags.

Descend north-west to the col at the head of Mosedale. Now an unused green path traverses across the head of Longsleddale. Cross the broad stony Gatescarth track to a gate at the corner of stone walls. Through this gate a green track leads up into the Wren Gill, alongside old metal pipe and other quarry debris. The track ends at a stream junction (GR471085). Now peaceful green slopes lead up onto Harter Fell. On the skyline above, walkers sweat up the eroded path from Gatescarth Pass.

Descend west to cross the rocky Nan Bield Pass. Nan Bield is used as a pass in the 'Lakes of Lakeland' chapter. It's just as good as a col between summits. The path winds below a rocky crest: you have to peer through the gaps for the long view over Small Water to the reservoir of Haweswater – a view that's particularly good if you've come

21

Above left: Thornthwaite Beacon; Above right: Yoke, Ill Bell and Froswick from the head of Kentmere

down out of the cloud to get it.

The path slants up right onto the crest of Mardale Ill Bell. At the top of the steep slope leave it at once, passing just north (right) of a small rocky knoll. Here find a small path heading west around the head of Hall Cove. Yes, it's another high traverse, the third; and it lets you miss the horizontal top of High Street. High Street's nothing: in another day or two we're going to miss Bowfell, Pillar and even Great Gable itself.

Where the path divides take the upper branch. This joins a broad track running down from High Street. Turn left to the monumental cairn of Thornthwaite Crag.

Follow the stone wall north along the long pleasant ridge of Grey Crag. At 530m the ridge-end steepens. Keep north-east to descend with scree on right, crag on left. Grassy slopes lead down to the track, which descends towards Low Hartsop.

After the sheep shed and before the car park turn left, ford the stream, and go through a gate onto a path along the right bank of the stream (Hartsop bypass). A footbridge on the right leads across into Hartsop if desired; otherwise take the track on the right a few yards further on, to emerge onto the A592 beside a phone box.

5: Hartsop to Grasmere over Fairfield
Distance/climb: 7 miles/2700ft or 12km/820m

This stage is classic Lakeland. It'd be a lovely high-level crossing even without the bonus of the gill scramble. Hoggett Gill lets you ascend three hundred metres vertical in the manner of a trout. Trout don't have feet; and if yours are sore ones, you'll forget all about them, your mind taken off your lower sorrows by the water falling on your head.

Turn right along the main A592 to a car park. On the left is a broad path along the bottom of woods. It passes along the side of Brotherswater to Hartsop Hall. Here pass above farm buildings but ignore the path slanting away uphill. Go horizontally forward through mud with fields on the left. The muddy track fords the stream from Dovedale

22

(footbridge 50 yards upstream – GR398118). Walk up the stream bank to enter Hogget Gill.

This ascent is a Grade 1 scramble. However, such difficulties as there are can be avoided by taking to steep but grassy slopes on the left (south) side, and indeed the entire gill can be eliminated in this way.

Go up the wide rocky stream bed under trees to the first fall. This is one of only two points of real difficulty. Climb up immediately to right of the fall on clean rock to half height. Cross the midway pool. Now finish up a steep groove to left of the water. A small tree growing in the groove provides obstacle and reassurance: your rucksack will let you pass it on the right only. Incut vertical handholds assist the ascent of the upper part of the groove.

Now the gill goes on and on, up and up. Clean, firm rock is always under the stream itself. Roll up trouser legs and sleeves and enjoy. At about the 450m contour a waterfall spoils the general character of the gill-scramble by being rather intimidating: escape onto those slopes on the left, returning into the gill down a narrow scree. Continue to where the stream divides, and take the left-hand branch to emerge on open fellside above the remains of a fence.

In mist it is best to continue up the stream onto the ridge south of Dove Crag summit (GR 375102), as the route next described passes among crags. That craggier route turns right from the top of the stream gully, crossing the slope, then descending a little to pass below the various small crags that stick out of the back wall of Hunsett Cove. Ascending again, pass along the base of Dove Crag on the small path made by rock climbers. Two large spiky boulders lie at the base of the crag: pass above these to get the full feel of the overhangs above. Slant up right to join the main Dovedale path, and go up it to the Dove Crag/Hart Crag col.

A broad rocky path leads over Hart Crag and onto the gravelly summit of Fairfield. A gentle ridge leads south over Great Rigg. Sixty metres below that summit the path divides: take the smaller branch-path on the right. It's a place to linger in the evening light to watch Windermere darken from silver to grey to black, except that if you do you'll miss the last bar supper in Grasmere.

We'd done everything as far as here in a single day, and the last bar supper in Grasmere was very much on our minds. We ignored the protests of the toes in favour of the demands of stomachs, left Windermere to darken on its own and made a real fell-running descent of these soft and gentle slopes. Whoever said runners are insensitive to the beauties of nature was quite right. But we do know how to appreciate the beauties of Cumberland sausage with double mash.

After the rocky ridge-end of Stone Arthur bear left slightly as the ground steepens, and descend to a stone wall. Turn left above the wall until the path descends, traverses back right, and becomes steep, eroded and horrid beside a plantation. Soon (but not quite soon enough) it runs out into a tarred lane that drops beside a little stream. At the road below turn left and walk down to the Swan Inn on the main Dunmail Raise road.

6: Grasmere (Swan Inn) to Langdale Head (Old Dungeon Ghyll)
Distance/climb: 5 miles/1600ft or 8km/500m

Hillrunners are greedy. Not just greedy for Cumberland sausage, but greedy for hill.

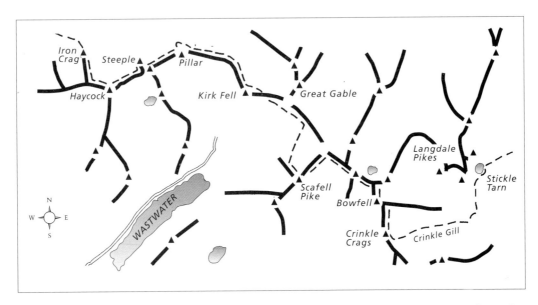

The moon was shining, or would have been if it weren't for the clouds. Apart from the bits under the trees, the path was just about visible. Grasmere, with all its facilities, has no designated bivvy bag site. We kept right on.

Cross the main road into the edge of Grasmere. The street crosses the Rothay. Now on the right a footpath runs through woods alongside the river. Under the trees it was, naturally, too dark to see, although an orange glow came in from the streetlights. In the middle of a wood, in the middle of a town, in the middle of the night, is a weird place to be, specially when you're quite tired.

The path trips over a few tree-roots, manages not to fall in the river, then skirts the north side of a wooded knoll to join another street. Turn right up this, north-west, not turning right again at the junction for the youth hostel. A footbridge on the left is sign-posted 'Easedale Tarn'.

Follow the broad, rock-surfaced path across fields. It turns uphill alongside the fine waterfall of Sour Milk Gill.

In darkness, the eroded path is no more, the waterfall itself seems to glow, and both its sound and its cold earthy smell are noticeably magnified. Above the fall the path may be abandoned in favour of the scrambling in the stream bed. (With midnight now passed, though, we had another sort of bed in mind to climb into.) Rejoin it to skirt the tarn.

Tarn? That's a bedroom, with a mattress of last year's dead grasses, dreamlike black-on-black decor and running cold and cold water en suite. And no clambering around at dawn to see what the weather is: you can feel it on your face. It's cloudy on the tops but it isn't raining at all. What more could you ask in April on a route that boasts of going topless?

Above the tarn the path continues westwards alongside Easedale Gill: once again, the enterprising may prefer the stream to the path. Above and to the right of the gill, the small rocky peak is Belles Knott. On Harvey's map it appears only as a grass knoll at GR 297085. Above it, the path from Codale Tarn comes in from the right, and here turn left (south-west) off the main path.

A typical scene at the Old Dungeon Ghyll Hotel

Cross the wide knolly ridge of Blea Rigg; it has one or two peat hags, shame on it. Drop gently westwards to Stickle Tarn. Cross the dam at Stickle's outflow and traverse onwards on a small path high above Langdale.

Cross the incised valley of the Dungeon Gill stream, and on the hind slope of the spur beyond find the clear path down towards Raven Crag. The path descends with many zigzags to avoid rockfaces. An energetic leap could lead to safe landing in the roof of someone's tent. Finally the path runs down onto the grassy spur leading to the New Dungeon Ghyll Hotel. It runs alongside Dungeon Ghyll letting you peer into the depths. Now a small path on the right slants down the base of a small but overhanging crag to a stile in the gap of a stone wall. Below this an open field leads down to the track where you turn right to the Old Dungeon Ghyll Hotel, a mile up-valley. A gate to a small streamside path bypasses the hotel if you don't want your companions to be tempted aside into episodes of beer-drinking.

The shop at the campsite may be small, but it has big, big opening hours.

7: Langdale to Sty Head
Distance/climb: 8¹/₂ miles/ 4200ft or 13km/1270m

Cosy tents lead to useful early-morning walking time lost in slumber. The campers of Langdale were still poking their heads out for that first groan at the weather as we set off westwards. Those campers, when they finally start to move, will do so in a circle; hardly out of the valley before having to turn back. Not for them the setting of the foot onto a ridge that'll end, thirty miles further on, at the flat land beside the Irish Sea.

We start with a gill scramble, and continue by not climbing Bowfell.

A track leads westwards to Stool End Farm. Pass through the farm buildings and follow the wide path into Oxendale (ignoring the larger path on the right up the Band). A footbridge crosses the bottom of Hell Gill; Crinkle Gill is the next stream round on the left.

Crinkle Gill is a long Grade 1 scramble, described by the guide as "very easy, almost a walk". One man's walk is another man's marathon and the same applies to women; and once embarked upon, the Gill can't be got out of. However, the point of least easiness is near the start and from this one can retreat; or having conquered, continue with assurance.

Walk up the rocky stream bed into the narrow gorge. One pool here may be problematic if the water is high, though there are large handholds in the left-hand wall. At the end of this narrow section the gill turns 90° left. Climb up on small holds beside (or under) the right-hand edge of the water: this is the rock climbing crux.

The gorge is now a wide one between impressive walls. Walk up for a long way over boulders. A twenty-foot waterfall can be avoided by gritty ledges on the left, but grassy slopes on the right are more in keeping with the easiness of the rest of the ascent. Above this fall, you pass through the hole behind a huge slab leaning against the right-hand wall. Finally, the gill divides into four streams. Between the left-hand and second-from-left is a sharp rocky rib.

The ascent of the left-hand stream is on good clean holds which are, to put it quite frankly, underwater. Those who are frightened of getting their feet wet (and legs, bodies, etc.) can use a path on the right-hand side of the little rock rib to reach the top of the same waterfall. A few more yards sees you on the open hillside above Langdale.

Go up steeply southwards to the floor of a tiny corrie, and continue southwards on grassy slopes to gain the ridge of Stonesty Pike (834m). A stony clamber, with sudden

Bowfell and Rossett Pike at the head of Mickleden

drops to Langdale, leads to the col before Long Top – this being the first and highest of several that make up the Crinkle Crags.

The path up Long Top ascends a shallow gully to a cave. Now good, well-scratched holds lead up the overhanging wall on the right. There is also, for the slender, a route up through a hole at the back of the cave; you won't get your rucksack through without a person at the top to lift it out.

Thread through the various rocky tops of the Crinkles. Though there is a path, the ground is complex and confusing in mist. The end of the Crinkle Crags is the col of the Three Tarns. The Three Tarns vary in number, sometimes being as many as five.

The way of avoiding Bowfell is by the Climbers Traverse, which is decribed in the Langdale daywalk(P36). For now here's an easier way. From the Three Tarns a clear scree path ascends the end of Bowfell. A band of clean rocks to the right of the path gives unalarming, easy scrambling. The path spirals to the rocky top of Bowfell, reaching it eventually from the north. You reach the cairn, raise your head to admire the new view ahead, and find yourself looking down onto the Three Tarns again. Jolly confusing.

A cairned path leads across west-facing slopes to Ore Gap, and over Esk Pike. (Esk Pike's true summit is a rock rib a few yards west of the large cairn.) The initial descent off Esk Pike is down a small gully, then the path runs along the left-hand edge of the wide ridge. After the first steep descent it traverses back right along flat slabs.

Esk Hause is the choice-point. Total purists will go by Sprinkling Tarn, avoiding not only Scafell Pike but also Great End and Ill Crag. But the Corridor is a traverse path within the meaning of the Act, and it's worth visiting Scafell Pike if only to see how nasty it is doing tops when you could be teetering along sides with half the rucksack hanging over the void.

From Esk Hause take the broad highway across the southern flank of Great End. Here there is a useful stream. Continue over the boulderfields of Ill Crag and Broad Crag to Scafell Pike with its huge flat-topped cairn.

The path off Scafell Pike descends north-west then, fairly steeply, north. 30m below a large oblong boulder with a cairn on, the path divides. Left, west, is for Wasdale and wrong. The Corridor Route traverses east, soon edging round the top of the deep hole of Piers Gill. The path continues north-east, dropping only gradually and on one rocky section reascending a few feet. Finally it divides, but both branches lead to Sty Head.

8: Sty Head to Scaly Moss, Uldale

Distance/climb: 12^1/$_2$ miles/3800ft or 20km/1100m

Now it's time to avoid climbing Great Gable.

Take the main path up Great Gable for 100yds. The Climbers' Traverse is indistinct at first, heading off along the left hand slope climbing slightly. If you're on a clear path descending, then you're on the lower path to Wasdale. The traverse path becomes clearer, and passes immediately below the small but famous rock climbing crag of Kern Knotts. The going is rocky, requiring occasional use of the hands.

A stream trickles through a cave just above the path. Now climb up some easy rocks (or avoid them on scree to left) to where the path rises slightly across scree. This is Great Hell Gate: the direct ascent from here is either the nastiest or the second nastiest route to Gable summit. Having crossed the scree, pass below a small overhanging crag.

Is it a trick of the light that causes all this white hair? Is it a local style statement to wear breeches instead of Rohan lightweights? Or is the average age of punters on this path really twenty years higher than what you get at Gable's top? As in the legend of the Young Bull and the Old Bull: the Young Bull says let's run up and get Gable. The Old Bull says let's walk up, and get Kern Knotts, the Napes, the Sphinx, and Wasdale from on top. Oh, and maybe Gable while we're at it.

The traverse path picks its way delicately through scree, crag and little grassy bits. Not one step of the way is plod. Being a traverse path, it goes uphill only occasionally, and then for no better reason than that it feels like it. It has views up to crags, and down to the field patterns of Wasdale.

Gable top is flat, with a view of other hillwalkers eating bananas.

The path onward is narrow, rising and falling among the rocks but basically following the 600m contour round. Thirty metres above appears the Nape's Needle, probably with rock climbers on. What we are on here is a traversing path, below the zone of continuous rock, crossing scree, avoiding outcrop, and marked with small cairns. Higher up, along the very base of the crag is the true 'Climbers' Traverse' which runs along the base of the crags.

> That route has many interesting moments of exposed Grade 1 scrambling. It could be reached by ascending either to the left or to the right of the Needle, and then following a scratched way along the bottoms of the rock climbs to pass behind a shapely projection called the Sphinx that is now above you on the skyline ahead. See the daywalk 'Not Climbing Great Gable'. Tired, with a middling-big rucksack, you may prefer the path.

The traverse path continues, small but followable, not ascending at all at this point. It descends slightly across the scree that comes down from the western side of the Needle and continues through, but not across, rocky bits.

The next nasty scree, Little Hell Gate, is either the second nastiest or the nastiest route to Gable, and even going across it, the path is lost through constant shifting of the stones. But it's found again on the other side. Finally it crosses the lower edge of the stable screes of Gable's western slopes. Rising slightly, with many cairns, it reaches the grassy col between Gable and Kirk Fell.

A col, a hill and a tarn: all named for the fact of being nameless. This may be all right for foreigners with their 'Pic Sans Nom' (or, as the Italians call it, 'Punta Innominata'). It won't do for logical Lakeland. If it's called Nameless then it's not nameless so it shouldn't be 'Nameless'. But if 'Nameless' isn't its name, because it's not nameless, then it doesn't have a name after all and so is entitled to be called 'Nameless'.

Such reasoning satisfied our grandfathers, but in the more pedestrian age of today, perhaps this col between Gable and Kirkfell is better as 'Beckhead'. Meanwhile the nameless fell has become Birkett's, celebrating one who agitated in the Lords on behalf of Ullswater. By being it in Greek, the Innominate Tarn has retained its Namelessness.

Actually, Innominate Tarn is a straight mistake: when it was originally named 'Nameless' it did in fact already have a name – the perfectly good, boring one of Loaf Tarn.

Descend northwards to find the contour path around the northern side of Kirkfell. This is a grassy path below impressive crags and gullies, and with fine views down into

Ennerdale. Descending gradually, it leads round to the Black Sail path, which is joined just as it's about to arrive on its own Pass.

The path towards Pillar out of Black Sail Pass starts slightly on the Mosedale side of the ridge, and bypasses Looking Stead on the left. After a flat section the ridge steepens, and at the foot of the rocky bit a cairn marks where the 'High Level Path' strikes off to the right.

The high path crossing to Cautley Spout was an Intimation. Bowfell Climbers' Path, the Gable Traverse were the Real Thing. But the Pillar High Level Route is the Platonic Ideal, the Archetype to which all traverse paths aspire. It has no right existing in the real world at all.

The path starts by descending to get round the bottom of a crag: a measure of improbability is essential to its nature. It's followed above (and below) impressive drops and in and out of various grassy coves to the large Robinson's Cairn. Here the monumental Pillar Rock suddenly appears ahead.

Wasdale from Little Hell Gate as seen on the traverse path around Great Gable

Although the summit of the Rock is visible, much of it is obscured by a lesser but still large crag called the Shamrock. The way forward will run along the top of this, by the 'Shamrock Traverse'. Walk forward across the bottom of a grassy cove, then turn uphill to climb loose scree to left of the Shamrock. At the top turn right to slant up along the top of the crag by a slanting ledge. This was once grassy but is now earth, scree and bare rock. The bare rock, newly exposed by the eroding feet of hillwalkers and climbers, shows scratch marks that are actually the imprint of the Ennerdale Glacier.

Having passed along the top of the Shamrock you look down into the 'Amphitheatre' between it and Pillar Rock. The Rock has three summits: Pisgah, on the left, is divided from the High Man by the Jordan Gap. On the right, below your standpoint, is Low Man.

(The easiest route up Pillar Rock can be assessed from here. It's a rock climb called Slab and Notch with formidable exposure. Below you, on the front face of High Man, is the gently angled Slab: above it, on the right-hand skyline, the Notch that's climbed into on large holds.)

Walk round the head of the Amphitheatre to the col between Pisgah and the main mountain. From here, Pisgah is a straightforward scramble (Grade 1) on good holds. The views down into Jordan gap are rock-scenery of the most thrillingly vertical sort.

Return to your rucksack in the col. The path up Pillar mountain slants up left, then back right to the crest of a small rib. It continues to the right, then up a short, easy rock groove to the summit plateau. More direct routes up the rocky hillside are possible.

From the trig pillar, a line of cairns leads south-west. Soon you're descending steeply over eroded jammed boulders into Wind Gap. A broad path leads up the ridge

Crag Fell and Ennerdale

towards Great Scoat Fell over a preliminary top. A wall appears, and you pass through a gap in it. The wall is now on the left, and sudden drops on the right; where the wall turns from slightly-north-of-west to slightly-south-of-west is the small summit cairn of Great Scoat Fell.

The out-and-back to Steeple is well worth while. Small cairns lead north-west; just over the edge is the narrow arete to Steeple. The path traverses to the left of the crest, but the rocky top edge presents no difficulties. Return the same way.

Going has been slow along the various traverse paths. Already evening is gathering among the pine branches of Ennerdale and seeping upwards towards the tops, while the colours of the sunset are peeping round the edges of the clouds and wondering if it's time to begin. Don't worry; just sit back and enjoy the show. The rest of the way to the end of Lakeland is easy: easy enough to do by torchlight or moonlight, or fast enough to finish before the end of day.

Follow the wall westwards down soft grassy slopes and up the gentle climb to Haycock. The going is slightly less grassy on the following descent, and if the wall is followed over Little Gowder Crag, it's possible to get a final scrambling moment: leave Little Gowder on the north side of the wall.

The wall guides you over Caw Fell, and turns right sharply (GR 126107) to lead you along the crest of Iron Crag. Iron Crag is dotted with little pink rocks, and the wall is high and pink, with a little green path alongside. (Aha! say the knowledgeable: Ennerdale Granite.) A gate lets you out and back to the summit cairn.

As the sun sinks so do the hills, each one smaller than the last. And the dark tide spreading up across the col of Black Pots isn't the rising dusk but the rising Christmas trees, coming up out of the valley like the creeping sludge of 1950s horror films. Some minor characters have already got swallowed up – Long Barrow and Heckbarley, we never got to know them and now they're gone, a heather elbow or knee projecting forlornly from the seething vile mass.

But already the Unlikely Rescuer in the shape of a clerk from the National Trust has removed his spectacles, leapt into the back of an open-topped Morris, and saved what's left of the world from the creeping greenery using a clever thing he thought up earlier. And now the film is finishing, it's time to shed a brief but manly tear for lost Long Barrow and Heckbarley, drop the popcorn under the seat and leave the cinema.

From the col, a wooden gate leads into the forest. Take a rutted track west, and then north, (left, then right,) to gain the end of a forest road. Follow this left for 20yds. A small cairn marks the start of a path that leads up unplanted hillside. After a stile the path continues to the summit of Crag Hill. It's a place to sit and look back wistfully: mainly at Ennerdale, for the great lumps of Pillar and Steeple are blocking the central fells, but distant Helvellyn peeps over the top of Haystacks.

Turn south-west into the soggy col. A stile beside the forest fence lets you through to Grike, a top with little but its name to live on. Descend westwards to a gate at GR 082140, and turn right along the forest road.

After about a mile the road turns right, and here a rough track leads up through the trees to a gate onto the open slopes of Blakeley Raise. Follow the forest edge to the summit and go straight down to the unfenced road below. This small road marks the end of Lakeland, the beginning of the coastal plain.

9: Scaly Moss to St Bees
Distance/climb: 7 1/2 miles/ 300ft or 11km/100m

No walk is exciting all the way. These seven miles to the sea are simply the quickest way to get from the great grey rocks of Lakeland to the sandstone of St Bees. (Just be glad it isn't the thirteen-mile linking bit on Wainwright's one!) There are a couple of moments along the Kirk Beck that could be nice enough if Pillar Rock and Langdale lay ahead in imagination in stead of behind in recent memory. After a fifty-mile orgy of solid rock, it takes more than the crumbling outcrop of Raven Crag Nannycatch to arouse the jaded appetite.

Cross directly onto the track for Sillathwaite Farm. Take the second track on the right to pass to the right of the farm and its small duck pond. Walk west with a field boundary on the left, then through two gates to continue with the field edge on the right. Descend steeply into the narrow valley of the Kirk Beck. Go through a gate to a broad track alongside the stream.

Turn downstream. Little crags overhang the grassy valley. "Who outside West Cumbria ever heard of Nannycatch?" asks Wainwright. Well, the ten thousand walkers

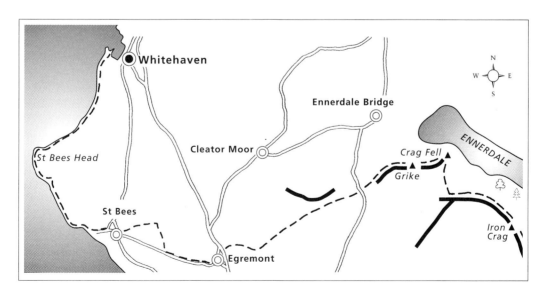

on his Coast-to-Coast – though a few, with a particularly law-abiding guidebook, are diverted onto a nearby road.

The bridleway fords the stream several times; footbridges are provided. After a final footbridge to the southern (left) bank a stile leads onto a forest road: go straight across this and continue by a muddy path along the stream bank to Uldale Farm.

Here ford the stream and take an old stony trackway along the edge of forest. Hawthorns blossom, and larches drop orange needles onto the mud for you, and shade your head with fresh green ones. Slippery mud underfoot is at least a change after so many miles of shifting scree.

After Moss Dalts (where you don't turn left) the track becomes tractor-haunted and puddly. River and playing fields appear on the right, and a wide footbridge crosses into Egremont.

Turn right on a path, which becomes a road to an underpass below the A595. Houses hem in the narrow passage beyond, eventually closing in overhead. It's a sinister dripping place used for various sordid urban purposes, but lets you out onto the charming main street of Egremont. The main street of Egremont is mostly pubs. It might be an idea to drink yourself into insensibility before the road walk; but then again it might not, as the road's only a couple of miles, while the sudden view of the sea at Loughrigg is better if you're sober enough to find the correct little gaps in the hedge to view it through.

Turn left, and right on the road for St Bees. The Castle, on your left, is a grassy mound with ruins on. The next fork is signposted left for St Bees: ignore it! Bear right for Orton Estate. Orton Estate has overwhelmed the northward footpath beyond, so walk out along this street (it's 'St Bees Road') for a mile. Turn right onto an unsurfaced farm road past Watson Hill.

At the 3-road 2-track junction, an ancient ivy-mantled footpath sign points through Loughrigg Farm to the mud track beyond. Stiles and waymarks lead along field edges over the crest of a low hill. Beyond the crest, the waymarks and footpath are diagonally across three fields; the next stile ahead is always visible. A stony sunken track leads down into St Bees.

10: St Bees to Whitehaven
Distance/climb: 7 miles/700ft or 11km/210m

Having looked down sneeringly from the mountaintops onto Wainwright's route through Lakeland, we now add injury to insult. For at St Bees we nip in and pinch three of his best miles - although, quirkily, we're doing them in the direction which on the Coast-to-Coast is eastbound.

If it should be raining in St Bees, turn sideways and look back with one eye, forward with the other (easier if there are two of you). Behind, the lump of grey nothingness you just walked out of suggests that it's raining much worse in Wasdale. And ahead, the clifftops of St Bees Head are at their best when wild and wet.

It would, admittedly, be perverse to linger in St Bees waiting for a worsening in the weather. Even though St Bees, with its cafes and chip shops, isn't a bad place to linger. St Bees is like one of those elderly great-aunts whose houses are full of the knick-knacks of an earlier age, all a bit faded from standing long years in the west-facing windows.

Opposite, top: Ullswater Morning; bottom: Two thousand feet out over the top of Upper Eskdale – photo by Roy Clayton; Overleaf: Langdale Evening, with Blea Tarn and a corner of the Blisco Wilderness

While in the kitchen cupboards are various nasty corners that great-aunts, once they reach a certain age, no longer consider important. (One of the nice bits is the sandstone arch opposite the abbey doorway. One of the nasty bits is the pebbledashed estate that's the view through the arch.)

Cross the railway at a level crossing beside the station. After 100yds, take a footpath on the left past playing fields. Go ahead on road to the seafront.

From the west end of the sea wall, a bridge crosses shingle (or there's a footbridge 20yds inland). There are many signposts: follow any except 'Public Footpath Rottington'. The clifftop path ascends on the seaward side of the fence; it is pink and sandy with wooden steps. After a mile, a ruined concrete structure is a good point for Coast-to-Coast walkers to stop and tighten their laces for the 189 miles ahead. At the first stile the path moves to the inland side of the fence. Soon it dips to a deep-cut grassy inlet, dropping to sea level or at least to just above the shingle. The beach below has damp sandstone caves, just the place for those too mean to seek proper accommodation at St Bees (where it was abundant). At times of exceptional tide the sea may come into bed with you at midnight.

Climb across the far wall of the inlet on flat sandstone which nostalgically recalls the rock ledge of the Shamrock Traverse twenty miles back and two and a half thousand foot higher up. Continue along the clifftop. At four points a stile over the fence gives access to cliff edge birdwatch points. The smaller sort of gulls are kittiwakes; the little black-and-white birds lined up on their ledges like gents at the opera are guillimots. Apart from the ones with big silly-looking beaks, which are razorbills.

At the lighthouse, a concrete track leads inland. Cross it beside the clifftop lookout station, and enter the next field by a stile. After the next stile, the footpath has been diverted to the seaward side. A notice invited those aggrieved by the diversion to complain to the Council. But all will be gratified by the extra clifftop exposure thus obtained.

The path returns to the seaward side of the fence, and dips to a grassy terrace below the highest tier of cliff. Here it leaves the Bird Reserve and runs up a little stone-floored gully. Waymarks in every possible direction indicate the start of a public footpath on the right towards Sandwith, but just stay along the clifftop. After another mile or so you skirt the inland side of a quarry to a long bungalow. Pass to left of the house and continue ahead even though multiple waymarks, including a rare black & white C-to-C one, point right.

The path slants gradually down along a terrace between upper and lower cliffs. A large signboard tells that you're on the Cumbria Coastal Footpath, sponsored by the NCB. Perhaps they supplied from their slag heaps the gritty path surfacing material. At the end of the upper cliff, a track and waymark pole point forward towards various industrial buildings including a pyramid-like the roof of a monstrous Lego-house. You don't want to go there. So turn left to a waymark pole, the first of a series leading down to lower cliffs. Walk along the tops of these on a well-made path.

At the edge of Whitehaven a fortress structure of barbed wire and railway sleepers stands across the path. (It protects some heaps of building rubble, as far as one can see through the cracks). Here a frightening red sign warns of dangerous cliffs: CCF walkers are to take the inland track.

Should the clifftop danger diminish or be repaired, a left fork will let you drop to a lower track, where the cliff-edge above conceals the chemical

imbalance of outer Whitehaven. Between cliff and sea is a lifeless little desert of heather, gravel, and fallen blocks of sandstone.

The path emerges at a deserted house above Whitehaven harbour. Drop to a stone chimney. Outstandingly gentle zig-zags take two hundred yards to descend fifty feet. Pass a cannon, an anchor, a huge pithead wheel, and a wall-portrait of the pirate John Paul Jones. (If you're American, read that as 'seaman and statesman JP Jones'.)

At an ornate 'Coastal Footpath' signpost turn onto the old, inner pier and follow it to the stone watchtower at its end. This has associations with pirate Jones, who staged the last ever seaborne invasion of England here. Associations don't mean bullet holes, just that it was around at the time. The end of an era for seaborne invasions of the British Isles (shucks Napoleon, shucks Hitler) and the end of a walk from Yorkshire.

The Lake District's out of sight behind the low swellings of the coastal plain. Whitehaven's sunlight lingers on pinkish sandstone. It smells of fish, and tastes of ice-cream.

Of Whitehaven's two railway stations, the northern one has more trains.

LAKES:EAST TO WEST

PLANNING MAP

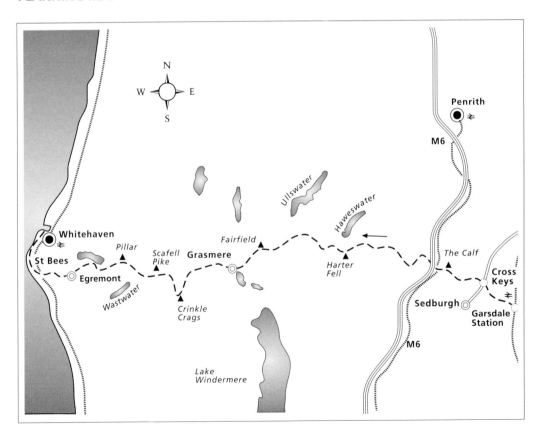

LAKES: EAST TO WEST

Distances and ascents

1: Garsdale Station to Cross Keys	8 miles / 13km	600ft/ 200m
2: Howgills: Cross Keys to M6	7 miles/ 11km	2000ft/ 600m
3: M6 to A6 High Barrow Bridge	5 miles/ 9km	2000ft/ 600m
4: A6 to Hartsop	12 miles/ 19km	3800ft/1100m
5: Fairfield: Hartsop to Grasmere	7 miles/ 12km	2700ft/ 800m
6: Grasmere to Langdale Head	5 miles/ 8km	1600ft/ 500m
7: Langdale to Sty Head	8 miles / 13km	4200ft/1300m
8: Sty Head to Scaly Moss, Uldale	12 miles/ 20km	3800ft/1100m
9: Scaly Moss to St Bees	7 miles/ 11km	300ft/ 100m
10: St Bees to Whitehaven	7 miles/ 11km	700ft/ 200m
Total	78 miles/127km	21,700ft/6500m

Transport:

The train rides, on two of England's best railways, are part of the holiday. Garsdale is on the Settle-Carlisle line, with connections to Leeds. Whitehaven is on the Cumbria Coastal line, with connections to Carlisle and Lancaster.

Facilities:

Garsdale: station only
Cross Keys: hotel
Lune Valley (M6 crossing): facilities at Tebay, 3miles (5km) north
A6: one B&B (Hollowgate)
Hartsop: B&Bs, no shop. Brotherswater Inn (bunkhouse). Facilities Patterdale 2miles (3km)
Grasmere: all facilities except a bank
Langdale: hotels, camp site with shop (opens 8:00 am)
Egremont: all facilities
St Bees: all facilities
Whitehaven: all facilities

Maps:

Large Scale:
Outdoor Leisure 19 (Howgills)
Outdoor Leisure 7 (SE Lakes)
Outdoor Leisure 6 (NE Lakes) or Harveys Eastern Lakeland
Outdoor Leisure 5 (SW Lakes) or Harveys Central Lakeland
Outdoor Leisure 4 (NW Lakes)
Landranger 89 (West Cumbria)
(Outdoor Leisure 33: Coast-to-Coast West gives some of the final miles at larger scale.)
The two Harveys maps are easier and cheaper than the OLs they replace.

1:50 000
Landrangers 98 (or Harvey's Howgill Fells), 91, 90, 89. A very small corner of 97 can be dispensed with by plotting the GR of Birk Knott onto your map margin.

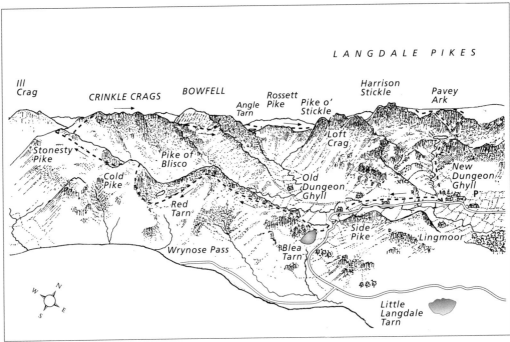

Langdale is the closest to the motorway, and so the most popular. Still, it's surrounded by Pike of Blisco and the Crinkles, Bowfell and Pavey Ark: and it has every right to refer to itself as "Great" Langdale. The surprise is that there are places, on the slopes above this busy civilised valley, where you can find yourself comparatively lonely, small and scared.

Blisco, now: Blisco is one of the great middle-sized hills. Blisco's paths are small, and wander among low crags. It has gullies, long scrambles, and a remote plateau on its eastern end that's a world apart, but just 20 minutes above the pub. Someday I'll circumnavigate Pike of Blisco around the 500m contour.

The walk start can be varied according to mood, legs and weather. A stream descending south-west to the outflow of Blea Tarn allows entry to the Blisco wilderness of Blake Rigg and Bleaberry Knott. Or forget Blisco, and go up the easy but interesting Crinkle Gill (scramble Grade 1) or the rather harder Browney Gill (Grade 1). The ascent by Crinkle Gill is described in the main chapter.

Start/Finish: New Dungeon Ghyll, GR 296064 (pay & display car parks)
Distance/climb: 12 miles/5500ft, or 20km/1800m by way of: Pike of Blisco, Crinkle Crag, Bowfell Climbers' Traverse and Great Slab, Pavey Ark
Map: OS Outdoor Leisure 6 (SW) or Harveys W Lakes or OS Landranger 90

From behind the hotel, a track leads west to the Old Dungeon Ghyll. Take the road heading south across the valley but leave it at a stile on the left into the corner of the camp site. A wall on the right guides you round to an uphill path with kissing-gates. Beyond a ladder stile you come out onto the road at the top of the steep pass, beneath the crags of Side Pike. Be nice: don't step out in front of the cars so they nervously stall and have to attempt a hill start under your critical eye. Blea Tarn is now visible half a mile away to the left.

> To explore the Blisco wilderness, take a built path left, passing through the pines of Blea Tarn's northern shore, and follow a stream up south-west. At the top of the bracken the stream steepens between juniper crags, and here a grassy rake leads up left to the skyline ridge. From here to Blisco summit is rocks, grass and tiny tarns. But the path taken by the main route is shorter, and almost as nice.

Cross the road to a small path along the Langdale flank: it climbs gently at first, then runs level around the slope. Yes, it's the first Traverse Path, offering elevated views into Oxendale and a foretaste of higher and wilder traverse paths to come.

All too soon it joins the main path alongside the Redacre Gill stream. Now you must turn your back on the Oxendale view and climb 250m (750ft) of steep pitched path. The stones and rocks of the Gill are a suitable setting for this austere task. The path reaches flatter ground above, and bends right, to weave among outcrops to the summit cairn.

The path to Red Tarn can only get down off Pike of Blisco by going sideways along the tops of outcrops. Near the foot of Red Tarn you join a much bigger path, which climbs north of Cold Pike onto Stonesty Pike (834 m). The view east is down the rocky slope to Langdale, now a satisfying 600m (2000ft) below. Southward, though, is a flat moor with many pools, with Coniston tops peeping over the rim. The contrasting views allow a moment of landscape philosophy. The bleak and the pretty are in collaboration. Lakeland's special quality is to be Civilisation and Wilderness, mingled.

A stony clamber, with sudden drops to Langdale, leads to the col before Long Top – this being the first and highest of several that make up the Crinkle Crags.

The path up Long Top ascends a shallow gully to a cave. Now good, well-scratched holds lead up the overhanging wall on the right. There is also, for the slender, a route up through a hole at the back of the cave; you won't get your rucksack through without a person at the top to lift it out.

Thread through the various rocky tops of the Crinkles. Even though there is a path, the ground is complex and confusing in mist. The end of the Crinkle Crags is the col of the Three Tarns.

A straightforward path leads up onto Bowfell (described in the main chapter). The less straightforward way is the Climbers' Traverse. Technically, this is a way of avoiding climbing Bowfell. But the avoidance is technical indeed, as you walk past the summit knoll at a distance of a few metres, pointedly ignoring one another as if it were not Bowfell but Beau Brummel and you were wearing the wrong colour socks.

It's not your socks that matter, it's where you wear them. Wear them along this airy traverse among the bilberries, then up the absurdity of the flat slabs overhead.

From the Three Tarns, start off down the path to right, which is the Band: rightly celebrated as the only comfortable way down to Langdale. But leave it almost at once, at the 750m contour, traversing forward towards a grass spur. The climbers' path leaves the Band 300 ft (100m vertical) below, to run up the near side of the spur. Join it as it quite suddenly stops ascending and traverses right, north-westwards.

The path is just right: well trodden but not eroded, narrow but not too narrow, even given the steep drops below it. Its severe fault is its shortness. Pass below the first climbing cliff, which is Cambridge Crag. The one in front, with slanty strata, is Bowfell Buttress and one of the great Lakeland rock climbs.

A spring gushes from the lowest corner of Cambridge Crags. Here the path goes forward over stones and vegetation but this only leads to the ascent of the scree gully in front of Bowfell Buttress.

So having rounded the corner of Cambridge Crags, turn sharp back up left. A rubble path leads upwards, and in the wet this is the way to take. But in the dry you can cross a brief boulderfield on the left onto the Great Slab. The Slab is broad and mossy, and drops away to nowhere at the far edge and at the bottom. But it's angled so that you can stand straight and walk up it; up and up, to the distant blue sky above.

Emerge at last onto the top of it, which turns out to be merely the path from Three Tarns to Bowfell. It turns out that you haven't avoided Bowfell in the slightest. Well, avoiding Bowfell's not everything.

A cairned path leads across west-facing slopes to Ore Gap, and here turn down right on the rebuilt path to Angle Tarn. The path crosses the outflow and climbs to a col: at your toes now is the Rossett Gill, the most horrible of the various horrible descents into Langdale; but turn left, onto Rossett Pike. Follow its unfrequented ridge down north-eastwards to a col after 600yds. Turn right, and slant down left to the stream at Sticks Pass.

Go straight up the slope opposite onto Martcrag Moor - this looks like somewhere from below, but is only the corner of a bog. The bog leads up to the pointy tops of the Langdale Pikes. These aren't quite the vast precipices they seem from Langdale. In fact they're merely rock knolls at two more corners of the bog: but big as rock knolls go. Scramble them and perch on their tops before continuing to Pavey Ark.

Off Pavey Ark by Jack's Rake:

The descent of Jack's Rake (Scramble, Grade 1) is for confident scramblers only. Dirt makes this one slippery when wet, and it is considerably more exposed than it feels. To find the top of the rake, return from Pavey Ark's summit south-west over gentle rocks for two minutes, to a cairn and a stone wall. Now go straight down south-east on scratched rock and little bits of path, to find the top of the Rake, a very clear groove slanting down left.

Once in the groove the way is plain, with vertical rock-climbs both above and below; and it slants all the way down to the bottom corner of the crag.

Off Pavey Ark by path and Easy Gully:

Leave the summit north-west, to find a broken stone wall after 40yds. A small path runs down right, behind the wall. After 200yds it joins a much larger one running down to the right.

This route was called North Rake by Wainwright, who says "it deserves to be better known". Better known it now is, an eroded way ten yards wide. Well, it is the top of the Stickle Tarn path, used by quarter of a million people a year – though one wonders why the quarter-million didn't turn left at the plateau to take in Pavey Ark's rocky top.

After ten minutes of descent the path levels briefly, and a few steps to the right will find the top of Easy Gully (see picture P133). A small path leads down between high rock walls. The rock wall on the right overhangs, and Stickle Tarn is at the bottom.

Walkers on Blea Rigg with Pavey Ark behind

There's an awkward moment on the way down, where jammed boulders block the gully. The short rock-step has a big handhold and is easier than the Bad Step you did on Crinkle Crags.

Near the bottom of the gully, large boulders are being undermined by footpath erosion and it would be well to stay out from under these. Paths lead round either side of the tarn: go round to the right for the sake of the evening sun-sparkle on the water. The tarn also reflects the black damp crags of Pavey Ark to perfection. From the out-flow rebuilt paths, one on each side of the stream, run down to Dungeon Ghyll.

Early Mist On Ullswater

When people say Lake District they usually mean the fells and not the lakes at all. And that's a pity. Walk alongside Ullswater at dawn in October – or even drive alongside Ullswater at dawn in October. The lake's been asleep, and its dream-world is a place that's silent, grey and dripping. Bare twigs make abstract patterns against the mist; the lake's been dreaming of Japan. There's the smell of dead leaves in water – a smell that has nothing in it of decomposition, but is what bonfires would be if bonfires burned cold instead of hot.

There may be a single orange buoy, floating in its own scattered reflection. The buoy acts within the scene as a cool plastic sun, giving out not light and flame but just a set of circular ripples. Somewhere out of sight a bird splashes down, changes its mind and splashes up again. An early tractor buzzes in the distance.

And then a new set of ripples shakes the orange buoy and and splashes the lake-edge boulders. A new sound comes out of the mist, a sound like the creaking wings of geese – but it's the sound of oars, many great oars pulling in rhythm. Almost close enough to see, the men from the North are passing along their lake in their boat that's made of overlapping pine and pointed at both ends.

The Norsemen are the first of whom we can say with certainty: they looked on this lake with love. The Briton crouched in his hollow hut around the corner of Dovedale. The Briton stuffed moss into the holes of his house and tried to shut out the rain and the mountains together. The Briton suffered as we suffer in stormy campsites, whether our tents are big family models that leak and blow over, or tiny lightweights that deform into a banana-shaped living space nine inches high with wet trickles across the groundsheet.

But now it's Ulf himself, who wears leather and doesn't mind the rain trickling down inside it. Ulf would say, if you asked him, that what he really likes is killing people and taking away their stuff. But in fact what Ulf really likes is this lake. Why else would he be cruising down Ulf's Water while the mist gradually dampens him and the longboat around him?

Ulf is facing a lifestyle crisis. The Patterdale pillaging's just about used up. Ulf could move on – but the Lake District's getting terribly crowded these days: it's hard to find anywhere unspoilt left to pillage. Or he could knock out the high seat-posts from his fireside, the posts with the carvings of the useful god Thor, drop them into Ullswater and follow Thor ashore. Build a hall, hack out some growing-land: in short, become an inhabitant. Which means enslaving the natives, with all the fuss and bother that entails...

The oars fade into the distance; across the lake the post van changes gear as it takes the sudden slope to Howtown. And then, in the space of a dozen steps, we walk out of the mist and it's like the moment in Wizard of Oz when it switches from black-and-white to glorious Technicolour and we discover that Judy Garland's been wearing cherry-coloured lipstick. It's the Present Day, as depicted in a thousand picture postcards. The bracken's all Autumn orange, the sky's that pale October blue, and the damp slates of Glenridding are gleaming in the early sun.

And in another time altogether, Ulf looks at that acre of flat ground where the stream comes down off Gowbarrow, and starts to consider the currents and calculate where to drop the seat-posts to make sure they'll drift ashore just so....

Ullswater

2: The Lakes of Lakeland

A walk of lakesides, ferries and high passes

A lot of the time in the Lake District it's Winter, and even when it isn't Winter it's raining. You could walk up into the mist and stay there until teatime, and there's pleasure to be got from sheer survival, not to mention intricate compass work and managing to keep the map dry.

More easy to enjoy, though, is the achievement of a high pass. The gradually increasing discomfort; the crags briefly glimpsed through swirls in the cloud; the sudden buffetting of the wind as you reach the col itself; the immediate relief as you start to descend; the emergence from the cloud to discover a new valley altogether lying below and the wondering whether it's the new valley you intended it to be or somewhere else; and then at last the warmth and shelter of the trees. Then spend the afternoon along some lakeside, and let the wind be merely a romantic sound-effect in the branch-tops and the means of making the lake itself splash around among the stones.

This, then, is a walk of passes, woods and watersides. The nine main lakes are visited, in clockwise order, starting and finishing at Windermere with its useful railway station. We start by taking the chain ferry across Windermere, and in Summer, when the Lake Steamers are operating, we have the chance of further boating on Coniston Water, Derwent Water and Ullswater. This, sadly, is to miss their lakeside paths, but there is consolation along the shores of Wastwater, Ennerdale, Crummock, Thirlmere and Haweswater.

Why not Bassenthwaite? The reason is both physical and metaphysical. The metaphysical is that Bassenthwaite's the only lake - the rest being meres or waters - so that natural perversity will exclude it. The physical is that it has lakeside road not lakeside path, and no high pass to Keswick.

Six of the high passes are above two thousand feet. The toughest is Levers Hause: a place where no Victorian traveller would venture in case Coniston Old Man fell on his head.

The summer route, using all the ferries, covers 82 miles with 22,000 ft of ascent. It can be divided into seven days, of which the longest will be Ennerdale to Derwentwater (14 miles, 3700 ft) to catch the boat to Keswick. You won't need a tent, provided you can find a bed at Kentmere where, at the time of writing, there is but a single B&B. Even there, a short diversion to the foot of Haweswater may solve your problem.

Elsewhere, either on or close to the route, inns, hotels, camping barns and youth hostels are plentiful - and all fully booked. Booking ahead means sticking to a prearranged schedule, which is a shame because if the weather's nice or you're fitter than you thought you'd like to press ahead. Press ahead sideways, and take the high diversions over various mountaintops.

In Winter, the route lengthens to 95 miles and 24,000 ft because of the extra lakeside paths.

Coniston Steamer

1 Breaking the Ice: Windermere

I stood on the lakeshore of Windermere at 6:45 am of a February morning. It was not altogether silent; a duck or two were splashing around among the rushes. It was not altogether dark. Indeed, the light was strengthening rapidly, allowing me to see several metres of grey water and an awful lot of early morning mist. Tourist Information has said that the first ferry is at 6:50, and does Tourist Information lie?

At 6:49 a man got out of a car, put on a peaked cap and accepted my 30p. It seemed that there was to be a ferry. "She'll be a bit slow," he explained. "She has to lift the chains out of the ice as she comes across."

The ferry was a distant rumbling, transmitted along the chains into the jetty under our feet. Now that I listened, I could hear, too, the cracking of the ice.
"Not coming back today, are you? Today's when we take the chains out and change them." The crossing then was to be irreversible. So much the better, for I didn't plan to come back today. I planned to come back in three days time at dusk, from the opposite direction, having visited the eight main lakes of Lakeland.

On such windless dawns you say very little, stand very still and think big. I thought of nuclear-powered Russian icebeakers heading for Archangel. The Windermere car ferry was a rusty box with no cars on, with no passengers on except me, grinding backwards and forwards through the mist to find, every ten minutes, another grey shoreline at the end of its chain. I looked overboard and wondered about the ice.

The ice was worrying. Lakesides were fine, but between the lakesides I'd planned passes, and some of them were high ones. To save weight I carried no ice-axe. Well, there was no turning back; they were stopping the ferry and lifting out the chains.

The sun came up slow and mauve, to show frosted fields, frosted trees, and scraps of mist, and several little valleys. I went up and down the little valleys, mostly under the trees. Some of the trees were pine plantations, and some were lovely Lakes woodland with mossed rocks, fallen branches, leafmould and deer. I'd arrived in the dark and hadn't seen Windermere or anything else: but suddenly, across a clear-felled area, Coniston Old Man was peering in, all snow-covered and disapproving. What are you doing walking over all that brushwood? You should be walking all over me.

About noon I emerged onto a pleasing little hill called Top o' Selside. How well-equipped is the Lake District with pleasing little hills. Top o' Selside has rocky knolls, and cairns. Below is Coniston Water, all surrounded with trees of the deciduous sort, and Coniston Old Man poses obligingly just where he'll get the best reflection.

I dropped to Coniston Water, where a boat takes you all up the lake to the village at the other end. Unfortunately the next boat isn't due for another three months. I walked up the Cumbria Way and along the waterside.

Walk along the side of a Scottish loch and what do you get? You get bog, and long tussocky grass, and wet bits reaching deep inland. But walk the side of one of the eight main lakes, and you get a lakeside path. Each lake has its own way of doing the Lakeside Path. Coniston is simple gorse and woodland, with more gorse and woodland to look at on the other side. No sudden slopes drop into Coniston, and it folds itself between low hills, one on the left, one on the right, all the way to the haze that hangs over the southern sea.

Coniston the village is altogether different. Various places in England are referred to as 'little Switzerland' - Hebden Bridge, which is just plain silly, or Church Stretton, where at least the shapes are right even if they do have golf courses up them. Coniston really does feel Swiss. This isn't altogether a compliment. In Switzerland, places of breathtaking beauty derive their effect from being concealed behind and above a certain amount of ugliness. Swiss valleys have chalet-style development; so does Coniston. Swiss valleys have more vertical than you really want, and Coniston has the dark crags of Yewdale suggesting that there's going to be quite a bit of uphill plod before you get anywhere you want to be. Between the meadow with the dwarf azalias and the glacier intervenes the moraine, a hideous land of rubble; Coniston too has its less lovely bit before you get to the mountain; Coniston has the old mineworkings.

And like Mont Blanc out of Chamonix, but like no other English mountain out of no other English town, the Old Man rises straight out of the back of Coniston. You think there should be long tree trunk barriers to keep the avalanches out of the streets.

2: Climbing over Coniston

On a real mountain journey you're off to the next valley for a wife or a bit of pillage. Real mountain journeys take the passes, not the peaks; and so did the early sportsmen. There's something satisfying about a pass, being the easiest way through between difficulties.

Sport is when you have to make up rules, and rules are arbitrary, and from arbitrary to absurd is a short stumble and slip sideways. The English have never been afraid to pursue sport to the point of absurdity (hence cricket), and by the 1850's the search for the hardest easiest way had Whymper and Mummery setting themselves at some very peculiar passes indeed. (Notably the Col du Lion: "it was brought home to my mind, that no more difficult, circuitous and inconvenient method of getting from Zermatt to Breuil could possibly be devised.") The name of Levers Hause suggests that it has at least been conceived of as a possible pass between Coniston and Duddon.

It certainly isn't a sensible one. The col is at 685m (2300 ft) although the mountains on either side reach only 803m (2700 ft). The approach is challengingly steep and so is the descent. Both approach and descent involve a dark crag-hung tarn.

And then there was the snow. I was reasonably confident that the sun would have softened the snow enough for me to walk up it. Either that, or else some other perverse pass-bagger would have made steps that I could use. Then again, I could go up, take a few photos, and be repulsed. What is a journey without adversity?

The approach through the old mine workings is tremendous. Piles of loose stone, both natural and artificial, rise to crags and then to high snow. A stream leaps down, more than half waterfall. Beside it a path edges up steep, loose scree below a gloomy north-facing cliff. At the top is Levers Water, one of the less visited tarns. High above is sunlight on bright snowfields, but Levers Water is grey ice and black rock and deep shadows at midday.

A few footprints lead round it, and the pass at the back corner is a simple snowfield between crags. I move upwards, kicking big safe steps in case anyone should suggest I'm being unwise without my ice-axe. Towards the top things steepen, and the snow gets harder. This always happens towards the top. But, just as it's getting to the point where everything is quite as hard and steep as I'd like it to be, comes a burst of golden sunlight and the ridge.

Levers Water and Levers Hause

The ridge is wide and easy and covered in helpful footprints. Indeed, it's covered in helpful people who are happy to be foreground for my attempts to shoot Coniston Old Man against the light. I look down the descent slope which is steepish snow without footprints. I look along the ridge, which is gentle and wide and leads between wonderful views to a peak I've never been on. I decide on the high-level alternative and wander across Swirl How and Grey Friar. These mountaintops lack the Victorian gloom of the pass, being wide white ridges close up under the sky. That firm snow provides the most delightful of easy walking, and the most delightful of easy running down the long ridge of Troutal Fell.

Just as well. There's three more bits of hill to cross before bedtime, and just two hours of daylight. This doesn't add up, except that it's going to be a bright night with lots of moon. A zig-zag path presents itself for the final steep drop off the moors to Duddon.

There are two routes onward. There's an unexciting bridleway through a forest, or there's a peak called Harter Fell to conquer on wide paths. I've rejected both in favour

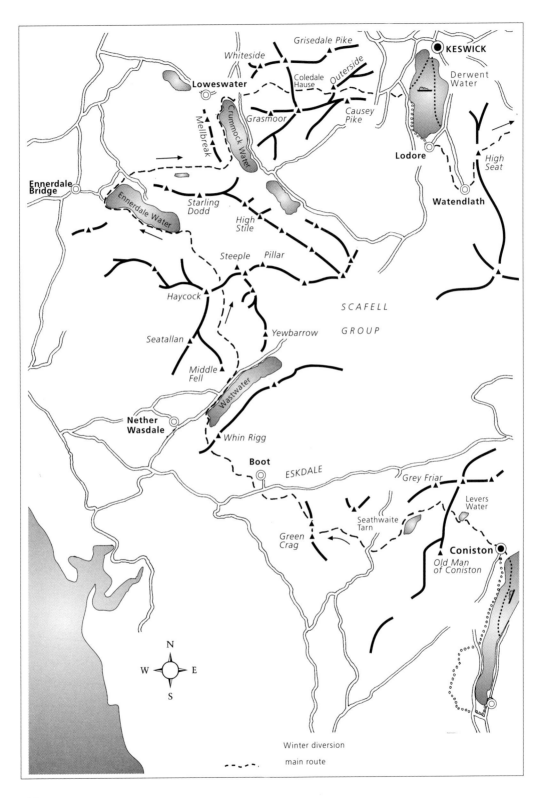

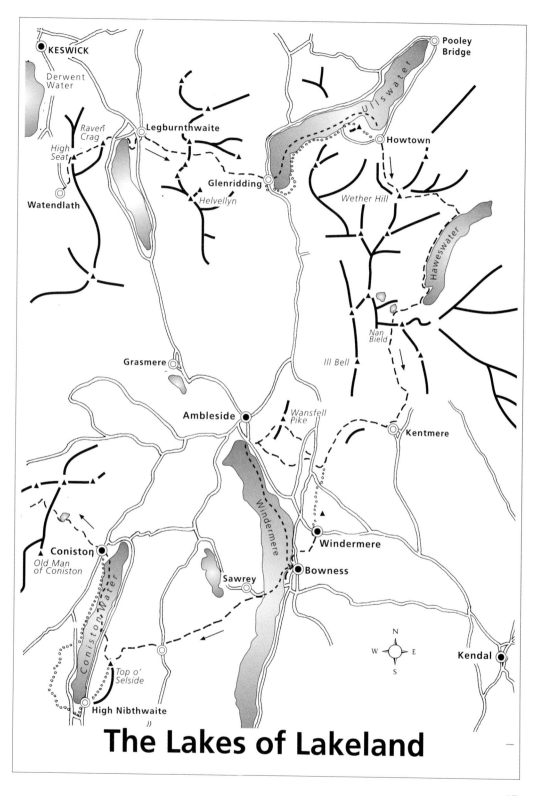

The Lakes of Lakeland

Grasmoor seen across the Buttermere valley

of two small summits to the south. When they'd finished the Central Fells they found two rocky tops left over: "no, we can't shove them into Langdale somewhere, we already squashed everything up to make room for Harrison Stickle." So they got dumped in this piece of waste ground south of Harter Fell and forgotten. Crook Crag is a black cone against the snowy Scafells, the snowy Scafells are pink and Green Crag is orange. It's a distinctly flashy sunset involving layers of multicoloured haze and disco-type reflections off Devoke Water and the distant sea.

I wander on dreamily through Eskdale and past a small dark tarn that's one of many Blea Waters. (Blea means 'blue': the Norsemen were a sturdy but unimaginative people when it came to names.) Miterdale offers quaking bog in the dark. Firm pebbles with only a few inches of water on top, the stream crossing is the driest part of Miterdale. And on Whin Rigg are narrow snowfields under the moon. Narrow snowfields are the best moonwalking there is. There's no peering at your feet or spoiling it all with torches when the ground's perfectly smooth and perfectly white. It's a quiet night and I'm enjoying the crunching of my own footfalls and the dream-feeling of having dropped into a black-and-white photo. Just how much I'm enjoying it I realise when the snow gives out half way down the Wastwater Screes and I have to stumble down the steep stony ground below.

Moonlight through bare branches is the waterside path of Wasdale: moonlight and silver water with the high intimidating face of the Screes above. Wasdale Hall is very grand across its dark lawns, but there's no-one there and I have to walk a mile and a half down the road to phone in and tell the folks at home I'm still alive so far. I unroll my bivvy bag onto deep and insulating leafmould.

3: Energetic in Ennerdale

Wastwater is wonderful; pass it in the dark before dawn to get the waterside road without traffic and Yewbarrow with no path visible. However, that is not the only invisible path. The bridleway along the Nether Beck is a fierce one to follow by starlight. Well warmed by the mile along the road, I could stop on a boulder and watch the light strengthening to grey. It was a dull day among interesting hills. Cloud was coming and

Opposite: The upper waterfall at Aira Force (daywalk 2);
Overleaf: From Scafell Pike: across the head of Eskdale to Bowfell – photo by John Gillham

going at summit level, but I'd go up onto Steeple anyway, and see if Scoat Tarn was as dramatic as Levers Water.

Scoat Tarn was a flat surface covered in snow, so not all that exciting, though the small window of visible view was Green Crag and Crook Crag looking like mountain-tops as they emerged from the morning mist. (Mountaintops they are, but standing on moorland rather than the usual mountain sides and mountain bottoms.) A sheltered snowslope rises easily onto Scoat Fell, and at the top there's a stone wall with a useful change of direction in it to indicate which way to turn for your summit.

Useful features end there. The small but tasty arete to Steeple was defended by steep hard snowslopes dropping into mist. Dropping into mist is fine for snowslopes but not for people without iceaxes, so I went back down the stone wall to the col. This is, after all, meant to be a route of paths and passes.

Path in fact is lacking on the descent into Ennerdale, and it was a rough half hour traversing heather until I found the forest trail at the bottom. Away from the Lakes a forest trail is a bit of a treat, getting you through the dreary trees with some to-and-fro over tree roots and the odd footbridge. Here it's a rare ordinary bit leading to the lake-side path along Ennerdale Water.

Step-kicking on the slopes of Coniston meant that I now had battered toes. I wandered along the lakeside path of Ennerdale wondering, as one tends to do on the morning of the second day, about the Point Of It All. Early alpinists have been an inspiration to me: my great-grandfather with his alpenstock, great-granny with her watercolour box. Their handbook was 'Peaks, Passes and Glaciers'. But here's me trying to leave out the peaks, and anyway where are the glaciers?

A primary school teacher and her class brought sudden enlightenment below Angler's Crag. Ennerdale Water is, in fact, nothing but an extinct glacier. Not even that: Ennerdale Water, and every other of the eight principal lakes, is a glacier in a dormant state. The glaciers retreated from the eastern slopes of Helvellyn even as early Egyptians were scratching marks on damp clay to work out if there was time for another rice crop before the flood. We're not at the end of the Ice Age, we're in a brief break at half-time. It's even possible that global warming may have the perverse consequence of bouncing us back into the deep freeze. Even as I walked, climatologists were tentatively ascribing the delightful snow cover I walked on to global warming.

It does make sense. Off Greenland, the icecap takes up fresh water and leaves the sea saltier than before. Salty water is heavier, so it sinks, and stays sunk to pass right round the bottom of the ocean to somewhere near California. This basic plughole effect powers most of the surface currents and if it stops happening so does the Gulf Stream. So Cumbria gets colder and the Lake District gets interesting winters.

I walked along the foot of the dormant glacier and took a wet bridleway past Floutern Tarn. Scale Force wasn't being very forceful, it was all that dry weather we'd been having (but tell that to the bogs around the head of Mosedale). Never mind. Grasmoor was appearing in front, rising out of the waters of the next of the dormant glaciers.

Crummock Water's path is not the nicest one: a boggy trod along the shore. What's delightful about Crummock Water is its hills. The best are by no means the biggest. Mellbreck is 512m, and a small thing called Rannerdale Knotts is just 355; but they're all you want in a mountain outline. And then you get them again upside down in the reflections. At the head of everything, Fleetwith Pike is actually a high corner of a moor but appears as a great rock lump with near-vertical sides. In all Lakeland, this is the place for shapes.

I phone my publisher to say I'm going a bit slow and this may take more than three days. He says never mind, it's such a lovely day. Is it, I say, and peer out of the phone box at the surrounding grey. There is indeed a patch of blue sky over Buttermere.

4: Diverted over Crag Hill

A writer called Jeremy Ashcroft suggests a route straight up the end of Grasmoor. I look up at this from the Liza Beck. Steep grass, then steep scree: in and out through some very scrappy-looking crags: and at the top a horrible rocky bit all covered in loose snow. I really will have to try this 'Grasmoor End Arete' some day. But for now there's the slot of Gasgale Gill leading deep into the hills: two thousand feet deep, and so narrow that the stream's taken all the bottom there is and the path has to go rock climbing along the side. The curve of the stream means it's a world of its own, with not even a view out the back, and the notch at the top end is very high and far away.

But eventually the bottom of the valley in its gradual ascent manages to reach the top, and that top is a sudden one of wide spaces and a view of Keswick and Skiddaw and Blencathra. It's a high perfect pass called Coledale Hause. So why do I spoil it all by wandering off sideways over Crag Hill?

Well, the sun's come out, the sky's gone blue all over, the snow is irresistible and I want to see over the top and say I've looked at the Pikes from both sides now. Behind, the sun sinks into yellow haze, and in front is a long ridge that's rather sharp. Not sharp in the sense that if you fell over you'd cut yourself on it, but sharp in the sense that if you fell over you'd go down a thousand feet or so rather quickly, and this on either the left-hand side or the right-hand side. A little cornice adds crispness and definition to the ridge as it swoops over Sail and Scar Crags, with the odd rocky twiddle to ornament the basic line. Excellent stuff, but slow going, very slow; there are so many photos to be taken.

Skiddaw glows in the sunset, and by the time I reach Derwentwater it's just preparing to get dark. Here's the Cumbria Way again, looking a bit tired after its long journey from Coniston through the middle of everything. It keeps trying to crawl away among the trees and go to sleep. But it's too early for that. The schedule says Thirlmere tonight, though it's not clear how I'm to manage down through Thirlmere's Christmas trees in the dark.

I reach the hotel at Lodore just in time for a nice bar supper.

The hotel at Lodore's the Borrowdale. It has three stars, it doesn't admit hillwalkers in boots and it doesn't do bar suppers. Beauty and cruelty unite in the young receptionist who intercepts me on the doorway and suggests I could try down the road. The road is dark with cars going up and down and a narrow stony pavement. Down the road is the Stakis Swiss Lodore. The Stakis Lodore has four stars, doesn't admit hillwalkers in boots and doesn't do bar suppers.

Never mind. There's still several Mars bars and a two-day-old sandwich. I climbed through moonlit woods below the grey precipice of Shepherd's Crag Borrowdale. The path dropped down the back and vanished, but I was drawn forward by a roaring noise

Thirlmere from Raven Crag. I was unprepared for the dawn view all the way up Thirlmere. From way up here, framed in dead larch, Thirlmere's almost pretty. I set the camera, wandered down into the fore-ground to find that Raven Crag is a huge precipice, starting just beside your right foot and dropping in a single swoop onto Thirlmere's dam.

among the trees. Everything's a bit confused hereabouts on my one-inch Tourist Map, so it was an unexpected treat to come suddenly upon the Lodore Falls as a great white patch between the trees, and that curiously brown smell you get when you drop leafy water suddenly from a height.

The path up to Watendlath's a good one under the moon, but I pass a large boulder and think that looks like a nice large boulder, and turn, and go back and shine my torch on it. And I find a patch of deep springy rushes under it, and enough of an overhang to keep off the frost. And really, I'm not going to get down through those Thirlmere trees in the dark, nor in the pre-dawn neither, and maybe it's not going to be three days after all but I know there's a nice wood at Mardale; and an extra night out won't do any harm with the sleeping bag not even damp yet; and really it'd be such fun to lie down now and go to sleep.

So that was what I did.

5: Shameful behaviour on Striding Edge

High Seat is not exciting. It sits in a wide wet moor and pretends, but unconvincingly. The way it pretends is by having real mountain for just the top ten feet. Photos are mostly taken on summits so why bother with the rest? The altitude of this hill is, pathetically, 1994 ft. I climbed it in the hope that higher would be drier.

At least the back side of it is downhill, and the forest plod beyond is short but has other virtues too: a glimpse of Saddleback in early slanting sun, and a sudden rock among the trees which turns out to be Raven Crag South Knoll. From here a bit of twigs-down-the-neck leads to Raven Crag proper. Twigs-down-the-neck is now an organised sport we call orienteering.

I read Wainwright afterwards; reading Wainwright beforehand spoils the fun. So I was unprepared for the dawn view all the way up Thirlmere. From way up here, framed in dead larch, Thirlmere's almost pretty. I set the camera, wandered down into the foreground, and found what else Wainwright would have told me. Raven Crag is a huge precipice, starting just beside your right foot and dropping in a single swoop onto Thirlmere's dam.

Looking through a hole in the boulders to miles of empty space: emerging from a forest to a sudden viewpoint: even riding up in the lift to emerge onto the roof of the Empire State Building – it doesn't feel quite right, but I like it. Everybody likes it, if we believe in the basic human instinct to grab another human's land. We love to survey much country while ourselves lying concealed, and according to this theory Raven Crag is the most gratifying viewpoint in the Lakes. Certainly it shows the long high ridge of Helvellyn, its snowfields backlit by the rising sun. Even the lowest pass across that ridge is going to be a high one.

Sticks Pass is a long plain plod up an ancient path, but at once arises the opportunity to embellish. Why be a person and go up a path when you can be a trout and go up a stream? Stanah Gill is not specially celebrated and starts with a slimy bit above a waterfall. But after that it's just clambering over rocks and deciding if it's really worth trying to keep your feet out of the water. If you really concentrate on placing yourself on the more inconvenient side of the stream it is possible to get some mild rock climbing. The main advantage, though, is that you have to look at your feet not the view: the view being anyway hidden by the grass banks of the gill. The secondary advantage is that you get to wash out your socks in complete privacy just 20yds from the path. ("A slow purification of the senses, a cleansing of the mind along with the socks;" Andrew Dempster on the approach march to the Mustagh Tower.) So when the gill does a final little waterfall and turns into an ordinary stream, you emerge to behold the slopes of Lower Man and Browncove Crag quite suddenly, with your first thousand feet already below you and pleasantly moss-scented socks dangling from the back of the sack.

Beholding the slopes is all very well, but on a still, golden morning those high snows will not be content with merely being looked at. It's clear that once again the pure line over the pass will have to be rejected in favour of some routine peak-bagging.

I catch up with a lady hillwalker and we strike an agreement to pose in each other's photos. The lady hillwalker has also been caught short without an ice-axe. The lady hillwalker has also been bewitched by the glamour of the snowfields, also plans to cross Helvellyn to Patterdale. This is unusual because most people who start from Thirlmere go back to Thirlmere. It's also unusual because both the ways down from Helvellyn to Patterdale are summer scrambles and not really sensible places to go without iceaxes.

People who walk over hilltops get tired, and often they get cold and wet as well. This may not seem terribly sensible, but hillwalkers are always ready to point to people less sensible than themselves: hillrunners, people who actually use their bivvy bags,

Striding Edge

people without ice-axes on Striding Edge. There are however some who, freely and with forethought, choose not to be terribly sensible. Still, it's always nice to know I'm not the only one.

The wander along the ridge to Helvellyn is just as nice as the Coniston one, just as nice as Crag Hill. It may be possible to get bored of high Lakeland ridges in the snow, but it'd take more than three days.

Swirral Edge has a snowslope at the top that's really rather steep, so we go and take a look at Striding.

Striding Edge is looking good. Indeed, Striding Edge is looking irresistible. The rocks of Striding Edge are warm and dry in the sun, and between the rocks lies crisp snow. The summer path is hidden beyond all hope of discovery. The various pinnacles stretch away into a piercingly blue sky and there isn't a breath of wind.

The start-off snowslope is slightly steep, with cliffs below it and Red Tarn below the cliffs. The lady hillwalker remarks that fingertips are of little use in arresting a slide on hard snow. "I know. I've left two of my fingernails on a mountain in Poland."

"That's terribly interesting; but perhaps you could tell me about it once we're off this ridge..."

Confidently stamped on, the steepish snow yields satisfactory steps. And below the snow are rocks that seem to consist entirely of handholds. We cross the first pinnacle and pause to regroup. "And look: here's two idiots coming up Striding Edge with no axes or crampons!"

Of course, I wouldn't make such a remark if I were in crampons myself. What do you take me for? We're reassured to see the upward idiots, as everything in front of us

53

they have already done. Equally, they're reassured to see us. So confidently had we stamped down the snowslope - facing outwards, naturally - that they'd assumed we were in crampons. How gratifying.

"Mind you, it wouldn't be much fun falling off here."

I agreed that getting killed isn't much fun. And then, how embarrassing when the Mountain Rescue find you without crampons on. He said he thought he could handle the embarrassment.

The trouble with the Lake District is that you can't commit your indiscretions in private. Young men in brightly coloured jackets and glittering crampons are working their way up-ridge one behind the other. "Are you going right along the ridge?"

I said that we were going to have a look at it.

"You'll fall off as like as not. See that chap over there? He's front-pointing, that's what he's doing."

Coming down off the next pinnacle was a steep bit between some rocks, and here the traffic had hardened the snow into something approaching ice. Coming down the steep bit, very slowly and tentatively, was a person in crampons. You come down steep hard snow backwards, and coming backwards you don't really know what your feet are getting into, and with a large drop underneath this isn't something you do while whistling 'Colonel Bogey' at the same time.

"And that's not the worst bit," he added. "Further along it gets very thin. Very thin indeed."

I have no intention of going forward over anything frightening. On the other hand, I have no intention of going back until I've actually arrived at something I have no mind to go forward over. Something I have no mind to go forward over is that steep bit of hard snow. Why bother, when just beside it is some sun-warmed rock which is extremely easy to climb up, specially when you're not wearing crampons?

We come to the thin bits. The thin bits aren't thin so much as narrow. It's just the same as walking along a frozen pavement. On a frozen pavement you do occasionally, through inattention, fall over. But a thousand-foot drop on each side does concentrate the attention wonderfully.

The photos show a sky of blue shading into ultraviolet, vigorously scribbled over with cirrus. I have to say that I didn't notice this effect at the time. There are no passing places on this highway, and we edge awkwardly round someone whose crampon has come loose.

The usual advice – and I'm not disagreeing with that usual advice – is that steep slopes and hard snow means crampons. I prefer to make up my own mind on the day: I had earlier turned back on Steeple. On Striding Edge I felt prepared to go on. Do we rope up for this scramble? Do I attempt this stormy mountain dressed as a fell-runner? Being prepared to stand or fall – particularly fall – by your own judgement, is part of the point of it all. The usual advice remains, of course, crampons.

The drops on either side become lower, so that one could almost contemplate falling down them. Two people without crampons come up the ridge and they aren't looking nervous at all: a sign that we're nearing the end of the difficulties. And then, in the space of a few yards, Striding transforms itself from wondrous arete to ordinary Lakeland ridge with rounded sides and a wall along the top. The lady hillwalker strikes off for Grisedale and that late bus through Dunmail Raise. I drop down onto Glenridding, looking for food, film, and the next lakeside path. Drifts of old snow and draining adrenaline give jubilant passage down a thousand feet of Birkhouse Moor. Then I hit earth and stones and suddenly remember about my sore feet.

6: Envy at Ullswater

Can you properly enjoy a sunset if your feet aren't sore?

Certainly after three days and nights of walking, even through busy urban Lakeland, you stop being a visitor and start being a part of it all. That hard chitinous exoskeleton you drive around in, that thing called car with its wind-up windows, its heater and its shiny painted exterior: you have to get out of it, and stay out of it for more than a day, before the land can press through to the skin. And if it does press more than you'd like on the underside of the foot, that's just the breaking down of the barrier so that you can flow down into the ground and the ground can flow up into you.

That's one way of putting it. The other way of putting it is that Spenco and Compeed are very effective, but only if they're applied early enough and the skin is properly clean and dry.

The mountains around Ullswater are mostly back over your shoulder, but this doesn't stop Ullswater's path from being the prettiest path of all. It's broad and walkable, and it goes up and down through small woods and behind knobs and across a slope of scree and hanging birch. And all the way it bends gradually round to the east, so that every headland gives new places to look at.

I veered up through a stony oakwood to see if I could get up Hallin Fell before the sun went down. I got onto the high shoulder of Hallin Fell as the sun sank in a glory of yellow beyond the head of the lake. Good; just in time. I took my photos of the sunset, relaxed, and wandered on to the summit.

I looked back, and realised that as far as the sunset was concerned I'd only caught the warmup. The glory of yellow had become a glory of deepest crimson, staining the clouds from the horizon right across Ullswater and overhead. It was one of those sunsets that makes you lower your voice and go all respectful, as in church.

Two other people were up on Hallin Fell photographing, respectfully, the sunset. One of them had a special sunset-exaggerator filter and let me take a photo through it. The result was striking, but not at all convincing. But then I took the filter away and the sunset was still rather hard to believe. Below us, Ullswater burned in the same sullen colours as the sky. A dark wedge across the clouds was the shadow of Grasmoor, thrown upwards from beyond the horizon.

Once it was all over we shook ourselves and blinked. Hallin Fell's a small but steep one where you hardly expect to meet people even at ordinary times of day.

Old Mardale church, now submerged by the enlarged Haweswater

Harter Fell and the head of Mardale

Its top is a grassy bowl and the photographer pointed out what a nice place it'd be for a bivvy. This I'd already noticed; but under clearing skies it was liable to be a very cold one. Besides, I was intending to walk through the night at least as far as Haweswater.

"Come off it," said the photographer's friend. "You've got a car at the bottom, like us."

"Return ticket from Windermere. Honest!"

But the photographer said "Gosh, I wish I was coming with you. Dammit, I've only got my sleeping bag." And he meant it too, I think.

"The force that through the green fuse drives the flower" says Dylan Thomas: and green Fusedale is where you feel that force. Even when it's dusk and all grey you can feel the greenness of Fusedale, so gentle after the stones of the Western Fells. The path is a kindly one even by moonlight, and moonlight leads me up onto a high flat lonely place of heather and snowfields.

The sizes of things change in the night, and the only way to measure them is to walk across them with a stopwatch. In mist you see nothing; in moonlight you see quite a lot but can't tell what any of it is. My mind hasn't caught up with my body and I'm still thinking that if I look out of the hills I'm going to see the sea. But I'm looking out east now, to Pennines faintly streaked with snow and streetlights along the line of the M6. I take my bearing along Low Kop and aim for the lights of Brough: the bright orange one in the middle must be to stop aeroplanes hitting the castle.

Haweswater gleams dully below. I descend beside waterfalls to the first tree. In order to break the long descent I stop and attempt a moonlight photo of it with a 30-second exposure. When I get up I discover that I'm already down; right beside the lakeside fence in fact, and must go back up to find the Coast-to-Coast path. Haweswater has various woods but I take the first one, which is of poplars and turns out to have uncomfortable roots rather than leafmould.

Weeping in Mardale

The path, marked along each edge by a neat row of upright slate slabs, veers left towards the Dun Bull Inn and the church. Lakeland churches do not strive for grandeur or decorative effect. In Lakeland landscape that kind of thing simply doesn't work. Mardale Church has a small square tower of slate lumps with the same rough texture as the surrounding barns, as the cliffs of Riggindale and Nan Bield. The church is so small, the churchyard yews so huge and old, that from the felltops you see only yews and no church at all.

A narrow stony road bends behind the yew trees, a road that's empty in the early light although a man and his dog have just gone round the corner and you can still hear him whistle.

Sit for a moment on the churchyard wall, and look up at the scar of the new road along the eastern fellside; the road built to be above the water level of the great Manchester reservoir. Feel the weight of earth and concrete as the dam rises across the valley five miles away. And on a quiet evening like this, when sunlight slants across the slate rooves and treetops, and glows along the ridge of High Street, walk away from Mardale and never look back. For who could bear to watch the water flow over the doorstep of the Dun Bull and rise slowly up the square tower of the church?

We know, we read in the papers, that there are too many people in the world; that year by year we're taking more and using it up. It's a simple mathematical calculation. But to see it with your own eyes just take up a book of old Lakeland photos. If it were just Mardale we could blame the greedy industrialists, the people of Manchester who insist on flushing good lake water down their toilets. But here's a corner of Langdale: a slate wall under a slate roof, a road with stones on and a dog asleep in the middle, a road whose vigorous angle nicely hides the next view but will hardly be acceptable to the age of the motor. Here's Wastwater, its little road unpaved and asking to be walked on. The familiar hillshapes are reflected in the water, except that there's something different about Yewbarrow. Yewbarrow's perfect cone, bracken-fiery between grey crag (except the photo's black-and-white), has the perfection of dream – because it lacks the scar of path down its front.

Does a simple trampled footpath matter so much? Yewbarrow is a very good-looking hill; but in 1929, Yewbarrow was perfect.

It's a mistake to look at those old photographs.

It's a mistake to look back to those days when, as landscape and as walking country, the Lake District was the music of Bach (and the paintings of Leonardo, the intoxicating rigours of Einstein's physics,) transposed into landscape for you to walk over. The days when you arrived slowly by coach, or even slower on foot; when paths were green and narrow; when every crag was a savage vertical desert that you crossed and still got back to Brackenclose in time for tea.

A hundred years ago the Lake District was perfect – and there to enjoy it were the Wordsworths, Samuel Coleridge and two hundred lucky shepherds. Today the lakes are very nice indeed – and enjoyed by millions. Very nice for millions must be better than perfection for the few. Still, it does no harm to look through those old photos. It can make you join the National Trust, pick up other people's litter, and make the effort to arrive by public transport.

Hope on Garburn

The Garburn Road is a river of stones between stone enclosures. Clearly the trail bikes met in the top of the pass have something to do with this.

And yet, experience tells me that next time I pass this way, or the time after, the footpath team will have been out and resurfaced the place with chunks of rock.

Lakeland has never been natural, not since charcoal-burning man removed the tree cover, and these rock-constructed roads are today's version of the copper-miner's pony track.

How safe is the Lakes? Is the National Trust trustworthy? Its Scottish sister, certainly, has learned in Glencoe some subtle truths. Closing off the land is bad: but so is its total opening up, for this destroys it. At Mar Lodge the Scottish Trust is showing itself open to the radical ideas of destruction for preservation: dynamiting footbridges, digging up tracks, resurfacing car parks with mud.

The next step for the Lakes must be the exclusion of the motor car. This must come, for tailbacks and traffic jams on the M6 are building up nicely towards the point where even the train can't be worse than the road.

Already it's being thought about: park-and-ride for Borrowdale, ticket-only entry to Kentmere.

Residents say they'll lose trade. But how much trade do you get from someone who leaves his litter in the bin and £2.40 in the pay-and-display? And what about the walkers? Well, if it's fun to do Scafell Pike from Seathwaite, then it must be twice as much fun from Keswick, no?

I'd start by closing off the Kirkstone. Who could object to park-and-ride when the ride's the lake steamer up Ullswater? This will make a day up Striding Edge something worth spending a night at Glenridding over. More money for the locals; more fun for the visitors; and a fine new footpath up the west side of the lake. It has to make sense.

And so by field footpaths to Orrest Head, where we stand at journey's end to look up and down the length of Windermere. There's a dusting of snow on the Old Man, and the Langdale Pikes beckon above the woods of the further shore. Behind, the Eastern Fells stretch green into the distance. Here stood Alfred Wainwright, and was inspired to write seven scratchy little books embracing every Lakeland fell. So what if he did it to escape his own domestic arrangements? He could have escaped into football hooliganism, or drugs, or golf; but he chose to escape to the Lakes.

Seats are provided on top of Orrest Head, and a great silence which is in no way broken by the squeaking of the small children who come up from Windermere to play. I got out my camera to find that the jiggling of a hundred miles had broken it.
Better, really. Why fiddle with machinery? Just stand, and this final scene will slide quietly along the optic nerve into the brain, and from there it will not easily be dislodged.

The children scampered down into the town, making the footsore backpacker feel somewhat slow.

The Route

1: Windermere to Coniston

Between Windermere and Coniston Water, the route wanders through woods and fields. Most of the woods are pleasant ones, with rocks, oak trees and deer. The rights-of-way are waymarked, but little used. Routefinding is fairly tricky and a compass bearing will often help in finding the stile in a distant hedge.

The 'Gondola', a wonderful steam vessel once inhabited by Captain Flint of *Swallows and Amazons,* will carry you across to Coniston Village. (See Chapter 9 for cruiser contact numbers.)

Start: Windermere Station

Turn left into the main road for Bowness. If you need a hillwalkers' shop, this street passes one on the way to Bowness. Otherwise, 400yds after the shops of Windermere town, a footpath on the right is 'Sherrif's Walk'. This drops through woods beside a stream. Cross a lane to the lakeside.

Levers Water

Turn left, into the centre of Bowness. Bear right past St Martin's Church to the jetties. These are the wrong jetties: do not board a lake cruiser! Turn right after the decorative ticket booths, on a lake side road, and onto a footpath 'private access: Cockshott Wood'. This leads round Cockshott Point, through a boatyard, to the small jetty of the car ferry.

⛴ WINDERMERE FERRY CROSSING ⛴

Walk the road round the first bend, then a footpath beside it up the hill ('Sawrey'). Return to the road briefly, to the brow of the hill, where a waymarked path leads off to the left. It descends by field edges to Sawrey Town End church.

Turn left along the lane past one of Cumbria's thousand Rose Cottages, and at once right on a signposted footpath south-west. Though waymarking is mostly good, here you must pass through an unwaymarked gate to find a waymarked stile immediately beyond. A track runs down through a wood of broadleaves, mud and rocks.

Turn left along the road below to a junction after a quarter-mile; directly opposite is a ladder stile 'High Dale Park'. The field footpath is unclear, but a compass bearing will find the ladder stile into the forest. A rough old stony track slants up right. A forest road at the top is crossed diagonally following waymark arrows. Descend through another nice deciduous wood.

At High Dale Park, the next signposted path starts to left of the buildings. This zigzags (to right initially, one less zig than on map) through leafmould and rocks. At the top it enters needletrees, crosses a forest road and is joined by a bridleway from the right. Descending, it reaches forest road at a tee-junction and continues straight ahead on needle-surfaced track to Satterthwaite.

Go straight across onto a track of decomposing tarmac. Once in the forest, turn left on forest road. Cross two old bridges below the road. Now the road bends right and climbs. At the brow of the hill, 10yds before a 'No Bikes' sign, turn right onto an old track of gouged wheelmarks. This track is only moderately delightful. It slants uphill, crosses a new forest road diagonally (GR 325923), and crosses a clear-felled area where the Coniston Fells look down disapprovingly on all this brushwood trampling. Beside some broken old stone walls the track almost disappears, but then recovers, firms up like an aged roué coming back for a second go, and crosses a forest road with two confidence-inspiring waymarks.

After another 300yds you emerge from the trees. Turn left along the forest edge, then bear away right for the summit of Top o' Selside. The walking is only moderately rough, on a hard-wearing heather mixture, to the rocky top. Here behold the Old Man and bits of his water. Here the Winter route turns left, to make its way round the foot of Coniston Water. The Summer route descends to Parkamoor pier for the lake steamer 'Gondola'.

Head down brackenny slopes west, beside a small stream, to a track running across the slope with views down to the lake. Follow this to the right, forking left onto a green track after half a mile. Just before the small white house of Low Parkamoor a permissive path turns down left beside a beck. It enters Dales Wood at a gate, and is marked with white waymarks. At the lakeside road turn left for a quarter of a mile to the jetty.

☛ CONISTON WATER ☚

Lake steamer to Coniston or

1A: (Winter Addition): Top o' Selside to Coniston

From the Top o' Selside descend south-west through bracken to a grass path (right-of-way on map) ambling nicely in a southward direction. It rises slightly to a col behind a rock knoll. Here leave it (if tired, stay on it though). Cross rough bracken and heather to the two cairns on the 228m spot-height above High Nibthwaite. This is an outstanding viewpoint: lots of Coniston Water, and the Old Man posing obligingly behind.

Descend steep grass eastwards to the edge of woods, where a good path (the one you never left if you were tired) descends to High Nibthwaite. Look up at Selside End, marvelling that timid Wainwright should have recommended the direct line of the skyline: a route half gorse and half vertical rock.

Turn left along the southward road. After 500yds, a signposted footpath on the right leads to the riverbank. Cross the bridge over the Crake into Water Yate. Cross the main A5084 onto a tiny tarred road.

At Greenholme Farm this becomes a green lane signposted 'Beacon Tarn'. It wanders around the side of the hill with a stone wall on its left, and diminishes to path. Just before a small stream the path branches; go straight ahead across the stream (not right). Follow the stream up to Beacon Tarn.

The route now follows the Cumbria Way to Coniston. (The Cumbria Way isn't waymarked.) The path leads through the col at the head of the tarn, to descend a little rocky valley. It wanders north-east across rough pasture to join a farm access track at a footpath signpost. Turn left, and after 50yds leave the track at a bridleway signpost (not at the third and final signpost, another footpath one). Work around the base of a knoll in tractor wheelmarks under power lines.

Behind the knoll a smaller power line appears out of the grass and strikes down a deeply-cut side valley. Follow this down northeast to a footbridge and the A5084.

Directly opposite is the footpath 'Coniston by Lakeside'. Follow this for two miles (don't leave the shore until after the stream crossing at GR 304959). Finally the path becomes a tarred track through a campsite. After the campsite pass along the front of Haws Bank Hall with its huge chimney stacks resembling World War One siege mortars. Coniston village is now in sight. Turn left after the hall and at once right onto a rough track. Where tracks branch go straight ahead by kiss and ladder to the road at the beginning of Coniston village.

2: Coniston to Eskdale

A high and demanding pass over the ridge of the Coniston Fells is followed by rough ground into Eskdale. This is the wildest part of the circuit.

Leave Coniston between the Bridge Cafe and the bridge. Just past the Sun Inn a track signed 'Levers Water' turns off to the right. After a green and sloping wood, turn right, across Church Beck. A rough track runs upstream and passes imposing slagheaps to the youth hostel. This is my preferred accommodation point at Coniston.

The track passes to left of the hostel (though the walker can also explore old mine buildings above the hostel and than contour leftwards). Fork right on a rough and ancient mine track to a wooden footbridge across the Levers Water Beck. The path ascends steep scree to left of the beck. With waterfalls on the right, crags above and the stony wastes behind, this is a bleak, imposing spot. Think Victorian and say 'dreadful'.

From the dam, a small path leads round to left of Levers Water. The path turns uphill, to ascend ever-steepening slopes between crags to Levers Hause. To use this high col between the Old Man and Swirl How is to make a romantic high crossing of the old fashioned sort. (If weather is clear, turn right at the ridge above for the high diversion over Swirl How.)

The direct descent onto Seathwaite Tarn is steep and relentless. Take a path that slants down northward (right) to gain slightly easier descent slopes. Pass along the northern side of the tarn to the dam, and cross this to a stony track. After 500yds the track bends left, and a single low waymark indicates the descending path. This goes down a small re-entrant to a gate, and follows a stream down to the flat fields alongside the Tarn Beck.

Turn left through a gate towards Troutal House, but after a few yards cross a footbridge on the right. A beckside path leads downstream, and to left of an abandoned building. Follow the bottom edge of a wood until a stile leads up into it. A path slants left through the wood, then emerges from the trees to bend right, west, through a low col below High Tongue, to the Dunnerdale road. Seathwaite, with its inn, is a mile down-valley. A few yards right, though, a bridleway sign points downhill. This leads to a river crossing marked 'stepping-stones'. The stepping stones are in fact stepping-boulders with a hawser to cling to as the current tries to sweep you away. (This crossing is not possible if the river is very full: footbridge at Seathwaite.)

A bridleway leads uphill through woods – not easy to see when covered with fallen leaves. The path carves its way through the odd rock, but ends up in forestry plantation to right of the stream.

A forest road arrives from the right; use the footbridge beside its ford to reach Grassguards. Above the farm, continue up to left of the stream. The path becomes

61

muddy, then swampy; trees are on both sides. Eventually a bridleway signpost points the path deeper into the trees, but here turn left up the stream to a ladder stile in 50yds out onto open moor.

The moor is at first no drier than the forest swamp. But ahead lies the arousing cone of Crook Crag, and to its left Green Crag. Green Crag is climbed first. It's a seriously rocky outcrop, a delightful thing to get your hands onto. Cross to Crook Crag and ascend it direct for a little pleasant scrambling.

Descend westwards over outcrops and heather. Aim for the slot to left of Kepple Crag. In the slot another forgotten pathway takes you down in well-graded zigzags into Eskdale. It was for peat sledges, originally.

Pass to left of Penny Hill Farm and onto its access road. Immediately before the bridge over the Esk, turn left on track to Low Birker. (But cross the bridge if you want the Woolpack Inn or the youth hostel). The rough track becomes a broad path that passes through sparse wood and scrub above the river. A bridleway sign points right, downhill to stepping stones (alternative footbridge 300yds earlier, GR178001). Cross to the small church.

Pass to right of the church and take a walled trackway on the left. Follow this to a lane and turn right to the road. Boot with its inn is a mile away on the right.

2A: High Diversion over Swirl How (extra 1 mile/ 700 ft)

The Old Man is a short stroll southwards; but to include the Old Man (or for that matter Wetherlam) on this crossing would be to deprive ourselves of Levers Water.

Having indulged in Levers Water, and the rigorous ascent to Levers Hause, turn right along the ridge and stroll to Swirl How. Behind, the ridge unfolds itself back to the Old Man like a musical phrase by Mozart. Look well, too, to the Scafells. By the end of this circuit, given seeing weather, you'll have looked at the Scafells from every direction there is.

Follow the crag tops round left to the perched cairn of Great Carrs, and turn west, downhill, for the continuing stroll to Grey Friar. The wide gravel ridges are the gentlest walking of the trip so far. Descend southwest, over Troutal Fell, on grass with rocky knolls. Delay joining the Troutal path until it's crossed its sidestream (340m contour). Boggy and indistinct in the flat upper valley, the path here becomes a distinct terraced zigzag as it drops the steep slopes to Troutal. The path descends to the highest building of the settlement at GR 236987. Cross above the building and slant down left, above the enclosed ground, to meet the Duddon Valley road. Follow it for a half-mile to the bridleway on the right for the stepping stones.

3: Eskdale to Wasdale

Miterdale is a deserted boggy place. It's worth entering simply for the sake of the leaving of it: the sudden arrival at the top of the Wastwater Screes promises rugged splendours ahead.

Walk west along the road to the bridge at Beckfoot Station. Cross the bridge, and turn right to cross the railway tracks to a public footpath sign 'Blea Tarn'. Cross a muddy field to find the path, which ascends in gentle zigzags up the harsh slope.

The path levels suddenly to pass along the foot of Blea Tarn and continue to the extended swamp of Siney Tarn, which it hits halfway along its southern side. Pass right of this tarn and proceed northwest to descend between two plantations. The right-of-way stays beside the left-hand plantation, but is not there in real life; following where it believes itself to be lands you in some exciting quaking bog where legs plop through the turf into liquid ooze below. It's a mystery how the stone wall stays afloat.

Steeple: the short but sharp arete from Scoat Fell

The stream crossing, on loose stones, is the driest part of Miterdale. Turn left along the bridleway track for a few yards, cross a stile, and turn right through a gate onto open fellside. Go up beside the plantation's boundary wall. This wall continues above the trees to guide you onto the ridge above. You thus reach it exactly at the head of Greathall Gill, which saves confusion in mist.

Walk 50yds up the ridge towards Whin Rig, around the gaping hole that is the head of the Greathall Gill. Now descend to the right of the gill on a small but steep path. It's a long way down and sore on the toetips.

At the bottom, cross the small and surprisingly tame little trickle that carved the huge gill. Walk down beside it to a track. Turn left here if you want Nether Wasdale: again my preferred accommodation is the youth hostel.

So turn right, and in a few yards left on a smaller track along the riverbank. Cross a fine stone bridge, and turn right on path signposted 'YHA'. This rambles through the wood, stumbling over the tree roots because it's looking up Wastwater instead of where it's going.

The front lawn of the youth hostel stretches down to the path. The hostel is slightly less grand than the one at Ilam in Derbyshire. In other words, it's very grand indeed, even if its morning sun is cut off by the big grey face of the Screes directly opposite.

4: Wasdale to Ennerdale

Are we just two miles from the busy central fells? The Nether Beck gives a high and remote crossing by way of a rocky valley with waterfalls. Remote means pathless: but high means that the going is reasonably comfortable. The high variant crosses Steeple, the sharpest summit in Lakeland.

The lakeside path runs past the youth hostel and after another quarter-mile takes you out of the wood and dumps you at the roadside. Now come a mile of road, which will be pleasant enough provided you get onto it before the hordes of hillwalkers vrooming their way to Wasdale Head. The road climbs slightly to a bridleway sign.

Wastwater Screes

Follow this along a rough path that climbs gradually to the Nether Beck, joining it just in time for some waterfalls and a bit of a gorge.

The small rough path runs along the quiet valley. The stream junction is marked by a rocky castle: Harvey's meticulous mapmaking has missed it, as its sides are too vertical to show on aerial survey - however they do mark the boulder decorating its summit! (GR 153102, 500m contour). Here the High Diversion turns off for Scoat Tarn.

Follow the main stream slightly west of north up rough grassy slopes to the col between Haycock and Scoat Fell. A cairn marks the col, and the descent slopes into Ennerdale are here, and only here, gentle and easy. Do not attempt to follow the line of the bridleway along the flank of Tewit How: thus you traverse steep heather half way up the side of Great Cove. Contour northwards until on the ridge above Tewit Tarn, and descend the left edge of this until you see trees below. Now drop into the vee-slot of the Deep Gill, to meet the stream where it enters the forest.

Go down the right bank, to where a stile leads to a woodland path above the gorge. At a Blue Trail waymark turn left to cross two footbridges. The path becomes a track leading downhill. A complicated set of gates opens onto open pasture at GR 131138.

Immediately turn left over ladder stile on path 'Lakeside'. This cuts a green swathe along next to the trees. It passes along the south side of Ennerdale Water, twisting among tree roots, sometimes terraced just inches above the surface of the lake.

Anglers' Crag plunges directly into the water: to fish from its top it's a long long line you'd need. The path traverses alarming screes that can be seen below, continuing below the surface of the green water. Then it takes to the very rocks in the most

Opposite: Striding Edge in winter; overleaf: Sunset over Ennerdale Water: from Pillar

exciting few steps of Wainwright's Coast-to-Coast. After Anglers' Crag all becomes tame and you are looking out into flatland. We'll need to take a sharp right hand turn before we get carried out of the Lake District altogether.

This we do at the corner of the Lake, crossing a green field between barbed wire to the bridge over the outflow. (The road ahead is the simplest way to reach Ennerdale Water if that is where you need to reach.)

4a: High Diversion over Steeple (extra 1.2 miles/600 ft)

On the map, Steeple is a little knob on the side of Scoat Fell. The map's got it back to front. Scoat Fell is a big knob on the side of Steeple.

Go up grassy slopes behind the castle knoll to Scoat Tarn. A stream runs up northward, giving comfortable and sheltered access to Scoat Fell. At the top, note the direction of the ridge-wall. If it runs slightly south of east, turn left. Slightly north of east, turn right. Just behind the wall's slight angle is the summit cairn.

Small cairns lead north. The ridge to Steeple isn't at all long. More significantly, it isn't at all wide. It's a narrow and exposed arete, and though rock climbing isn't required, in high wind you may prefer to crawl.

Steeple's north ridge is sharply defined, with drops on the right. When it becomes a broad grassy slope, take the left edge. 200ft (60m vertical) above the trees a path slants off to the left, crossing the Low Beck at the 400m contour. Now a path leads west along the top of the fence, to drop into an unplanted slit above the Woundell Beck. Keep next to the trees on the left, and enter them at a gate following 'Blue Trail' waymarks, to join the main low-level route.

5: Ennerdale to Crummock Water

The crossing to Crummock is a gentler one, passing a peaty tarn and a high waterfall.

From the outflow stream, continue around the foot of Ennerdale Water. The path becomes a track, with a gate at GR 097163. Go through the gate, and at once turn left across a muddy corner to a ladder stile. Follow the right-hand of two waymark arrows, up the field edge by a stream, recrossing the stream at a plank bridge and another waymarked stile. Turn uphill to exit onto the road to the left of a big green shed.

Turn right along the road for 100yds to a tee-junction. Directly opposite is the signposted bridleway 'Buttermere Loweswater Floutern Tarn'. It's a clear path that starts muddy between hedges and then climbs into the hill pass. The steep slopes of Great Borne, to right, are forbidden by various notices.

The path becomes less obvious as it starts to descend. Floutern Tarn is in a grassy hollow on the right and may not even be noticed. As the ground levels, keep to the right hand side of the pass to skirt the boggy headwaters of the Mosedale Beck. The beck runs away northwards, while we make a slight rise over a further col. As the new stream dips into a vee-slot, keep to its right, thus ending on the path that traverses to the footbridge at the bottom of the impressive Scales Force. Descend to cross two more footbridges but not the stile beyond, and go down the left bank of the stream to Crummock Water. Follow the lakeside footpath to the foot of the lake, where multiple

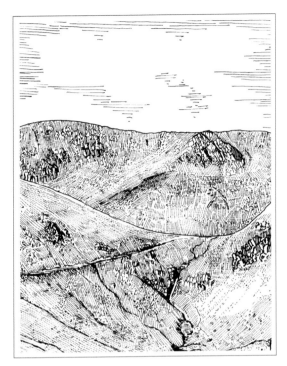

The miners' track in upper Coledale, with Eel Crags above

footbridges cross the River Cocker.

6: Crummock Water to Derwent-water (Hawes End)

On a long walk like this one, we get to find out how Lakeland fits together. Across Crummock, the place has new shapes. We have left the lumpy landscape of the central fells for the tall slopes of the Skiddaw Slate country. The mountains of the Grasmoor Group rise in steep straight lines to narrow ridges of grass and rock.

When we return to the knobbly scenery of the Borrowdale Volcanic, it will be in the gentler East. The very harshest parts of the journey are now behind us.

Cross the Cocker at the foot of Crummock Water to a forest track in Lanthwaite Wood. Cross this to go straight up through trees and turn right on a higher track. At a gate, it becomes green way across a field. At a tee-junction turn right, and bend round to left of Lanthwaite Green Farm to the road. A footpath sign points across rough grassland to the footbridge over Liza Beck at the entrance to Gasgale Gill.

This deep narrow slot is followed to its very top. The path fits itself in where it can, taking to rocks on the sidewall where necessary. The pass at the top is Coledale Hause: here turn right for the High Diversion over Crag Hill.

Otherwise descend ahead into the head of Coledale. The valley suddenly drops to a lower level, and the path finds itself contouring on the right wall. It turns downhill more steeply at a cairn. Here, look for a little-used green path, climbing to the right in zig-zags. It joins a much bigger path near the top of the slope. Turn left on this, to pass through the high col between Outside and the main ridge. The broad stony track leads down to the bridge at Stoneycroft.

Turn right to cross that bridge over its juniper bobbled gorge. The road down left leads into Stair. After the bridge, go straight across a four-way crossroad (phone box on the right). The road bends left through Skelgill Farm, and past the bottom of the very popular path up Catbells. Beyond this path foot the road forks: take the left, and after a few yards take a path ahead through trees. The track ahead is signposted to Hawes End jetty.

6a: High Diversion over Crag Hill (no extra distance/300 ft)

At Coledale Hause turn right (south). The direct ascent over Eel Crag is steep and stony: more gently, follow stream from Gasgale Gill southward through a high hollow to the Crag Hill/Grasmoor col. Gentle slopes on the left lead to the rounded dome of Crag Hill. Views south to the Central Fells are outstanding, specially late or early in the day.

The rounded dome conceals the ridge to Sail, and a compass bearing may be required. This ridge is a good one, steep on the left and very steep on the right with a narrow crest that's occasionally rocky. It swoops over Sail and Scar Crags, and continues to the five lumpy tops of Causey Pike. Beyond Causey Pike is the steep rocky descent that makes this hill into such an overbearing cone when seen from Newlands Valley. And see it from Newlands Valley you eventually will, turning left at the col before Rowing End for a descent path that drops those last thousand feet rather more suddenly than you'd like.

DERWENTWATER FERRY

Hawes End - Keswick, Keswick - Lodore

6b: Winter Extension from Hawes End to Lodore (2.4 miles/no extra ascent)

At cross-tracks before the jetty, turn right to pass below the Hawes End outdoor centre. After 100yds, a waymarked gate on the left opens onto a wide gravel path. This leads down to the lakeside and the Victoria Bay landing stage. The path continues along the lakeside to a final landing stage at Brandlehow Bay.

Here a clear track leads up right, away from the water; it is trying to tempt you away up the hillside for some unnecessary roadwalking. Instead, follow the shore round below the white house, to a track that enters woodland through a gate marked 'No Bikes'. Ignore a track to the left, but at a grey house bear left 'Public Footpath Lodore'. Work southwestwards through the open pinework, and at the second bay look out for a stile down on the very beach. Emerging from the wood, you find long plank walkways. If it were allowed, what fun here on a bike; the slightest wobble would dump you into the marsh so you'd have to do it very very fast. The plankways are so long and narrow that they've even been provided with passing places.

After the footbridge over the Derwent, turn right up the riverbank to the first stile. Then strike off diagonally across the field to a track that debouches onto the narrow Borrowdale road just north of the Borrowdale Hotel.

7: Lodore (Borrowdale) to Legburnthwaite (Thirlmere)

Watendlath snuggles into a fold of the hills. It has packhorse paths, swimming geese and little bridges. You can get to Watendlath by car - but how much nicer not to!

Fifty yards south of the Borrowdale Hotel, a path leads up to right of a B&B farmhouse. It is confused by climbers' trails going to and from the Shepherd's Crag which rises out of the oaks on the left. Go directly uphill, past a convenient seat to rest on. Down the far side, the way ahead is indicated by the racket of the upper Lodore Falls.

Having trembled at the ferocity of the falls, work southward through the woods upstream to emerge by the footbridge. Don't cross it, for from here a well-built path leads up the west bank to Watendlath. Enter Watendlath by a stone packhorse bridge

Ashness Bridge, Watendlath with Skiddaw behind

beside the tarn, and turn right towards the discreetly concealed car park. Bear left to avoid entering this depository of the horrid automobile and head uphill on a rebuilt path. At the top of the steep rise (400m contour), footpath signs point in various directions, but squelch off north-east. A fence along the crest of the moor runs north to High Seat.

The summit trig point is perched on a very slight rocky bit, useful foreground for the splendid mountains to be seen everywhere else. Apart from the views, the reason for taking in this dreary peak is simply that the top has to be slightly less wet than the sides.

Descend carefully westwards. You aim for the point where stream reaches forest at GR 298182: for here there is a high kissing gate through the deer fence. (There is also a ladder stile 300yds north where the track turns into the forest, but only reached by a clamber down and up through the stream.)

Turn left along the track. It enters the trees, with surprising views through the slot of Shoulthwaite Gill to Skiddaw. After 500yds the rocky south knob of Raven Crag appears above, and here a side track turns back right, uphill. This option is for orienteers, preferably with a better map than the 1:50,000. Others should stay on the main track to the track junction with the two brown signposts. Then they can drop sacks (but not cameras!) for a quick up-and-down to the summit.

The orienteers' side-track circles south of the South Knob (GR 302184) to end high on its further, eastern, side. From here you can work north through the open forest to the main, northern top of Raven Crag. This main top is a sudden emergence from the trees to the brink of a huge crag and a splendid view.

A well-laid path with steps descends north-west to reach the main track at two brown signposts: east for Castle Crag ("disappointing" says Wainwright) and west, downhill, for Thirlmere. The Thirlmere path descends steeply, crossing new forest road at two points and letting you look back up at the huge crag you could have fallen off the top of, and even perhaps retrieve your dropped camera.

At the road turn right and in 100yds left onto Thirlmere dam. The road bends left after the dam, and here is a permissive footpath on the right ('Swirl, Dalehead'). It runs through woods between Great How and the steep edge of the lake. The stretch of Thirlmere lakeside is nice, but short: after all, Thirlmere's only a reservoir.

The footpath bends round to the corner of open ground at GR314185. Here a broad path on the left is the out-and-back for the summit of Great How. At half-height branch right on a smaller path 'Great How summit'. You thought you went up Great How to look down, once more, on Thirlmere. Great How's rocky little top is deeply afforested and the current view is restricted to Raven Crag. Chainsaws may soon carve a wider outlook.

Return to the lower path, which becomes a track as it continues westwards. The obvious exit to Fisher Place is intimidated by a 'No Path' sign, so stay on the track until it reaches the main road just north of Legburnthwaite. A field path leads over to the lesser road beyond.

8: Thirlmere to Glenridding

Now the longest and highest ridge of them all lies across our path to Patterdale. The pass across it rises to 750m, but was still the one used by miners and their ponies to carry lead ore to the smelt mills around Keswick. How much lighter will be the mere rucksack, containing no rocks at all, to be lugged up from Legburnthwaite.

The descent is by a high and little-visited green valley – or else by the high and much-visited Striding Edge. The Edge deserves its popularity – but Green Side is good too in its gentler way, and certainly does not deserve its lack of popularity.

A short lane runs uphill just south of the youth hostel, leading to the stone stile at the beginning of the Sticks Pass path. After 200yds the path crosses the Stanah Gill on a small footbridge.

Here the path can be left to trudge its weary way up hill. The route up the stream bed is an easy scramble (Grade 1) by small waterfalls and pools where you can enjoy informal bathing in perfect privacy just yards from the busy path.

The first small waterfall must be bypassed by a greasy and rather exposed ledge on the right-hand side. Tree-roots and flying leafmould are the means of progress here. Don't be discouraged: the rest is not like this, being on clean boulders or grass unless you really want it not to be. These rocks hold no terrors, so if you do become uneasy it must be from poisonous snakes, angry anglers or inconsiderate gill-scramblers stopping to wash their socks. In which case you can simply walk away up the grassy slope on the right.

You gain about 600ft (200m vertical) by a boulder clamber and grassy walk. Finally a real waterfall of about 20ft appears. Go up the scree to the left, and back right onto dry rock beside the waterfall. The adventure is now over and you leave the stream-slot on the right to regain the Sticks Pass path above all its dreary steep stuff.

The path slants up right to the rounded col between Stybarrow Dodd and Raise. It's impossible to see Helvellyn from here without wanting to climb it, so in clear weather the High Diversion will now be turned to.

Otherwise descend eastwards beside Sticks Gill (East), keeping to the left hand side of the boggy upper valley on a small path. Directly below the huge holes of the Greenside quarry, the path turns right to cross the valley below extensive spoil heaps. A footbridge is downstream from all the heaped rubble, and the path slants away from the stream, south-east, to descend the steep zigzags of Stang End.

Turn right down the main track alongside the Glenridding Beck for three quarters of a mile. A path turns sharply back through a gate on the right, and leads to a foot-bridge. The small path joins a track descending from Helvellyn. A sign 'To Car Park'

Badger Stone, Kentmere, with the parish church in the distance

leads you into Glenridding along the beck's right bank, which is not through the car park at all but past the shops.

8a: High Diversion via Helvellyn and Striding Edge (extra 2.2 miles/1400 ft)

OK, so Helvellyn is Britain's most popular mountain and Striding Edge its most popular ascent - but rightly so. If you're tired of Striding Edge you're tired of Life: in which case, Striding Edge is as convenient a place as any from which to fling your weary carcass. (However, for the truly jaded, the alternative is the east ridge of Nethermost Pike and the Nethermost Beck. It's almost deserted and really rather pleasant.)

At Sticks Pass turn south and follow the broad path over Raise and White Side. Airy drops and bits of old cornice on the left embellish the steep ridge to Lower Man. Helvellyn's stone trig point is followed by its shelter cairn. Walk the rim to find the pointed memorial cairn at the top of Striding Edge. Or simply walk back along the stream of people coming up off it.

Descent will be a slow business unless you time your journey to avoid the upward crowds. The ridge is not equipped with passing-places. It's possible to do Striding Edge without touching rock, with an exposed gritty cop-out path (on the right-hand side, mostly). Even so, you'll have to walk the crest in places: just a few inches wide, with long lethal drops both ways. The rock, if you do decide to use it, is altogether satisfactory: firm and entirely composed of handholds. Snow on Striding Edge quickly gets trodden into ice, and in wind it's to be treated with respect.

Once past the interesting rocky bits, continue along the ridge to Birkhouse Moor. Descend beside a stone wall, ignoring the turn-off at Hole-in-the-Wall. At the wall corner on Birkhouse Moor a new path, marked by poles, leaves the wall to zig-zag down the face of the Nab into Little Cove. At the bottom turn right at the 'To Car Park' sign.

ULLSWATER LAKE STEAMER TO HOWTOWN

8b: Winter Addition from Glenridding to Howtown (4.8 miles/1500 ft)

You can sit in a plastic chair on a vibrating surface with a tepid drink in your hand and watch the scenery go by: or you can walk the Ullswater Lakeside Path. The plastic seat makes a nice change, but the Lakeside Path is a delight.

There's no need to walk the A592 to Patterdale as permissive paths are alongside it; first through the wood on the right and then on the Ullswater side of the road to

Patterdale. With the shops and hotels of Patterdale still ahead, turn left on the lane to Side Farm. Go through the farm and turn left onto the Lakeside path 'Sandwick, Howtown'. This rambles along through various woods, some pretty, some very pretty, and some quite ravishing. After crossing steepish slopes below Long Crag, the path skirts inland of some pasture and reaches tarred road at Sandwick.

Turn left for a few yards, then right on a broad path that soon enters Hallinhag Wood. Fifty yards into the wood is a gate through a stone wall. An ancient warning sign has lost all its paint and is being raised ever higher and swallowed up into its tree. Heed well its mysterious message, and then turn uphill. A stile leads out of the top corner of the wood. Ascend through bracken and outcrops onto Hallin Fell. Its top is a suspended grassy bowl where you may want to lie and linger.

The direct descent to Waternook is a very steep gully of grass and blocky scree. Your battered toenails may prefer the grass path southwards to St Peter's Church.

9: Howtown to Haweswater (Mardale Head)

Fusedale is green and peaceful. Here are not the rigours of the Western Fells but a gentle ascent up steep but rounded slopes, with a high moor at the top to stride over.

The road past the Howtown Hotel becomes a concrete track. A waymark points right; the right-of-way, not all that clear on the ground, climbs to right of the stream. At the end of the enclosed ground descend to recross the stream at a footbridge.

The path goes up Fusedale to left of the stream. It's an old path, laid for the hooves of Lakeland ponies but little-used in boots. It rises gradually above the stream, passes a ruined building, and crosses on a stone slab the top of Groove Gill.

Follow the path for another couple of hundred yards, then strike up grassy slopes for the northern summit of Wether Hill – GR 456167, 'White Bog' on Harvey's. It has a small cairn. A path leads south to the main top. Now work eastwards along the broad ridge to Low Kop: wheelmarks of a quad bike make passage pleasant.

Descend the south-east angle of Low Cop (the line marked as right-of-way is not helpful). Drop to Measand Beck and before it goes all waterfalls cross to its right bank. This is the line of the right-of-way and also gives views of the falls and lunch places. At Haweswater turn right onto Wainwright's Coast-to-Coast (Westbound).

The lakeside path is clearly marked and enjoyable, passing under crag at Benty Howe and rising to a low col between rock knolls below Birks Crag. The subsequent short descent is unpleasantly eroded, though. A handsome stone bridge crosses the Randale Beck, a plain wooden one the Riggindale. The next path is marked with little stone uprights on either side, but the way thus marked veers off towards the underwater village of Mardale. Cross the forested peninsular of the Rigg: here turns off a nice route up High Street (Daywalk 6). Work round the head of the bay to the path junction above the car park.

10: Haweswater to Windermere 11 miles 1800 ft

The eastern Lakes are, on the whole, less exciting. However, Nan Bield is an exception: it's a mountain pass of the old school, with a path winding up through the crags to a jagged notch on the skyline. Gentle Kentmere is the start of the end, and from the Garburn Road you see the mountains of Coniston once more before you.

At the signpost above the Mardale Head car park, follow 'Bridleway: Kentmere' not 'Public Footpath: Longsleddale'.

The rough path slants up the narrowing valley, to arrive suddenly at the foot of Small Water. This is a dark cold hole, and the upward path circles the tarn anticlockwise so you can peer into its chilly depths from various directions. The feeling of light and space is intense and sudden as you reach the wall-like cairn in the pass of Nan Bield. (If you don't have a wall-like cairn you're slightly too far west).

From here to Windermere the way is downhill - if not literally, at least in the metaphorical sense. To come are still some delights, as well as the discomforts of the Garburn Road, but nothing quite as excellent as this classic pass. If you've reached the pass without noticing Small Water at all, don't attribute this to the thickness of the mist. You're in the wrong pass, that's all, and about to descend into Longsleddale. Well, Longsleddale's quite nice; and you've only given yourself an extra two miles.

Steep eroded zigzags start you down the Kentmere side, but soon the path slants away gently and easily along the east side of the dale. It climbs a little to cross to the eastern side of a spur called the Tongue. At the bottom it becomes a stony track along the east side of the valley, crossed by many streams.

After a mile you come through an unmarked gate and can drop a few yards to a farm track running parallel. At Overend Farm is a choice of blue bridleway arrows; bear right onto a rough track between walls. After another three quarters of a mile you pass under power lines and see a large split boulder on a knoll on your right. Behind the boulder, turn right through an opening in the wall (right-of-way: no waymark) to a footbridge over the green water of the River Kent. Cross the corner of a field to a gap-stile in the stone wall and turn left along a track.

At the first house yellow footpath arrows point ahead and right: keep right. Just before the next house bear right again without benefit of any arrows. This, the Kentmere Bypass, takes you round above the small village. It emerges onto the road to Hartrigg Farm. The phone box is down opposite the church, 200yds further away than Harvey's map suggests.

Kentmere to Ambleside (Waterfoot)

Walk up the Hartrigg road to the open gate and the sign saying 'Hartrigg Farm and Please Close this Gate'. Turn left, and in 200yds right (signpost 'Troutbeck'). Take the broad stony Garburn Road up to the pass. The pass has fine views, but the downward road is nothing but a river of stones between confining walls.

The river of stones starts to show you Windermere as it descends below a wood of high pines and through a gate. Here it forks: take the lower branch, and in 400yds, at another wood, bear right, downhill. (Here the Winter variant, heading for Windermere town, keeps ahead.) The track passes above caravans – the site has a useful shop and cafe – and bends back right to reach the A592. Turn right for 200yds.

There is now a choice to be made between Nanny and Robin. The main route, by Nanny Lane, will cross Wansfell. For the tired, there's a lower way lacking the excellent view along Windermere that you get from Wansfell. From Robin Lane the Windermere view is merely very good. A minor road leads up left to Troutbeck Post Office: Robin Lane is the stony track continuing opposite. After a kilometre (three quarters of a mile) it bends right, uphill, and here a gate leads onto a path continuing at the same level. A tarred track leads into High Skelghyll, and a path beyond contours into Skelghyll Wood. At the Stencher Beck, turn downhill to the lakeside.

For the Nanny Lane route over Wansfell, continue up the A592 a little further, and turn left, just past the church, onto a bridleway. At the upper road, turn right for 150yds. A bridleway sign on the left indicates the start of the Nanny Lane. At the top of the enclosed ground is a stile on the left and a sign for Ambleside. The path leads gently up Wansfell Pike.

From the summit, ignore the large path westwards. Descend on a small path south-west, with a stone wall on the left. The path, with occasional waymarks, is small and grassy. It descends southwest, with views along the full length of Windermere. Go down to left of a downhill wall to a ladder stile at GR 386032. This lets you into the top of Skelghyll Wood.

Go down alongside the Stencher Beck to a complex path junction. The lower path, rightwards but descending, takes you down to the pier.

LAKE FERRY TO WINDERMERE

10A: Winter Diversion Kentmere to Windermere town - no extra miles, 300ft less ascent

Follow the Summer route over the Garburn Pass to the second track fork above Troutbeck. Here take the uphill fork, ahead. The track is now much pleasanter and leads gently out to road near Latrigg.

Turn right, downhill, and in 100yds a gate (doesn't open: stile on the right) is signed 'Public Footpath: Far Orrest'. Follow tractor wheelmarks around the hill to a track between walls. At Far Orrest, waymarks point around to left of the buildings and through a gate. Head southwest across fields, crossing two ladder stiles and then two stone stiles marked with faded white paint. Waymarks lead round to right of Near Orrest.

Turn right along the road for 200yds, and turn off left, through a gate, at a foot-path sign. Head uphill with a stone wall on your right until a stone stile lets you out onto the open top of Orrest Head. Here are seats and long slow views of Windermere.

Descend the broad path westwards into a wood of laurel. Go down just inside the wood to a white footpath arrow. The indicated path leads across to the opposite (southern) edge of the wood. Descend to a serpentine lane that lets you out on the streets of Windermere just 200yds from the railway station.

FACILITIES ROUNDUP

Miles	Km		
0	0	Windermere	All facilities
2	3	Bowness	All facilities

CHAIN FERRY TO SAWREY PIER

2	3	Sawrey Pier	Inn
7	11	Satterthwaite	Inn

LAKE STEAMER TO CONISTON

11	17	Coniston	Shops, accommodation
12	19	Coppermines	YHA
14	22	Troutal	
15	24	(Seathwaite)	Inn
21	34	(Boot)	Inns, YHA
25	40	Wasdale Hall	YHA
25	40	(Nether Wasdale)	Inns, phone
35	56	(Ennerdale Water)	Shops, accommodation
40	64	(Buttermere)	Cafe, hotel, camping barn
42	67	(Loweswater)	Inn, camping barn
43	68	Lanthwaite	phone
47	75	Stair	Phone, B&B, camping barn

FERRY TO KESWICK

48	77	Keswick	All facilities, climbing shops

FERRY KESWICK – LODORE

49	79	Lodore	Hotels, B&B
56	90	Thirlmere	YHA Legburnthwaite, phone
57	91	(Thirlspot)	Inn
61	97	Glenridding	shops, accommodation

ULLSWATER LAKE STEAMER TO HOWTOWN

62	99	Howtown	Inn
71	113	Mardale Head	Bus to Penrith
76	121	Kentmere	B&B, phone
77	123	Troutbeck	shop, cafe, inn
80	128	Ambleside	All facilities

LAKE STEAMER TO WINDERMERE

82	130	Windermere	All facilities

MAPs

All four Lakeland OS Outdoor Leisure Maps (ie Nos 4 to 7): make sure you get the new, double-sided version of sheet 6 if using the Winter route at Coniston. Alternatively, OS Landranger nos 89, 90, 96 and 97.

DISTANCE/CLIMB SUMMARY MILES/FEET

		High Route if Different	Winter no Ferries
1 Windermere To Coniston	10/1500		
Coniston Lakeside			6/500
2 Coniston To Eskdale	11/3200	12/3900	
3 Eskdale To Wasdale	4/1100		
4 Wasdale To Ennerdale	10/3200	12/3900	
5 Ennerdale To Crummock Water	8/1100		
6 Crummock To Derwent Water	7/2600	7/2900	
Derwentwater Side, To Lodore			2/00
7 Lodore To Thirlmere	7/1300		
8 Thirlmere To Glenridding	6/2000	8/3400	
Thirlmere Side, To Howtown			5/1500
9 Howtown To Mardale Head	9/2500		
10 Mardale Head To Ambleside	11/3500		
Mardale To Windermere			11/3200
Totals	82/22 000	87/26,000	95/24,000

DISTANCE/CLIMB SUMMARY KM/METRES

		High Route if Different	Winter no Ferries
1 Windermere To Coniston	16/500		
Coniston Lakeside			9/200
2 Coniston To Eskdale	17/1000	19/1200	
3 Eskdale To Wasdale	6/300		
4 Wasdale To Ennerdale	16/1000	19/1200	
5 Ennerdale To Crummock Water	12/400		
6 Crummock To Derwent Water	11/800	11/900	
Derwentwater Side, To Lodore			4/ 00
7 Lodore To Thirlmere	11/400		
8 Thirlmere To Glenridding	9/600	13/1000	
Thirlmere Side, To Howtown			8/400
9 Howtown To Mardale Head	14/800		
10 Mardale Head To Ambleside	17/1000		
Mardale To Windermere			17/900
Totals	130/6600	140/7600	150/7200

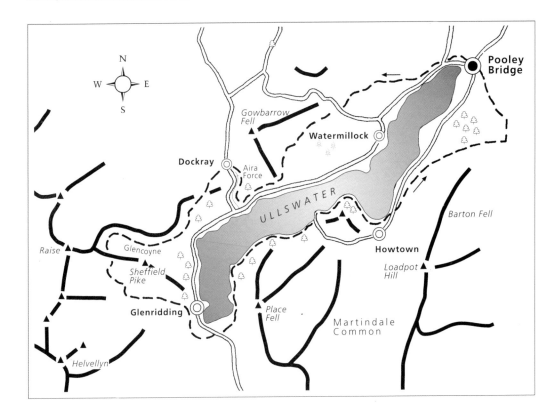

Which of the lakes of Lakeland is the loveliest? Such arguments tend to go on for ever. Let's just say that if you don't like Ullswater then maybe you should take up billiards; Lakeland is obviously not for you.

The path along the eastern shoreline is quite well-known. But just as good is the high traverse-line along the western side, curving away into Glencoyne before dropping like a loose rock into the back of Glenridding. Link them for a long, long circuit: or just go as far as Glenridding then take the lake steamer back to Pooley Bridge. (Steamer details in Chapter 10)

Start/Finish: Pooley Bridge
Distance/climb: 23 miles/3500 ft or 37m/1000m
Map: Outdoor Leisure 5 (NE) or OS Landranger 90

Leave Pooley Bridge by the bridge itself, which crosses the Eamont to a car park, and take a wooded footpath above the road. At the end of the wood, signs point both ways to Pooley Bridge. (And yes, our journey will eventually bring us back to Pooley Bridge: but not quite this quickly!) Continue on the path close to the road. Cross the A592 at its junction, to a field near a boat house (GR 462243). On a thorn tree is the first way-mark for the new Environmentally Sensitive Area Footpath (green arrows). The route slants back right to a fence end near Waterfoot Hotel Farm and back up left. It is marked as tracks on the OS Outdoor Leisure map, but is barely visible on the ground.

Hallin Fell and Howtown Pier seen across Ullswater

A stile leads into woodland at the 200m contour.

The path slants up through woods of ash, almost overwhelmed by foxgloves but otherwise clear. After a stile across a higher fence, the path slants back sharp right for 150yds, then back left again above the trees but still on the Ullswater flank of the hill. Small posts mark the way to a stile.

Head westwards along the fence at the top of a pine plantation. At the stile at the plantation's end, slant slightly right to join a tractor track above. This descends gently, curving round right, to meet a gravel track beside a restored field barn (GR 450242). The gravel track leads down left towards Bennethead, crossing Ramps Beck. At the farm sheds, turn off right, through a gate. A track, or the field edge on the left, leads up to road.

Take the road left through Bennethead. Fork left, and after 200yds take a kissing gate on the left (footpath sign). Two more kissing gates lead to a stream: do not take the stile on the left here, but work alongside the stream to a distant stile under two trees. Field edges and stiles lead to a gate at the corner of Crag Farm. Here go to left of a shed that's been built over the right-of-way, and through the farmyard. It is a vile place, with dismembered vehicles of many sorts, piles of tyres, ill-natured dogs on chains and heaps of mud and slurry.

You're passing below Little Mell Fell, which is a lump of geological concrete ('Mell Fell Conglomerate'). There's an obvious contrast with the small Priest Crag, which is

the authentic Lakeland lava. Turn right, up the road, for 100yds, and at GR432233 pick up a path encouragingly signposted 'Aira Force'.

A track, then a clear path lead below the wooded rocks of Priest's Crag and up right to a gate. Traverse round the head of Swinburn's Park. The valley has been smothered in spruce, but the path is in lovely broadleaf wood of mud and tree roots. These well-placed tree trunks hide the needle trees, and also Ullswater.

The wood was nice, but things get even better as you enter the NT land. The path climbs a little, and you're traversing a steep flank of Gowbarrow. The path passes below a small waterfall, and takes to a wooden bridge to avoid tumbling into the treetops below. Before the Yew Crag viewpoint it divides: take the lower one. There's a big cairn at the corner. Ullswater looks good from anywhere, but best of all from this cairn.

Slant down the flank of Gowbarrow to reach the edge of the wood at GR 403204. Here is a gate on the right, which is the line of the right-of-way, and a stile on the left. Cross the stile, and take the second path back right, half-way up the side of the gorge. It leads to the fanciful Victorian bridge below the Aira Force. Cross, stand, and admire: sweaty walkers will be pleasantly cooled by the spray that flies up out of the cauldron. Climb high steps to the western bank, but don't recross the upper bridge, which is only there to be part of photos from below. Instead, cross a wooden footbridge 400yds upstream, just below another waterfall. After a third fall you've rejoined the right of way, which leaves the woodland to make its way across open fields to Dockray. If looking at all that water's made you thirsty, here is the Royal Dockray Inn.

Cross the river to a short lane beside a phone box. Follow a rough track for 100yds, then head south-west beside a stream to pick up the path on the flank of Bracken How. This slants up, crossing the Pounder Sike, to join a stone wall for a mile. Where the path leaves the wall to strike across grassy moorland, it's marked by the occasional cairn. Once again, we're to be taken on a contouring trip across steep slopes that'd be nasty indeed without the path. This one, made presumably by miners on their way to work, circles the head of Glencoyne. If you're doing this flat walk because the day's too wet for the tops, you'll be impressed by Glencoyne. White water splashes down on every side; the path wades ankle-deep in froth. Wind lifts the ends of the waterfalls and whirls them round the curve of the glen end.

The path rounds a corner to the bottom of the two big quarry holes at Greenside. At the foot of the lower hole, turn downhill to meet the Sticks Pass path at a corner with a clump of six cairns. Cross the valley floor along a terrace of mine tailings. Dropping onto the top of the zigzags at Stang End, you remember Ullswater again, seeing the head of the lake all blue at the end of the cosy valley of Glenridding. The old track drops down a stony slope of junipers with the high triangle of Birkhouse Moor overhead. The place is somehow un-English, almost Corsican.

On joining the lower track at the former mine buildings, turn right to a footbridge. A path traverse along the south side of the valley: the lower branch, at the top of the stone walls, is the right-of-way. Gate and ladder stile on the left open onto an unsurfaced road. Follow it downhill for 200yds, past the house of Miresbeck. A footpath sign for Lanty Tarn points right, across a footbridge. The path turns uphill, and is waymarked through the field beyond.

It joins a bigger path that threads behind an upstanding boulder as it rises to Lanty's Tarn. 'Lanty' is a useful way to make your name sound friendlier if you have the misfortune, as the builder of this little reservoir had, of being called Lancelot. His tarn looks out from its little wood along the length of Ullswater. The wood isn't necessarily a sheltered one. The wind funnels down Grisedale, and stirs the waters of the tarn into a green leafmould soup.

Descend beside the outflow to join the westward track below. Go through the lower of two field gates and turn downhill to the bridge over the Grisedale Beck (GR 383157).

Turn left down the tarred lane beyond. The beck's below, rushing through deep woodland. It's a place to see red squirrels. At Home Farm turn right onto a footpath round the corner of a football pitch. It's waymarked with white-topped poles. Cross a wall and turn down to Patterdale.

Turn right, out of Patterdale, to the Rooking track end (no sign, 6'6" width limit). Cross the valley and go through gates onto the open fell, to turn left through quarry terraces.

Above Side Farm it's possible to drop to a lower track. This upper one is rougher, but has even better views, and is slightly more exciting in other ways. Water falls into a quarry hole, to emerge below the track: a chance for some dangerous caving exploit. A mile further on, the upper path goes through a tiny pass at the back of Silver Crag. It's a dramatic hollow, with more of the junipers that look so good against the grey. The upper track drops to join the lower and pass below Birk Fell. Wooded slopes drop steeply into Ullswater. While the views down and across Ullswater are good, the very best views are back over the left shoulder.

The path turns slightly inland, to pass above Scalehow Wood with a stone wall on the left. At Sandwick turn left down tarred road for 100yds. The path continues through a succession of wooden gates through the leafmould and oaks of Hallinhag Wood. Pass above Waternook, and look out for the gate and wooden steps down left to Howtown pier. (Again, you can now finish the walk by boat.)

Walk past the pier to the road and cross to a field gate with footpath sign. Cross the field, with white-topped posts for waymarks. Go up steps to right of a house to a gate ('no cycling' on the back). It opens onto a track above.

The track offers easy walking on firm grass along the top of the lakeside cultivation. A small stone bridge crosses the Swarthbeck below its fine gorge. At Auterstone the track slants uphill below the crags. A sign is for 'Moor Divock'. Below Long Crag, a tall cairn stands above the track (GR 461213). It's a place for a pause in the progress, for here is a fine final view back to the head of Ullswater.

The track passes along the top edge of the trees of Barton Park, and dips in and out of the little limestone gorge of Aik Beck. Continue forward on the same level: the track is many-rutted and muddy, and not distinct from other wheelmarks across the moor. It becomes clear again as it rounds the curve of the slope to the ford of the Elder Beck. Just beyond the beck is a fallen stone-circle set in short green grass: this is the 'Cockpit'.

The main track continues northwards, paddling through another branch of the Elder Beck. At a large cairn and four-way signpost, turn downhill on a stony track for Pooley Bridge. This becomes a tarred lane at the 200m contour.

Pooley Bridge has all the facilities for a slow enjoyable afternoon tea.

England's Eiger

England's finest mountain is Scafell – and when I say Scafell, I don't mean Scafell Pike.

Originally there was no such place as Scafell Pike. There was Scafell; and there were some odd bits stuck on the side. When it was discovered that the odd bits rose higher above the sea than the main mountain, they needed a name. Hence, Scafell Pikes.

That was Pikes, in the plural. But then the two lesser odd bits got names of their own by the simple process of looking for the nearest bit of writing on the map and assigning it to the whole hill – thus, Ill Crag and Broad Crag; and thus, by depletion, Scafell Pike. And it's useful, in its way. I say "I'm off up Scafell, best hill in the Lakes" and you think I'm actually talking about the lesser, higher one next door. So you go up and join the queue for the cairn on the Pike, and I get Lakeland's finest to myself.

Scafell is England's Eiger. Like the Eiger, it's not quite high enough. The Eiger is 30 metres too low to be an Alpine Fourthousander. Scafell is 41 feet too low to be Scafell Pike. The Eiger has one great grim North Face with a famous rock climb up the middle – and so does Scafell. The Eiger climb is well-known, with its Difficult Crack, its Hinterstoisser Traverse, its three ice-fields and its Death Bivouac. Almost as well known, among those of us without a hope of climbing the thing, is Central Buttress, with Jeffcoat's Ledge, the Cannon, and the Great Flake with its crucial chockstone. Here in the heroic thirties, the second man climbed up the crack and held onto the chockstone, and the first man climbed up the second man until he could just reach the crucial holds on the top of the flake. And let us not forget that the boot planted in the second man's hair was a tricouni-nailed one. The crucial chockstone has fallen out, but today's rock people keep climbing Central Buttress – indeed, they climb it in winter. Have they no sense of history and tradition?

Both Scafell and the Eiger have a walkers' way up through the middle of their great north faces. The Eiger's one is a tunnel, with an underground railway inside it. Odd it is to ride the thing, feeling like a commuter but dressed in shorts and a lurid tee-shirt, and dashing up the platform at Eigerwand Station to look through thick plate glass, down, down those horrible boilerplates, smooth and black, each one topped with a square foot of grey dirty ice.

Scafell's version, though self-propelled, is almost as surprising. A path, quite a wide and comfortable one, strikes out below the largest of the crags, above others only slightly smaller, and leads to a loose gully that's a horrible place to be but a wonderful place to see out from. Above, another path called the West Wall Traverse leads back above the tops of the large crags you just went under, to a place where everything except what you're actually standing on is pretty well vertical. Here you look down onto Mickledore. Almost, you think, you could leap out and slightly sideways, and land safely on Mickledore. Almost, you think, you'd like to. For on Mickledore they're wandering around in any direction that takes their fancy, telling each other about the weather and deciding not to have the mint cake now but save it for the summit.

Ah, but the summit they're saving it for is merely Scafell Pike. And the rock-faces that loom so large around you are doing so to guide you around to a second loose gully that rises like an escalator and lands you suddenly on the very summit plateau.

Half a mile away eastward, a hundred people are eating mintcake on a flat pile of rubble beside several large but shapeless cairns. Scafell proper is less promiscuous. Indeed, Scafell proper can be accused of playing hard to get. The Lord's Rake route I've just described. The route by Foxes Tarn is a gully scramble on well-jammed boulders to a bog hollow that crouches among vast screes like a frog in the corner of a dungeon. It's not such a difficult route; merely a complicated and roundabout one. And then there's Broad Stand...

Broad Stand, the logical direct line between Scafell and its Pike, is a rock-climb that's brief but beastly. It was descended in classic lost-climber style by Coleridge in 1802. Coleridge used the traditional method of hanging from one small cliff in order to drop to the next. His account of the adventure doesn't quite say "yes, I was being a bloody fool, you don't have to tell me," but you can tell that's what it's thinking.

But listen; being a Romantic Poet must count for something, surely? And where better to be a Romantic Poet than on the summit of Scafell.

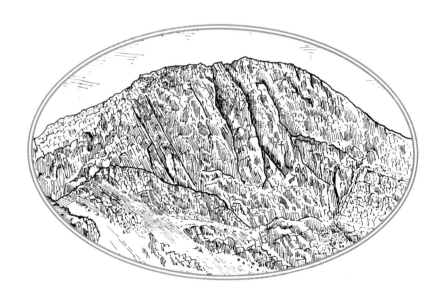

3: The Lakeland Threethousanders

An Introduction to the Art of Excess

Variation in moderation we approve. A bit of valley and a bit of ridge; a smooth place and a rocky place; and the path through the wood beside the little stream. But do we really want an exposed rock climb graded Moderate taken in descent? And do we really want 12 miles of road and pavement?

For the matter of that, do we really want 45 miles of anything at all, together with 12,000ft of ascent? Do we really want Skiddaw, Scafell, Scafell Pike, and Helvellyn, all in one walk?

David suggested that we did. David and I had been walking the Southern Upland Way for ten days and felt lean and fit enough to eat mountains, let alone walk them.

Skiddaw is easy, and Skiddaw isn't terribly exciting, so we start off by doing Skiddaw in the dark. We start off, actually, through the ruins of the station, surmounting crumbled walls with the help of some ironwork. David compares this passage with the famous *via ferrata* of the Dolomites: crag pathways above huge drops protected with metal cables. The excitement of the day ahead is already getting through...

At 3am the mind wanders into strange fields of dreams, but walking into a low-slung barbed wire soon brings us back to earth. (Recent earth movements have rendered this masonry section impractical. See route notes at the end of this chapter.)

The path starts off under trees, which is a bit spooky; but after passing a high car park it sets off up the open hill. Once our eyes have got used to the starlight and the beginnings of dawn it's like walking in extremely grey daylight, except for the solitude. On this cloudless midsummer night I expect to see other people undertaking this famous walk, but no. We have Skiddaw's stony summit and the surrounding yellow sunrise to ourselves.

The strengthening light allows a rapid descent to the valley, and that's the first bit over.

The roadwalk up Borrowdale ought to take the smiles off our faces but it doesn't. At 6 am in Borrowdale there's no traffic on the road but us, and for much of the way not even us as paths have been laid out behind the stone walls. For the first four miles there's Derwentwater to look at, and then the wooded slopes and precipices of this valley that keeps turning corners so you never have to see just how much Borrowdale still lies ahead.

Our sacks are light, we're feeling fit and walking fast; except when we're peering up through the branches trying to work out which bit's Troutdale Pinnacle where we once

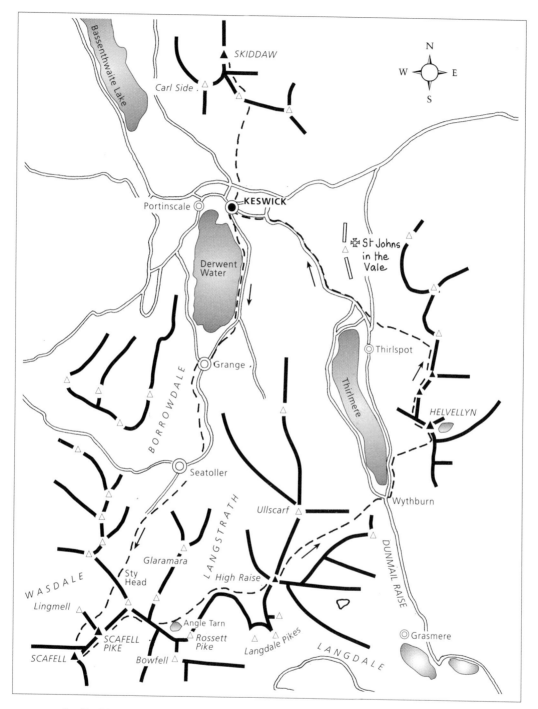

went rock climbing.

Still, the world is beginning to wake up, and a mile past Rosthwaite it's a relief to branch onto a path called Allerdale Ramble. Short grass and sprinkled grey rocks came just in time – we'd had to work quite hard to persuade ourselves we were enjoying that

Skiddaw summit to Grasmoor

seventh mile of road.

At 9 am the day's traffic is just unloading at Seathwaite. These people think they've made an early start – but we've already done Skiddaw and nine miles of Borrowdale. While they're still fiddling with their rucksacks we're off across the packhorse bridge, and we're the day's first humans at Styhead Tarn. We strip down to shorts and pose in front of the sparkling waters.

The Corridor Route rambles up the side of the Pikes, clambering in and out of streams and being altogether amusing. Lingmell's big and rocky, but it's only been put there to conceal Scafell, which is much bigger and much rockier.

"I expect we go up there," says David, pointing to a steep scree-fan coming out from among the crags.

The scree leads up into a gully where there's nothing to hold on to that isn't resting loosely on top of something else. I'm wondering if this is fun but David's scrambling ahead confidently so it must be. Anyway, I've got to stay close behind in case he knocks down a stone.

The gully leads onto a grassy ledge with a path. Above, below and in front is what has to be the famous Central Buttress of Scafell. Seen through gaps in the rocks, the arid stonescape of Mickledore is positively friendly by comparison. The path is comfortable, the surroundings are overpowering, but I'm wondering if there's going to be another horrid loose gully.

There is. And the steepest, loosest bit of all is the final few feet; while David on the plateau above has already started saying "Wasn't that great?" and "Blimey, look at that view."

At least he's not looking downwards to see me emerge, as good climbers don't, on hands and knees. I straighten up, wait for a gap in the word-flow, and start saying "Wasn't that great?" and "Blimey!" too. The nasty gully has spat us out onto the summit plateau itself, a brief flat stroll away from the cairn.

"I'm not going back down there," I say. "Let's do Broad Stand. It's all right; I've been on Broad Stand before."

We find our way down to towards Broad Stand, passing a preoccupied solo walker coming up. "You've done it," we tell him. "There isn't any hard stuff further up;" and he relaxes very noticeably. We peer down Broad Stand. It's all very well if you know there's a route, and the holds are scratched, and it's graded moderate, and you already came up it once when you were still a rock climber; but you can't help wondering about the poet Coleridge making the first descent, solo. Actually, a stiff dose of laudanum wouldn't go at all amiss, even if it is a known route and all that... not all that known, either. I descend the steep little wall and try to remember the lower difficulties, the bent slab, the chimney behind the block, the other bits.

There are no lower difficulties. We've already completed Broad Stand, and a jolly little scramble leads down onto the eroded airy crest of Mickledore. We stroll up to join the lunchtime crowds on Scafell Pike.

After Angle Tarn it's nicer, as we branch onto the smaller path across the head of Langstrath to Stake Pass. Suddenly, surprisingly, the friendly lumps of the Langdale Pikes pop up from behind some moor. I'd always thought of the Lakes as a whole lot of different places; today, though, we're going to be everywhere.

All talk about the sudden occurrence of Langdale stops abruptly as we hit the slope to High Raise. It's 300m of moderately steep grass, which is very very tough and very very high to climb. For a while the map didn't bother to name this unexciting hill, and the nearest writing to the summit was a sheepfold called High White Stones. Almost, the hill managed to grab for itself this much better name... what a shame.

The summit photos show an interesting deterioration: breathless on Scafell, somewhat jaded on the Pike, and definitely tired on High Raise. It's a fact, though, that you can feel exhausted uphill and still find walking in your legs when it flattens out at the top, and we go down the soft squashy grasses of Wyth Burn quite comfortably. We can't help remembering, though, that the next hill is twice as much climb as High Raise. This walk we're on must surely be the one that put the Hell into Helvellyn...

Putting one foot in front of the other and not thinking of anything in particular, we gradually get a small part of Helvellyn underneath us.

"Is this the right way for Helvellyn?"

The writer Harry Griffin was surprised to be asked this, on a perfectly clear day, on this wide and popular path up Britain's favourite mountain. It was the day when the Ramblers' Association organises a walk around this route of the four threethousanders. "Have you much experience of hillwalking?"

"Not really; this is my first time."

As he studied the man's unsuitable and scuffed footwear, his obvious exhaustion, the writer's disapproval started to give way to sympathy. "And how have you been finding it?"

The man smiled. "It's been the best day of my life."

Humbled, Harry pointed him the way up Helvellyn.

One or two people pass us coming down, and then we're again on an empty mountain. Clouds have been gathering for an afternoon shower, but can't quite make it work, achieving only a sulky haze. The ridges across the valley have retreated into what resembles an early and badly stained sunset, and Thirlmere gleams a nasty brownish colour. It's unattractive, but at least it's different: counting darkness, this is the fourth lighting effect we've had during the long day.

Without really knowing how we've done so, we reach the top of Helvellyn.

Stand up? We can barely sit. The summit photo shows us flat on the ground, propping our necks against the trig point. Behind us there's a rather pretty view – the sulky clouds have gone up to their bedrooms and slammed the door, a golden evening light drops gently over the eastern fells. We recover enough to eat our last sandwich and

Scafell Crag seen from Mickledore

start down the path to Thirlspot.

The path off Lower Man is cruelly steep and stony, but at least it's downhill. Gentler slopes lead to the white hotel at the bottom. Now it's all over – all over, apart from the five miles of road back to Keswick.

We never expected the final road section to be fun, and it isn't. Fortunately we're too exhausted to realise quite how nasty it is walking along the dirty verge with cars whizzing past our ears. There are milestones, letting you know just exactly how much more of this you've got to go through. I count paces: a thousand double stumbles and that's another milestone.

After a while there's a pavement. Then a bit of uphill, which makes it slightly better because it's all right to feel tired going uphill. And at the top of the hill there's Keswick all lit up, and the little side road that lets you get there half a mile sooner than the milestones. I look at my watch and a madness seizes me: if we arrive by nine we've done it in only eighteen hours! So I swerve out into the street and break into a shambling run, and so does David; which is most peculiar as we certainly are very tired indeed.

Actually there's a sensible reason for getting back to Keswick by nine: that's when they stop serving bar meals. But by the time we've done the celebration photos it's two minutes past and we're too late anyway.

Never mind. They're still serving beer and there's an excellent chippie.

Route Notes

Leave the Moot Hall through the covered passageway beside the Old Golden Lion Hotel, cross a car park diagonally, and enter Otley Road (24-hr car park on right). A lane on the left leads to a path on the right. A footbridge crosses the Greta river into Fitz Park. Cross diagonally left, then turn left along the far side of the park, beside the disused railway embankment. At the road, double back right under where the railway isn't, and in 100yds take the broad path signposted 'Skiddaw'. This crosses the dual carriageway and proceeds unmissably up SKIDDAW. Descend by the same route and pick up the rucksack you left in the car park.

Leave town on the Borrowdale road. Straight after the roundabout pick up the path on the right. This ambles through woods, looking out across Derwentwater. Towards the end of the lake, the road is recrossed to a path in woods above – this passes above the Lodore Hotel and under the Lodore Falls.

Road edges lead up Borrowdale, but can easily be avoided by crossing the double-arched bridge into Grange and turning left on the track to Hollows Farm camp site. Just past the campsite, a bridleway sign offers a right fork to Seatoller. This takes you behind Castle Crag to look back along Borrowdale for what is in Ruskin's opinion the third-best view in Europe. But the riverside route is also very pleasant, and flatter.

Cross Folly Bridge (251138) and the B5289 for the 'Allerdale Ramble' path to SEATHWAITE.

Take the huge path southwards, and turn right over the packhorse bridge to Sty Head Tarn and Styhead Pass. The Corridor Route, a lesser path, runs south up the flank of Scafell Pike. The start of it is a little down on the Wasdale side of the pass, and may be hard to find in mist.

Seatoller

Cross the col between Lingmell and the main mountain and continue south, losing at least 100m to pass below Pikes Crag to Hollow Stones. Hollow Stones is a momentary flattening in the path from Wasdale, marked by a 5m boulder. The scree fan would be the first one on the right if you'd come up this path from Wasdale Head.

It leads up into a narrow, loose, and very well-used gully (Lord's Rake). The only actual danger is that stones may be knocked down by parties above. At its top the gully passes to left of a pinnacle. Here a groove leads back left onto a stony ledge. This is the West Wall Traverse. At its end turn right up another narrow loose well-trodden gully, Deep Gill, which shoots you out onto the summit plateau of Scafell. Walk forward away from the cliffs for 200yds to the cairn.

Alternatively: from the top of the Lord's Rake gully continue in the same direction (ie with uphill on your left) past the pinnacle, then descending along the foot of crags and climbing a scree to emerge some 200ft down the west ridge of Scafell.

From SCAFELL SUMMIT descent is possible by same route, but BROAD STAND is quicker – the fact that it's a short but exposed rock climb graded 'Moderate' may be a bonus, or maybe not. If it's not, the FOXES TARN route is no longer than Lord's Rake, easier, and very attractive in its own right.

BROAD STAND: return to the top of the northern crag. You should be looking down Deep Gill (top of West Wall Traverse) with Scafell Pinnacle projecting into the void on your right. Turn right, and move away from the cliff edge for 30yds to the right-hand of two small cairns. (But such cairns tend to divide, multiply and even sometimes subtract spontaneously). Descend eastwards. The well trodden way is over scree and rock. A small gully appears below: the way goes down its left brink to a sloping rubble platform. The Rescue Box on Mickledore is now in sight, only 50ft below but some 50yds round left.

Move left to a sprawling cairn. Descend a short groove immediately below; here a rock-spike may bear a sling from someone else's abseil. This is the top of Broad Stand. A short wall leads down onto a sloping triangular ledge. The wall overhangs slightly. At its outer (right-hand) edge good holds lead down to the platform. Less exposed, but with less convincing holds, is the inner (left-hand) edge.

Descend the slab below, going round a corner to the left (if you've turned and are facing inwards, then the corner is on your right). A deep crack behind a block slants down to Mickledore.

FOXES TARN: to avoid the rock climb altogether, use this alternative descent. From the cairn, return NE for 150yds to a cairn where the path divides. Turn downhill, SE, on rebuilt path to the tiny 5m tarn GR 209064 (not on Landranger). Follow its outlet trickle for two minutes, then move 20yds left into the top of a boulder gully. (Very easy scrambling: not loose). At the bottom of the gully turn left up the foot of the crags to Mickledore.

Walk up the broad scree/boulder path to the huge crowded cairn of SCAFELL PIKE.

Follow the broad path east from Scafell Pike, to drop along the southern side of Great End. Here a useful stream crosses the path. At the path junction at Esk Hause turn downhill (NE), and at the shelter cairn below slightly right (SE) to Angle Tarn – the paths are wide and clear, but there are many enough of them to be thoroughly confusing in mist. Before starting the descent to Angle Tarn, check that you have enough daylight for the crossing of High Raise, as Wythburn is not amusing in the dark. If time is too short, a left turn at Esk Hause is a convenient escape back into Borrowdale.

Cross ANGLE TARN'S outlet and contour NE below the long low ridge of Rossett Pike to the tiny tarn in the Stake Pass. Continue east, crossing the top of the Stake Beck, then NE up grassy slopes to the stone trig point on High Raise.

Take the path north for a mile to the col, then turn right and go down the valley of the Wyth Burn to STEEL END at the head of Thirlmere. (The small path is to the right of the valley-bottom bogs.) Cross the main Dunmail Raise road onto a footpath that runs through the trees, just above the road, to Wythburn Church. Here is a useful phone box for a safety check-in call or even taxi summons. Given warm clothing, reserves of food and energy, and reasonable weather, Helvellyn's wide paths can be followed in the dark. It's a straight 2500-foot climb to the summit of HELVEL-LYN.

Striding Edge and St Sunday Crag

Rather than descending over Lower Man, stay on the ridge northwards over Whiteside and Raise to the Sticks Pass. Then descend directly to the crossroads at Legburnthwaite. This gives a few metres of extra climb, but a gentler descent and less road.

The ambitious can follow the Dodds ridge to its end, and include Blencathra by its clambery Halls Fell Ridge. All right – silly idea.

The first three miles of road, before the pavement starts, really are unpleasant. There's a slightly longer, but considerably nicer, alternative on paths by the church of St John's in the Vale (GR306225). But since it's dark by now, what's the difference? The quick way into Keswick is signposted 'Keswick, via Manor Brow'.s

Walk Facts

Distance:	45 miles
Ascent:	11 000 ft
Terrain:	Good paths and no serious navigational difficulties APART FROM THE CROSSING OF SCAFELL.
Maps:	OS Landranger 90 covers the route, but isn't really adequate across Scafell. Supplement with Harvey's Western Lakeland or OS Outdoor Leisure 6 (SW Lakes).
Event:	The Ramblers' Association organises a walk around the three-thousanders in mid-June. As well as a jolly day out, they offer refreshments at Seathwaite and Steel End.

Daywalk

During the introductory daywalk on Helm Crag I promised a daywalk of the rockiest mountain and wildest dale. Helm Crag is a fine walk for children. This is the version for grown-ups. I have praised Eskdale and Scafell at many points in this book: and offered a route of two days with difficult scrambles, and a 24-hour running version. Now, one of the first principles of writing books is that you shouldn't tease the readers. So here's a walk, without rock climbing and of a sensible length, to Eskdale and Scafell. Since we're right beside it, we may as well have Scafell Pike while we're at it.

Start/finish: Brotherilkeld, Eskdale GR 211011.
Distance/climb: 12 miles/3600ft (18km/1100m)
by way of: Scafell, Lord's Rake and Scafell Pike; Esk Pike; Ore Gap
Map: Outdoor Leisure 6 (SW Lakes) or Harveys Western Lakes

Lower Eskdale ends at the Brotherilkeld track end, the cattle grid and the warning notices about the Hardknott Pass. Two hundred yards south of the Brotherilkeld track is a small grass parking area (and there's another just above the cattle grid).

Follow the track to Brotherilkeld, and pass to left of the buildings onto a riverside path. This becomes a rough track through the fields, rising right to a ladder stile.

This mid-section of the valley runs as a deep hollow to the stream junction and packhorse bridge (Lingcove Bridge). Now a straightforward path crosses the bridge and runs up to right of the Esk river.

So why should we want to cross the river before the bridge, to go up to left of the

The Scafells and Mickledore from Bowfell

90

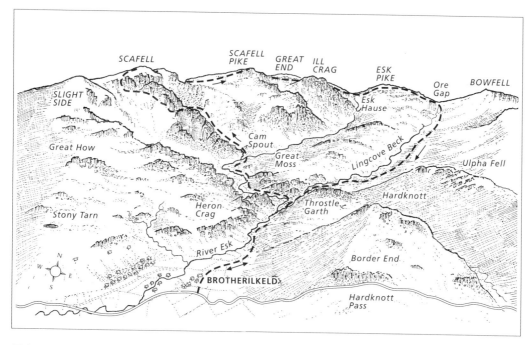

Esk River? There are, it is true, views into the gorge. However, the river crossing is difficult, even dangerous in spate: the path up the west side, under the cliffs, is narrow and crosses a steep slope: at one point it becomes an exposed rocky scramble that isn't technically difficult but does have one or two loose handholds.

For those not tempted across the river by the previous paragraph, the path up the east side shrugs its shoulders and crosses the packhorse bridge. It then keeps a little way to right of the river to avoid the gorge and the gorge views. At the top of the gorge the path and river bend left, in front of a low crag called Scar Lathing, and then right again into Upper Eskdale.

You will probably pause here to admire the magnificent mountain cirque. After you've appreciated the various crags, look at the first of them on the left, which is Cam Spout. Our route will go up beyond this, then slant back left to reach its topmost point.

Cross the river, and go up to the right of Cam Spout Crag on a path that clambers over bare rock beside the waterfalls of the How Beck. At the top of the falls the angle eases as you enter a secluded stream valley. Cross the stream, and go up slopes on the left, with the crags immediately to left. (This is some 300yds to left of the path optimistically marked on the Outdoor Leisure map.) The slope is grassy, with occasional rock-slabs of gentle angle to walk up or round. It culminates in a small knoll at the top of Cam Spout Crag.

A narrow spur of grass and rocks leads up onto the ridge of Scafell, which is reached at Long Green. Turn right, on an unfrequented ridge of scree and stone to Scafell's summit.

There are various ways from Scafell to its outlying Pike, and none of them is dull. The most straightforward is by Foxes Tarn, and was described in the main chapter. The second most spectacular is by Lord's Rake: a slanting fault-line, behind pinnacles and

91

Top: The Upper Esk Valley at Brotherilkeld with Bowfell dominating the head of the valley. Above: Esk Buttress fronting Scafell Pike (left) and Ill Crag (right)

down a loose bouldery gully, through the middle of Scafell Crag. (The West Wall Traverse is even more spectacular, but its gully is even looser and more bouldery, and slightly dodgy in descent.)

From Scafell's summit head north-east for 400yds, to the top of Scafell Crag. The deep hole of Moss Gill opens below, with Scafell Pinnacle on the right. Turn left, and go down alongside the crag for 100m vertical – about ten minutes. It is crucial to identify the point where Lord's Rake turns off into the crag. This point is immediately to right of a small rock-tower with a double top, and is marked by a cairn. The initial descent is of a fine scree, with a clear path running off to the right after the first short descent. If you don't see this path below, then you are about to descend at the wrong point.

The path ascends, to pass behind a pinnacle, and then drops and ascends again to the back of a second pinnacle. Behind this, it goes down a steep and loose gully. Great care must be taken not to knock down stones, though there is little that can be done to prevent others from knocking stones down onto you.

At the foot of the gully, screes descend towards Hollow Stones, but a path runs forward horizontally below the crags. Above is the very famous rock-climb of Central Buttress. The Flake Crack can be picked out; there may even be a brightly-coloured intrepid rock climber clinging to the face. In Lords Rake the water drips, the sun never shines, and anything you try to hang onto falls off. Lord's Rake seems a bit intimidating until you see the climber in his pink tights clinging to the Flake Crack of Central Buttress.

The path runs out onto the loose eroded scree, and the very nasty ascent to Mickledore just makes the narrow sunlit ridge of Mickledore into an even nicer place than it is anyway.

The serious part of the day is now over. Scafell Pike is a mere outlier, and broad popular paths lead on over the boulderfields of Ill Crag. The path drops across the flank of Great End to the complicated pass of Esk Hause. You look down into Eskdale, and then bear right (south-east) to climb Esk Pike. The path, though perfectly easy, weaves its way among the sunlit rocks and traverses to the right along a ledge.

After the following col of Ore Gap, one could continue over Bowfell and the Crinkle Crags. Bowfell and the Crinkles are fine mountains – but not quite so fine as Scafell – and anyway there's probably not enough daylight. While below on the right is a branch of Eskdale that's yet to be explored. So turn right at the pass, onto a small grassy path that soon has a stream beside it. The path stays beside this stream as it drops into Green Hole.

Lingcove is a peaceful place. Not many leave the mountains this way. They should, of course: but the Band into Langdale is more convenient, and so what if the sunset is turning the crags of Scafell all pink?

The path follows the stream all the way, descending beside waterfalls to rejoin the outward route at Throstle Garth. Remember that nice packhorse bridge? You crossed it this morning; but a lot seems to have happened since then: Scafell – the rockiest mountain; and Eskdale – the wildest valley. If I ever get sent to prison, this is the walk I'll be doing in my head every morning.

Long Days Of Summer

June the twenty-first. The Sun reaches the highest point in its year's itinerary, flops down behind the cairn, gets out its sandwiches and calls up its friends on its mobile. "I made it! I'm at the Apogee! What d'you mean, what's the weather like up here? I am the weather!"

The Solstice... doesn't it just bring out the druid in you? Doesn't it make you want to wander round the bottoms of some ancient rocks, peering into your sacred writings and mumbling "according to R Brian Evans there's a scrambling route up here somewhere?" Doesn't it make you put on your longest Goretex robe and walk round in solemn circles on some misty deserted moor? And at various special points on the Earth's surface, points where the Coast-to-Coast meets the Old Straight Track, special ceremonies take place. Visit Keswick's Moot Hall at midnight, at the time of the midsummer moon, and you'll see the votaries of the order of Bob Graham. Half-naked, trembling, they gather below the clock. Theirs is a ritual that brings new meaning to the phrase 'long days of Summer'. It leads them through the darkness of Skiddaw Forest to the knife blade at dawn. (Well, Halls Fell Ridge is pretty knife-like.) At Dunmail Raise they'll be anointed with the sacred embrocation and feed on the ambrosial banana. At high noon they'll cross the tops of Bowfell and Scafell Pike, and suffer the terrors of Broad Stand. At Wasdale head they'll bathe their feet, and torches will escort them in triumph down to Newlands.

Meanwhile, below Borrowdale's dark crags, dawn sees the sacrificial victims of the Three Peaks Attempt as they stumble down into the daylight with pebbles in their shoes. Not for them the crouching beneath the altar-stone in a foetal position; instead, they'll squeeze themselves into a minibus and attempt to remove their socks.

Long days of Summer don't necessarily have to be quite so long as that. Lie in the campsite till noon. Let the sun beat down and turn the inside of the tent into a delicious oven while you flick idly through this book. Save washing up the first saucepan of porridge by boiling up a second. Leave the socks on the guyrope until they really are dry; ease into your boots; and wander up onto Gable just as everyone else is going off to the pub.

Then stride along the heights while the warm earth breathes gently into the cooling air. Drop into Eskdale – Eskdale, which is full to the brim with golden slanting sunlight. Since there's nobody left to see, you can take a dip in the waterfall without benefit of bathing suit.

Climb back up onto the Crinkles, and that'll warm you up nicely after your swim. Time it right and you're there as the sun sinks into Mickledore, and Scafells stand blue and even bluer against a purple sky.

Saunter down the Band to Langdale, watching the stars appear even as the lights at Old Dungeon Ghyll go out. The bar is locked and silent, a few crisp wrappers blow slowly under the moon, but the bottle of wine you left under the flysheet is still nicely at room temperature. Avoid the druids by sleeping through to noon, and do it all again tomorrow.

This we could call the 'Slugabed Strategy'. But there's an opposite way. If you follow the adventures of Asterix the Gaul you'll know that there's one really useful thing about Druids. That's their Magic Potion, brewed from mistletoe, tealeaves and exotic herbs, plus a few dozen cloves of garlic. This allows you to run up steep hillsides, leap over precipices, and do the Corsican GR20 in three days.

Us Brits don't eat garlic, so we have to make do with the same tealeaves, brewed in chilly half-light, and a big swig of morning dew. Walk through fields covered in wet cobwebs and watch the mist rise off the lake. The roads are empty, the houses are silent, and even the cows are lying asleep in their fields.

From now till breakfast you can dream of ancient days when the Lake District hadn't been invented, Skiddaw was 4000 ft high and only shepherds, escaped convicts and the cast of 'Wuthering Heights' wandered the dangerous hilltops. And with 18 hours of daylight stretching ahead, anything you can think of you can do. (Well, maybe not the GR20 in three days...)

So sleep out the shortest night on Steeple. Start on Skiddaw and follow the sun clockwise round Derwentwater. Develop the Druid in you. Let out some midsummer madness. Go a little bit over the top - or even over several tops.

This year, do the Solistice in style.

4: Bob Graham Round 1992

O ne dark night in 1932, a man wearing rubber gym shoes and a pyjama jacket left the Moot Hall at Keswick on the way to 42 Lake District fells. "We thought it great fun," he reported afterwards; and added: "any reasonably fit man can do it."

At the beginning of this century, to run 26 miles and 300yds along a road was almost impossible. Only the toughest and most gifted athletes even attempted it, and they tended to collapse before they got to the end. Women weren't allowed to try at all. This year 25,000 people will start the London Marathon and most of them will finish it.

The Marathon is no longer a superhuman feat, but the Marathon still matters. For an ordinary day-to-day jogger, the Marathon is a big dream, but not unreasonably big. It's hard – it's very hard – but if you really want to do it, you will. For the fellrunner, or for the vigorous fellwalker, the big dream is Bob Graham's round.

The distance, measured on the map with a piece of string, is 61 miles or a nice even hundred kilometres. The total ascent is 27,000ft or 8000m: the height of Annapurna from sea level. The time limit is 24 hours. By 1970, a total of five had done the thing. In 1992, however, over a hundred attempted the round. About 50 of them were to succeed. My friend Glyn and I thought we'd give it a go.

The Round comes in five sections. At the road crossing points between the sections the runner receives encouragement, sugary drinks and fresh food supplies from friends in cars. We decided to start at 1:00am and go clockwise. We'd do the first, Skiddaw, section carrying our own supplies. For the second, Helvellyn, section we were to have a single support runner. Thereafter we'd have two support runners, allowing the party to separate, if appropriate, into slow and even more slow sections.

By normal standards, we were low on support: three runners and my cousin Oliver in a car. Last minute nervousness recruited an extra support runner. Gordon had kept our weekend free to support someone else on the Round, but they hadn't explored the route or gathered enough supporters. We had the knowledge; we had the help; we invited Gordon's Someone Else to come along, get to know the run, see how far he could get.

Section 1
Skiddaw, Great Calva, Blencathra

There's only one full moon Saturday in June, and we aren't the only ones to think that Skiddaw in the dark is the clever way to start. A dozen runners are standing around

96

Opposite: Helvellyn's other ridge: Swirral Edge (chapter 8)
Overleaf: Loft Crag and Gimmer from Pike of Stickle – photo by John Gillham

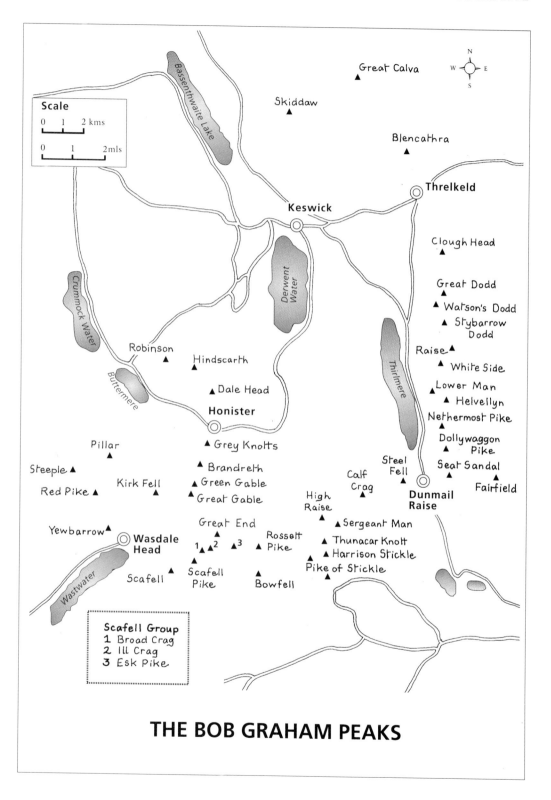

Scale

0   1   2 kms

0   1   2 mls

Great Calva ▲

Skiddaw ▲

Blencathra ▲

N
W ✦ E
S

Threlkeld ◎

Keswick ◎

Clough Head ▲

Great Dodd ▲

▲ Watson's Dodd

▲ Stybarrow Dodd

Raise ▲

▲ White Side

Lower Man ▲

▲ Helvellyn

Nethermost Pike ▲

Dollywaggon Pike ▲

Robinson ▲

Hindscarth ▲

▲ Dale Head

Honister ◎

Pillar ▲

▲ Grey Knotts

Steel Fell ▲

Seat Sandal ▲

Fairfield ▲

Steeple ▲

Red Pike ▲

Kirk Fell ▲

▲ Brandreth

▲ Green Gable

▲ Great Gable

High Raise ▲

Calf Crag ▲

Dunmail Raise ◎

Yewbarrow ▲

Wasdale Head ◎

Great End ▲

1 ▲▲ 2   ▲ 3

Rossett Pike ▲

▲ Sergeant Man

▲ Thunacar Knott

▲ Harrison Stickle

Pike of Stickle ▲

Scafell ▲

Scafell Pike ▲

Bowfell ▲

Scafell Group
1 Broad Crag
2 Ill Crag
3 Esk Pike

THE BOB GRAHAM PEAKS

shivering under the clock tower. It's the Bob Graham machine of Ambleside. Like most athletic clubs in northern England, Ambleside have a team of guides, porters, cooks, sherpas and liaison officers; Ambleside are mounting a Himalayan-style assault on the Bob Graham. And why not – it is an 8000-metre peak, after all.

Glyn and I pop down the road to avail ourselves of the Convenience. The place is open, but unlit: a considerable Inconvenience to the Public, but not to us who are wearing head torches. We return to find Alan alone and bewildered. "The clock struck one and they all ran away!"

We follow them, diving into a covered alley beside a pub and orienteering furiously across Fitz Park. Once on the open hill, we slow down. Not running any of the uphill bits is sensible discipline, if you want to get all the way round this Round.

The lights of Keswick twinkle merrily below us, with pale moonlight on the path, and on Derwentwater if we care to take two seconds to glance back. We don't. An hour and thirty-two minutes to the top of Skiddaw. Four minutes behind schedule: that'll do nicely. Going too fast to start with is a good way to fail on the Bob Graham.

Other good ways to fail are getting lost, getting too hot, not eating enough, not drinking enough and getting severe damage in the knees.

The radio masts at Aspatria form a gay pattern of lights; across the dark Solway I can see my local race-hill, Criffel. No time for that. On with the torches, and down into the heathery Back o' Skiddaw. Below us, the lights of the Ambleside party are spread "like an airport runway," says Alan. Moonlight is better than mist, and we find the best line across the valley bottom, the line that we never quite hit off on our two wet-weather reconnaissance trips.

In front, Ambleside choose a less good line and trample unnecessary heather. Poor things: they're not used to heather, these English runners.

Grey dawn seeps down the rough sides of Calva. We reach the top having got back two of the lost minutes. This is pleasing. We've got through our first night section without real loss, which confirms our idea that steep uphill and heather are the stuff to do in the dark. Blencathra's next, with the sun really almost up now, and that sudden view of all Lakeland as you come over the top. Most of that view, we're now intending to run around on.

We switch the torches back on as a signal to someone called Keith, who we hope may be lurking below. Descending the rocky crest of Hall's Fell with the rock dry – what a treat. I get carried away, leap from rock to rock, slither down the path, and overtake some Ambleside runners. It only means I have to wait for the others at the bottom.

And at the bottom: "are you Keith Wilson? Are you Keith Wilson?"

"Ronald and Glyn!" Yes, the seventh parked car is Keith Wilson; and he has small tins of pork and beans, opened on the tarmac, together with Ambrosia custard in the tub.

We met Keith back in February, Back o' Skiddaw. It was the day we saw the Brocken spectre on Blencathra and the helicopter lifted a body from below Sharp Edge. There were two ice climbers looking for ice in the Whitewater Dash:

"Off up Calva? Sounds like a Bob Graham recce. When's your attempt? I'll come and support you if you like."

And here, a dozen letters and phone calls and four months later, is Keith: driven from Cleveland to meet us at dawn for a run over Helvellyn and points beyond. And even more altruistic, here's his friend Tim with a twisted ankle who's come anyway to

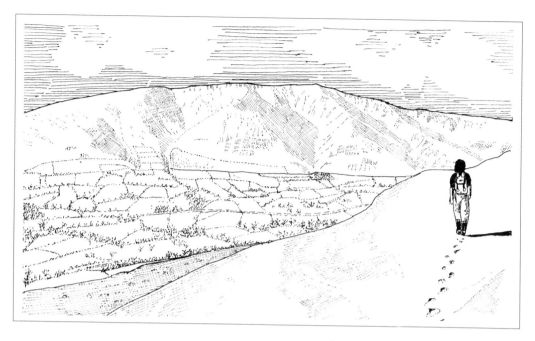

Snow-covered Blencathra from Clough Head

drive the car and open tubs of custard.

Threlkeld: arrive 0436 (schedule 0448)
Threlkeld dept 0453 (schedule 0503)

Section 2
Clough Head, Great Dodd, Watson's Dodd, Stybarrow Dodd, Raise, Whiteside, Lower Man, Helvellyn, Nethermost Pike, Dollywaggon Pike, Fairfield, Seat Sandal

So off we go up Clough Head with the sun rising. Clear air, a lot of Lake District to look at, and breaking into a run as the slope eases: this Bob Graham thing is supposed to be the challenge of a lifetime, they never said we'd actually be having fun...

Great Dodd, Watson's Dodd, Stybarrow Dodd: up here it's just one Dodd thing after another. And, as we reach the top of each, Ambleside are just leaving the one in front.

"Take no notice of them," says wise Keith. "If anything you're going a shade too fast. Here, have a Tracker bar." And another Tracker bar. And a very jammy sandwich Keith's wife made. We'll catch Ambleside after Bowfell when they start to get all weak and exhausted. Or else we'll be getting all weak and exhausted ourselves, and shan't be caring about Ambleside any more.

Away in the east, Gable looks distant and big. Gable, still half a day ahead, is where we clockwise Bobkins attain our absolute heights of suffering.

Keith entertains us with his own Bob Graham story. He and Tim were road-runners, invited to join the club's hard hill men just for the run. But one by one the hard

99

hill men backed down. Left on their own, they decided to start their anticlockwise round at 9pm so as to finish before the pubs closed.

This gave them the horrendous rocky crossing of Great Gable in the dark. Still, they made it, in a respectable 23 hours; and they haven't run the roads since.

"And did you have that pint of beer?"

"We did. And when it hit our stomachs, it turned round and came right back out again."

At the end of the long ridge comes the sudden drop and thousand-foot climb up the loose stones of Fairfield. Fairfield is where, according to tradition, we feel the first twinges of the despair to come. But no; we're still feeling chirpy and irresponsible. Even the descent of Fairfield's rubble path can, if you really put your mind to it, be enjoyed.

At 8am, Fairfield's ridge is waymarked with stationary runners admiring the view. These are Ambleside support, taking a break while their principals do the up-and-back to the cairn. It's hotting up now. On Seat Sandal we dip our heads into a peaty pool, expecting the usual tepid bathwater. But no; it still holds the invigorating chill of night.

It's the rush hour on the dual carriageway at Dunmail Raise; but the traffic is all at right angles to the roadway, and on foot. And there in the lay-by is Oliver with his folding chairs. Can this really be a serious-feat-of-endurance thing? All my life I've been despising people with folding chairs in lay-bys. At least Keith didn't tell them to bring stretchers...

Somewhere among the supplies Oliver has entertainment for this interval: the slides of our trip across Knoydart. We've been taking the training for this run rather seriously, Oliver and I – three days from the West Coast to Fort William, with an impulsive bivvy on top of Sgurr na Ciche. But already the momentum of the occasion has swept aside such frivolous ideas as lay-by entertainment. We receive instead dry socks, sandwiches, and sugary drinks. And a rebuke from Tim, as schedules are transcribed from bits of chocolate wrapper.

"You're twenty-eight minutes ahead," he says sternly. "You've probably blown the whole thing already."

"But it's only on the descents that we're gaining!" is my plea in mitigation.

Dunmail Raise arrive 0855 (schedule 0923)
Section 4 hrs 02 (schedule 4 hrs 20)
Dunmail Raise dept 0912 (schedule 0938)

Section 3
Steel Fell, Calf Crag, Sergeant Man, High Raise, Thunacar Knott, Harrison Stickle, Pike of Stickle, Rossett Crag, Bowfell, Esk Pike, Great End, Ill Crag, Broad Crag, Scafell Pike, Scafell

Two new pacers now, and a chance to get to know Gordon – met yesterday for the first time. But yesterday we were too busy lying on sheets of foam pretending to be asleep while some young people kicked a coke can round and round the tent. All I know about Gordon is that he beats me in races, though not by a lot. Today he's enjoying the weather, the slow running and the hills that are new ones to him. Our other pacer,

Peter, is a more sensible second-half-of-the-field sort of runner and seems to be along with the attitude: it's a bit silly, but after all, why not?

Why not indeed.

Peter reports that the campsite livened up considerably after we left. A party arrived with five ancient tents and spent the rest of the night hammering in the pegs.

But as we rise up the slope of Steel Fell the gay chatter dies away. Alan is feeling sick and I am feeling sick and Glyn is being sick.

On theoretical grounds it's almost impossible, but perhaps we have been overdoing the food input. We stop eating for a bit, and start struggling. A helpful hillwalker suggests that the reason I have to keep stopping to squat behind a bracken frond is potassium deficiency. Good sources of potassium are grapefruit and bananas. Neither of these useful trees grows on Steel Fell.

Keith has come up the inter-Stickle stream and is reclining against a boulder in the sun. Keith doesn't like to be away from the running for long. The green liquid in his bottle is, according to the label, little else but sugar and potassium. Certainly, it seems to sort my digestive problem.

But now on the rough descent to Martcrag Moor comes the first injury: a nasty knee-hinge twinge returning from several years ago. Still, it only hurts on the downhill; and the section ahead has lots and lots of uphill.

Here we cross Bob Graham runners of the anti-clockwise persuasion coming the other way. All that we have yet to do, they have already done since we left the midnight clock tower. They look energetic and fresh; do we look as fresh to them? One of them is the 13-year-old Ben Squibb. He doesn't look as if he just ran 30-odd miles of rough hill. Mind you, he doesn't look much like a 13-year-old, either.

My detailed sketch-plan of the face of Bowfell is quite wasted. We just follow the red jerseys of Ambleside all the way up. The thousand feet of rough boulders is good relaxation for my knee, and we reach Bowfell, half-way round the 24-hr schedule, nearly half an hour ahead.

We treat ourselves to a little cautious optimism. The schedule expects misery and exhaustion to start at Bowfell. Every non-miserable, unexhausted mile from here on is pure profit. And the miles from here on are long ones.

We are entering the rough bit. From Bowfell over the highest tops of England to Great Gable it's scree and boulder and bare rock, with hardly a blade of grass or patch of earth to plant a foot on. Fully seven hours are allowed for these sixteen miles. Sixteen miles: ah, but also eight thousand feet of climb.

We run this arid stony landscape at the heart of Lakeland, with the central valleys sliding outwards into blue distance in all directions. Skiddaw is a shadow on the horizon; Gable gets closer – and bigger – all the time. Nobody's worrying about Gable: we're looking along the ridge to Scafell, and worrying about the rock climbing section.

The rock climbing section is Broad Stand, on the eastern face of Scafell. From here it looks very big, and very steep. This impression is somewhat false. Broad Stand is only a dozen feet of climbing. And it's not steep: it's overhanging, with a sloping shelf below and a lot of empty space below that. Surveying this section in the February snows and damp, we decided that Glyn certainly wasn't going to do Broad Stand; I was almost certainly not going to. The alternative, by Lord's Rake, is only eight minutes longer; kicking steps up the snowfilled gully had been very pleasant, even if our shoes had got us funny looks. ("I know they look like trainers: but these are actually fell running shoes.")

Mickledore, showing Broad Stand

But someone says Oliver's got a friend with a rope on Broad Stand. This is hard to believe. Oliver is a member of the Scottish Mountaineering Club. Folding chairs in lay-bys, maybe, but ropes on Broad Stand...?

At Esk Hause, Oliver encourages us by being obviously excited to see us another five minutes ahead. His morale-boosting presence is valuable, his soup less so. I manage a small cupful; Glyn doesn't even bother trying, and Alan's small cupful turns right round and re-emerges onto the gravel of the pass. Ecologists of the future will be mystified by the fertility of various bits of Scafell Pikes, caused by Bob Graham contenders who fail to retain their carbohydrate.

We reach the cairn on Great End, where some Ambleside runners send us to another cairn a bit further away. "But Wainwright says this one's the top!" Alan protests.

"Too bad mate," say Ambleside. "This isn't the Wainwright Round you know. This is the Bob Graham Round."

Ambleside have a man with a rope on Broad Stand; but will they let us use him? And won't he be getting rather tangled up with Oliver's Friend and Oliver's Friend's rope? On these crowded fells we slip past Ambleside without noticing where. Ambleside's efficient support system has brought them up lots and lots of sugary drinks and sustaining snacks, and they keep having to stop to consume these.

Up the great path of Scafell Pike, we zip among the hillwalkers like motorcycle messengers in a busy street; then dodge off to the side to pick up a couple of small peaks. Walkers don't bother with Ill Crag and Broad Crag. But if we're to get forty-two, some of them will have to be little ones. The pacers Keith and Peter stroll along the main path in pleasant conversation. They are probably discussing the Boat Race. (This isn't the one in London: the hillrunners' boat race is the high points of three western islands and a hundred miles of stormy seas between.)

When we came up here in the snow, the footprints were so obvious that we failed to observe that the way off Scafell Pike isn't directly towards Mickledore. This, our route-finding error, costs us several seconds. Glyn is puzzled to see us tiptoeing among the boulders with a perfectly good path round to the side.

We must have been looking at Broad Stand. Broad Stand is covered in a gay multi-coloured throng. I begin to wonder if allowance should have been made for queuing time at the bottom. The Lord's Rake is now a vertical scree, covered in people dropping bits of it onto each other. Even the absurd route-choice of straight up Central Buttress is out: full of rock climbers from bottom to top.

We scramble up to Broad Strand. "Make way for the Bob Graham people please," says a helpful voice, and the crowds suddenly part. The rope snakes down. Oliver's Friend and the Ambleside Man are one and the same – in my run-down condition I'd not been capable of this simple deduction.

The difficult rock climb takes about twelve seconds. This even though I ignore the sling placed for direct aid (ie grabbing hold of) and take care to keep knees off the rock face. There are certain standards to maintain: I may be a mere hillrunner but my ancestors were members of the Scottish Mountaineering Club.

At the summit, Glyn too has surmounted the difficult rock climb and is just behind us. Eight more minutes gained! We're definitely rather pleased. We're over half an hour ahead now, and could almost think of arriving before midnight. Twenty-two hours something to get round: that doesn't just sound like doing it, that sounds like doing it comfortably!

But this idea my knee disagrees with on the long, long drop to Wasdale. And Alan's stomach agrees with my knee. Pain and frustration, and five minutes off the schedule, are the cost of getting back down to sea-level.

Twelve minutes later Glyn limps in, looking sad. One of his shoes has fallen in half on the screes.

Wasdale arrive 1520 (schedule 1544)
Section: 6 hrs 04 (schedule 6 hrs 06)
Wasdale dept 1533 (schedule 1604)

Section 4

Yewbarrow, Red Crag, Steeple, Pillar, Kirk Fell, Great Gable, Green Gable, Brandreth, Grey Knotts

"But Oliver is there with his folding chair, together with the Spirit of 1932 in the shape of Ivan Waller:" so I wrote in my original account of the run, and Ivan wrote back saying the phrase was truer than I knew.

Ivan is what we call a Grand Old Man of the Scottish Mountaineering Club. You see his blurry black-and-white photo in old books. In 1930 he was on the first ascent of a

103

famous rock climb called Mickledore Grooves, just round the corner from Broad Stand. He's done all the Munros, he's walked a Scottish coast-to-coast or two, and at the age of 74 he completed the Cuillin Ridge twice in one month. And now he devotes himself to searching out small peaks with silly names (Maiden's Pap, Faugh, Great Cockup).

And on New Year's Day of 1932 he was with one Eustace Thomas on the upper slopes of Ben Nevis. Thomas was then the holder of the most-Lakes-Peaks-in-a-day record. But there was this chap Bob Graham.... As the wind howled in the crags and their hempen guy ropes sagged under the accumulating snow, they played the fascinating game of telling each other names of Lakeland peaks.

Despite the seduction of the folding chairs and the bowls of hot water for the feet, we manage to snip a few minutes off the rest time. It's off to Yewbarrow for 2000ft of really nasty ascent. It's a shame we overtook all those Ambleside; they could have trampled some of this bracken for us. Then on to Steeple, hanging in grey air over Ennerdale: 'a fairytale summit', Glyn wrote in his route-notes. Gordon supports us now, and will do so all the way to Keswick... encouraging thought. There's less than twenty miles to go...

After a long despondent break at Wasdale, Glyn found some shoes and started the heartbreaking slope of Yewbarrow. He asked if Keith knew of any Bob Graham attempt next year that Glyn could join in on.

"You're not doing the Bob Graham next year," Keith told him. "You're doing the Bob Graham today."

"I suppose so," Glyn agreed unhappily as he overtook a couple of Ambleside runners. He stopped to be sick on Red Crag; he was encouraged to find that this didn't actually make him feel any worse.

The real people have drained off the hills into pubs. We have the grey evening Lakeland to ourselves. Oliver is waiting in Black Sail pass, under the towering crag of Kirk Fell. He offers coffee, but we mustn't take too much: it's reserved for Glyn.

The towering crag of Kirk Fell is a help rather. A bit of hand-on-rock distracts from increasing tiredness. And here comes Gable now, looking very big indeed. The screes of Gable pass under our feet. The boulders of Gable pass under our feet. We're over Gable! And really the sufferings have been very moderate, very moderate indeed. Merrily we scamper down to Honister.

Honister arrive 2030 (schedule 2107)
Section: 5 hrs 05 (schedule 5 hrs 18)
Honister dept 2038 (schedule 2122)

Section 5
Dale Head, Hindscarth, Robinson

Meeting the support team only when it's sitting quietly in car parks, we don't appreciate the frantic activity that's going around on the edges of the Lake District. Peter has been having an exciting time driving my Polo, with its gentle Polo brakes, up and down the steepest roads in England.

We're just leaving when Oliver arrives suddenly from Buttermere. Reluctant to retrace even a single step, we shout across a few yards of grass. Glyn was only 25 minutes behind at Black Sail. Also, he really enjoyed his coffee – so it's just as well we didn't finish it up, isn't it?

Glyn was encouraged by the coffee, but encouraged even more by the 25 minutes. He'd only dropped five minutes; and most of that was spent being sick. He was not, in fact, going slower and slower. He was actually going reasonably fast.

Up the rocks of Kirk Fell he went then, continuing to go actually reasonably fast: so much so that Keith was left behind, and Glyn had to stop for him at the top.

On Dale Head looking to the Grasmoor group of hills

Meanwhile, we were climbing onto the Derwent Fells. The Derwent Fells are long ridges of short grass, with deep craggy valleys gradually filling up with night shadow. The Derwent Fells are, quite simply, lovely running. And run we do, tearing great chunks off the schedule. The schedule expects us to be exhausted, lame and half-asleep; but in fact we're not.

We even enjoy the long gentle run off Robinson. Here we overtake the last of the Ambleside runners, and then a couple of people who started an hour before us. And even the people from an hour before are going to make it to the Moot Hall in time.

Being, by now, a good hour ahead, the truly sporting thing would be to grab ourselves a couple of extra hills on the way in – Causey Pike, say – and cut out some of the road bit. We're not enjoying ourselves so very much as that would imply, and no-one even suggests such a thing. We drop onto the tarmac just as darkness is dropping on us; and there are our road shoes laid out on a mat beside a completely strange car.

For now all the support teams have rolled together into one big support team, and it's mostly supporting Glyn. Glyn has impressed friend and stranger alike with his stubborn determination, and also with his rayon pullover with all the holes in. A leading hillrunner called Martin Stone offers him a long-distance homeopathic pill.

"Haven't I seen your face before?" Glyn asks.

"Oh, around the fellrunning scene," replies the self-effacing Stone. If I'd known it was Stone, I'd have asked him why his book says the Bob Graham's only 60 miles...

Gordon and Alan set a brisk ten-minute mile pace along the road, but it doesn't last. Soon we're jogging, and walking, and shining our torches at the signposts. If we kill ourselves along the road we can make it to Keswick for 11:30 but there's enough death on the roads already and we make it for 11:34.

We sit on the steps and look at the parked cars. An Ambleside runner arrives and starts splashing champagne into the gutter – he's the only one of their large party to complete the Round. Two half-naked runners get out of a car, glance at the clock, and dash into the alley beside the pub.

The support team arrives. "Ah, you've got here. Good. Listen: Glyn's already at Church Bridge!"

I drive out with Oliver. The headlights catch Peter and Glyn coming into Portinscale. They are jogging where we walked. They are looking slightly smug.

They deserve to carry those smug expressions all the way to the clock tower. But under the streetlights of Keswick, just beside the Pencil Factory, Glyn goes over in a pothole. Wrenched thigh and twisted ankle will spoil his running for months to come. However, nothing can spoil the final bit of very slow road running through the car park to the clock.

Who says the camp site's noisy? I didn't have any trouble getting to sleep.

Afterthoughts

Bob Graham said that any reasonably fit person could do it (odd, then, that no reasonably fit person turned up for the following 30 years...) We were lucky with the weather: no mist, no wind, dry rocks; just a bit too hot. That certainly helped us, and so did our support team; in particular Keith on the Helvellyn ridge. (We forgot the schedule, but experienced Keith led us at exactly the correct speed for this section. Leaving aside the downhill sections, the times were what they should have been, to the minute.)

We were lucky with injuries. Our injuries were few, late in the run, and bearable. On the other hand, we are not champion hillrunners. I once got First Veteran in a race with only 22 runners; but that was only because the race was over deep tussocks and peat – my speciality.

The Bob Graham is, then, the correct challenge for the ordinary hillrunner (or even hillwalker). Gather a good support team, explore the route, and train to the limit and, given luck with the weather, you'll get round – provided you don't get injured too early.

And it's about the best day (and night) you'll get on British hills.

Distance

In a logical world, you'd measure the distance with string or a little wheel. (In a logical world, would there be hillrunners?) Thus measured, the Bob Graham has 60-62 miles.

However, factors can be added 'for wiggles', or 'distance up the slope', or 'to make it more exciting'. The generally quoted figure for the Bob Graham is 72 miles.

I've used the distance as measured, of 62 miles. The climb of 27,000ft is found by counting contour lines.

THE BOB GRAHAM ROUND SCEHEDULE

The schedule is derived from calculations of height and distance, from the experience of previous runners and from our own training and reconaissance runs. In the light of our experience on the day, my only criticism of it is that it is unnecessarily generous on the final (Honister-Keswick) section. The most important function of the schedule is to stop you going too fast in the early part of the run: specially on the Helvellyn ridge.

	SCHED	ACTUAL		SCHED	ACTUAL
KESWICK dep	0100	0100	Rossett Pike	1223	1210
Skiddaw	0218	0222	Bowfell	1300	1240
Great Calva	0308	0310	Esk Pike	1325	1301
Blencathra	0418	0415	Great End	1350	1334
THRELKELD arr	0448	0436	Ill Crag	1406	1347
			Broad Crag	1417	1357
THRELKELD dept	0503	0450	Scafell Pike	1431	1408
Clough Head	0601	0544	Scafell	1509	1438
Great Dodd	0633	0614	WASDALE HEAD arr	1544	1517
Watson's Dodd	0641	0621			
Stybarrow Dodd	0654	0634	WASDALE HEAD dep	1604	1538
Raise	0709	0649	Yewbarrow	1701	1622
White Side	0718	0657	Red Pike	1748	1704
Lower Man	0731	0710	Steeple	1805	1724
Helvellyn	0738	0716	Pillar	1841	1754
Nethermost Pike	0745	0724	Kirk Fell	1929	1852
Dollywaggon Pike	0758	0736	Great Gable	2011	1930
Fairfield	0838	0812	Green Gable	2026	1943
Seat Sandal	0903	0837	Brandreth	2041	1958
DUNMAIL RAISE arr	0923	0855	Grey Knotts	2049	2005
			HONISTER arr	2107	2024
DUNMAIL RAISE dep	0938	0918			
Steel Fell	1003	0941			
Calf Crag	1023	1004	HONISTER dep	2122	2040
Sergeant Man	1056	1040	Dale Head	2158	2110
High Raise	1106	1052	Hindscarth	2220	2127
Thunacar Knott	1118	1103	Robinson	2251	2151
Harrison Stickle	1126	1111	CHURCH BRIDGE	2338	2236
Pike of Stickle	1138	1124	KESWICK arr	0049	2336

One of the most popular walks in Lakeland is the Fairfield Horseshoe, starting and finishing at Rydal. Why? Is it the views? Everywhere in Lakeland has views. Why look at Windermere when you could look at Windermere and Ullswater as well? Is it exciting Dove Crag, the most overhanging rock face that's climbed? Because it's below you, and because it's overhanging, the only view you'll get of Dove Crag is if you should happen to fall over the edge. Is it the long rocky ridge to Scandale Fell? Well, no. The ridge to Scandale Fell is wide and stony when it isn't being wide and a bit of a bog, and it's not even all that long.

So it just has to remain one of the mysteries of Cumbria, along with why they don't sell ice-cream at the bottom of Blencathra, and why the Romans made a road on High Street. There is an even worse way up Fairfield, and it's described in the main chapter - Fairfield has an important part to play in the Bob Graham Round, and that part is First Taste of Agony to Come, and the scree path from Grisedale Hause is just right for that particular purpose.

However, there is also a good way up Fairfield, and that way is by St Sunday Crag and Cofa Pike. There is a good way down Fairfield, and it's Dovedale. And there's an end-of-day wander home along the Goldrill Beck. On some occasions, agony is what we're after. But the rest of the time, why settle for any worse way up Fairfield?

Start/Finish: Glenridding's big Pay & Display
Distance/Climb: 12 miles/3700ft or 20km/1100m
By way of: St Sunday Crag, Cofa Pike, Dovedale
Map: OS Outdoor Leisure 5 (NE), or Harveys Eastern Lakes, or OS Landranger 90

Return to the road and turn right, up the south side of the Glenridding Beck. All signs from Glenridding say 'Helvellyn'; follow the ones that add 'via Lanty's Tarn'. At once there's a view down Ullswater that you scarcely deserve after a mere hundred metres of ascent.

Pass the tarn and, at the track below, turn right to the lower of two gates. Descend a field to cross the Grisedale Beck. Turn left on the tarred lane for 400yds to a footpath sign. This is the path up St Sunday Crag. It climbs rather steeply between oaks. The oaks are far enough apart to let you see out to that view down Ullswater, and then to a rather better, longer view, and then to an even better view than that. Fallen tree trunks supply foreground, and seats to rest on.

Above the oaks, the path stops being steep and contours round onto the Grisedale flank. It's a narrow traverse across a steep slope, and then a green shelf above Grisedale.

That gets you up St Sunday. While if you really want ridge, there's ridge down to Grisedale Hause: not at all wide, bumpy, and with big steep drops on both sides.

After Grisedale Hause the ridge gets even better. The crest is scree-covered rock, and the path's mostly on the scree though the rock provides safer footing (with a little need for handing!). Cofa Pike's a peak that does deserve to have a name of its own even though it has only a single contour ring. It's a rather small name, and Cofa's a rather small summit – just a narrow crest overlooking two deep corrie holes, and a small rock that can be climbed over for stunning photographic effect, or else walked

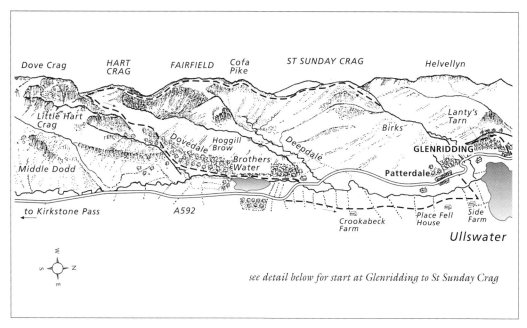

Dove Crag HART CRAG FAIRFIELD Cofa Pike ST SUNDAY CRAG Helvellyn

Little Hart Crag

Lanty's Tarn

Dovedale Hoggill Brow

Birks

Deepdale

GLENRIDDING

Middle Dodd

Brothers Water

Patterdale

to Kirkstone Pass A592

Crookabeck Farm

Place Fell House Side Farm

Ullswater

see detail below for start at Glenridding to St Sunday Crag

under on the path.

The continuation to Fairfield is more rock with scree on, which is quite fun provided you stand upright not low and clutching, and stay off the scree. Otherwise, there's a path traversing right to join the west ridge.

Fairfield too deserves its own name as it's utterly different from Cofa Pike. Fairfield is flat, stony and crowded. Where you get stones and crowds you get cairns, and Fairfield's summit has half a dozen, while the flatness is such that you can't tell which

of the half-dozen is the top. Hurry off eastwards, as the huge Horseshoe path gradually forms itself underfoot, to the col before Hart Crag. Here the views have proper rocky bits for foreground, and among those rocky bits are sheltered lunch spots and even a small walled-in bedroom.

A short rise leads to Hart Crag. At the col beyond (GR 371108) a path drops off left into Dovedale. This descends gently at first, with the formidable overhang of Dove Crag gradually appearing on the right.

In the rocky ground above the crag and close to the path is a well-known cave, the Priest's Hole. It's very easy to find, they say – and I'm not going to spoil your fun by

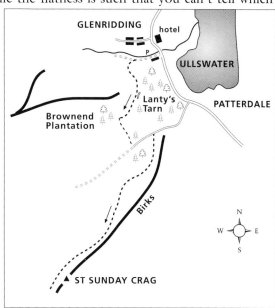

GLENRIDDING hotel

ULLSWATER

Lanty's Tarn

Brownend Plantation

PATTERDALE

Birks

ST SUNDAY CRAG

giving any grid reference.

The small path keeps to right of the stream, and descends a steep little gully with some rock and scree – an awkward descent for five minutes or so. Upper Dovedale is a dramatic hollow that shows you what you miss on a walk (like, for instance, the Fairfield Horseshoe) that's all ridge. The path slants down to descend to the left of the main stream. It then leaves the stream to pass

Cofa Pike

along the top of the field enclosures, looking down onto woodland and then entering the trees for some root-hopping. (This path, though generally used, isn't the right-of-way. That descends to right of Dovedale Beck to a footbridge at the junction with Hogget Gill.)

Pass to left of the buildings at Hartsop Hall, for a broad path that runs through woods alongside Brothers Water. At the car park turn right along the road (away from Glenridding!) Take the side road at the phone box, towards Hartsop village, but at once turn left on a farm track. The bridleway path runs along the valley floor, with a particularly nice moment at the crossing of the Angletarn Beck: this lively stream is in keeping with the fine tarn it's tumbled out of.

Dovedale with Dove Crag and Hart Crag on the horizon

A permissive path on the right avoids the farmyard of Crookabeck. At Rooking take the tarred lane ahead for the bridleway to Side Farm. Take that farm's access track to Patterdale.

If night has fallen, headlamps will illuminate the path to Glenridding: this is to right of the A592, then crosses to run through the woods just above the road.

Eskdale

It happens to rock climbers, as often as not. Even to the occasional ice climber on Great End. Tussle with the vertical, trot down off the summit in a bit of a snowstorm, come to this flattish place with downhill in lots of different directions and various huge paths.

"All right, who's got the compass?"

Nobody's got the compass. Compasses are for hillwalkers. But it's all right because that's the path to Sprinkling Tarn and so this - this is the slope down to Angle Tarn. And they go down, and they don't get to Angle Tarn, and then they come out of the mist and there's this big river winding away into the bog, and the bottoms of lots of crags, and not a pub or a car park or even so much as a litter bin; just four hours hard walking back out and two hours left of daylight to do it in.

It happened in 1916 to a man my grandfather knew. How good to live in times when the sensible, the rational, the quick way from Wasdale to the rest of the world was Sty Head, round the back of the Pikes and down to Langdale for the bus. My grandfather's man was due to join the army and he needed the rational, the quick way out. So up he went into the mist and rain, and round the back of the Pikes, and Langdale was longer than he'd thought it was going to be but he got to the hotel and dropped his sack and left his big hobnailers under the horsetrough; and did he have time for a whisky-and-soda before the Ambleside bus?

"The Ambleside bus, Sir?"

"The Ambleside bus... this is the Dungeon Ghyll, isn't it?"

"I'm afraid not, Sir. This is the Woolpack."

Mist helps, certainly; but it can be done in daylight. For who can believe there's a place in the Lakes, just a brief wander down from the Scafell-Rossett highway, that's six hard miles to civilisation or else two thousand feet out over the top? Not the man I met at Three Tarns in the middle of a multi-coloured sunset, the man who asked for the quickest way to Langdale and then amended that – "no, the easiest way down to Langdale..."

He'd planned to come down to Mickledore, but come down to Upper Eskdale instead. It's hard to enjoy Upper Eskdale when your car's in Langdale, it's getting dark, and you ate the last of the chocolate two hours ago.

But come down into Upper Eskdale on a golden Autumn afternoon, come down in Summer with the rain beating the cliffs black and the bogs awash, come in Spring with snowclouds and sunshine chasing each other across the face of the Crinkles - and Upper Eskdale is not at all hard to enjoy.

Walk the long ridge north from Glaramara, on the peat path that dodges among the boulders and crosses the occasional outcrop though it could just as well go round, and generally plays at being a fairly rocky sort of place. Step straight across the Rossett-Scafell highway, looking carefully to left and right for a gap in the traffic. Walk forward and realise you're using Esk Hause the way Nature intended – as a pass. Drop across its grassy col and down into a deserted re-entrant that narrows to a gully with an overhang. And come into the place that's not playing around, that's rocky and really means it. Gimmer Crag's impressive, Bowfell Buttress is pretty big, but in Upper Eskdale crags like these are scattered around for decorative effect like pot-palms in a hotel lobby.

Cam Spout Crag doesn't even have rockclimbs. Cam Spout Crag's just there because there was a spare bit of hillside. Esk Buttress on the other hand does have rockclimbs: high and breezy Severes and VS's with no climbers on because it's too far from the car park to carry in the chalk. Thor's Buttress has a huge cave, and then there's Ill Crag and Horn Crag...

Rocks going up into the air, and rocks going down into the water... the Esk river runs out through a fine gorge with a dangling path to look down into it from. And so downstream in a deep valley on a path that's long – but too long? Only if you meant to be in Langdale three hours ago.

Eskdale Green has stone walls with roses growing over them and the dear little train to Boot. Eskdale Green is one of the lovelier Lakeland villages, if only because it's damned awkward to get to in your car. But... Eskdale Green is green. It's not the grey crag, and yellow grass, and silver river running through.

It isn't Upper Eskdale.

Eskdale

5: Scafell Scramble Circuit

Your standard Lakeland day goes up that big path from Langdale to Esk Hause and Scafell Pikes; and then goes back to Langdale. The Scafell Scramble Circuit does the exact opposite.

It circles Esk Hause about six miles out. It visits seven valleys and only a couple of summits. It doesn't go along the tops of the crags and so not see them; it goes underneath to where the crags can drip their black slime on its head, and it goes through. It goes down waterfalls and gets wet, it goes over Pillar Rock and gets scared. Here and there it even manages to suffer a little loneliness.

You can treat it as a test or you can treat it as a treat. As a treat it can be savoured over four days; even more with a tent or bivvy bag. We did it in two, in May of 1996. That was greedy, and meant we didn't have room for Attic Crag and Dovedale Combe.

But those who are particularly fit, fearless and rock-competent can attempt the single-day circuit. For this is the Lakeland's attempt at a Cuillin Main Ridge Traverse.

The attempt fails, of course. Lakeland isn't Skye. The Cuillin Ridge has 10,000ft of scrambling up, 10,000ft of scrambling down, and no damned hillwalking. The Scafell Scramble Circuit has a mere 7,500ft of scrambling, counting up and down together, and 30 miles of hill and lakeside in between. Skye has the Inaccessible Pinnacle, but actually I've spoilt the argument there as Pillar Rock is bigger and more interesting than the Pinnacle. On the Skye Ridge you have to carry drinking water the whole way; the Scafell Scramble Circuit has four pubs.

On the Cuillin you get thrillingly exposed gabbro ridge; and then more thrillingly exposed gabbro ridge; and then more thrillingly exposed gabbro ridge. On the Scafell Scramble Circuit you get: -

A pretty waterfall at the head of Newlands. The scree and tree hollow in the side of Robinson. The cave path beside Buttermere. The High Level Path above Ennerdale. Wasdale Head Hotel. The crag amphitheatre of Upper Eskdale. The grey-on-green field-patterns of Langdale. Jack's Rake. The high knoll-hidden Tarn at Leaves. And the oak-hung golden pools of the Derwent.

And you don't get that path from Esk Hause to Scafell Pike.

One person's silly little scramble is another's terrifying rockclimb. Anyone undertaking this circuit will be a competent rock climber prepared to drop to the forgotten bottom grade of Moderate; or they'll be scramblers who know just what's meant by the grade of 3S and can handle a rope, a nut and a couple of slings.

The rock climbers will probably want to go ropeless. We carried 25m of 9 mm rope (the minimum for the Waterfall Climb to Pillar Rock) four nuts and two slings. All of

the Grade 3 sections can be well-protected, but this does require nuts on Chockstone Ridge and the West Waterfall. One of us wore cross-country type fell shoes, the other lightweight walking boots.

To enjoy the two gill-descents to the full you need to enjoy them empty: which they won't be after heavy rain. The harder scrambling is on rock that's intrinsically clean or else well-used: wet rock won't add greatly to the difficulties though cold fingers may. Wind increases the seriousness of all face scrambles.

Account of the Two-day Trip

The tape you play in the car goes round your head for the whole of the trip. So perhaps I shouldn't have chosen that particularly Lutheran bit of Bach. 'Mann, du must sterben' – Man, you gotta die. For these were to be my first days on Lakeland rock for

24 years: my first, in fact, since that embarrassing failure on Scout Crag Route 2 (Grade: Moderate).

Unsure of myself, I was happier about my companion. Keith's a fellrunner who's only recently made the transition from adrenaline to endorphine, from scary sports to exhausting ones. He's been doing climbs graded Severe and even VS as recently as two years ago. And the weather looks OK, even though the Met Office says it isn't, and the first scramble looks just about possible...

1: Borrowdale to Buttermere

The first scramble starts just 30ft above the camp site. Nitting Haws gets the nothing-to-it grade of 1, and not a single star for quality. But nothing-to-it is just the grade we want. What there's nothing to is rough grey rock rising out of the bracken but not rising very far, with a little path to show where to go,

The first scramble of the circuit: Keith Wilson on Nitting Haws

and great big firm handholds for just in case we don't feel altogether happy with the great big flat footholds. And no stars for quality is nonsense when you're in Borrowdale under the newly risen sun, with Borrowdale's lovely woodlands all backlit and Derwentwater in the distance...

We spend time on Nitting Haws, trying to rearrange things with large frightening drops for the benefit of the camera. Cheating, rather; but later on, when things really will have large frightening drops, we'll be feeling far too small and frightened to take photographs.

We drop into the Upper Newlands vallley. This is one of those places you don't usually drop into because it's not really tops and not really bottoms either - but should, because it's crags all around and a long narrow view down to the Bassenthwaite Plain and Skiddaw. The Lake District isn't great for waterfalls. One of the few is here in Upper Newlands. There's a neat little shower cubicle at half height, but careful you don't tread on the soap or you'll end up ten feet lower down in a pool with rocks.

This initial section is good on scenery, good on situations; and also good on psychology. For it gradually gets less easy without ever becoming truly difficult. Far Tongue Gill has awkward moves, but only if you go out of your way after them, and

115

higher up it's a boulder-walk between high walls. We're in a rocky place without actually having to do any rocks.

Above lie Hindscarth Slabs and Hindscarth Slabs represent the Unknown, or at any rate the Not In Guidebook. If scrambling's to be something other than pathetically easy rock climbing, then scrambling should involve loose rock, moss and the Unknown. Hence, Hindscarth Slabs. So I'll leave Hindscarth Slabs ungradedvague and mysterious, even in the Route Description at the end of the chapter.

Instead I'll rabbit about the Alps. There are routes in the Alps over high spiky ridges where the rock is firm and grabby, and the sun shines on the glacier 1000 metres below. And there are routes that are just a great wide slope, and nothing's really loose and nothing's really firm, and it's a bit damp and a bit dark because the sun isn't up yet, and it's a long way to the bottom except that if you did manage to fall over you'd grind to a halt in a shower of chippings, and the place isn't difficult but there's a certain awesome awfullness about it...

And so having climbed in imagination the Ordinary Route on the Wetterhorn, we emerge onto Hindscarth. And since one can't avoid ridges altogether, wander round onto Robinson and start looking for the top of Hasness Gill.

It's another Grade One No Stars, but the rocky entrance drops us into a steep hollow of screes and trees that's very, very different from the path up Great Gable from Wasdale Head. All right, after the rocky entrance the scrambling's really only careful treading on grit. But the view out to Buttermere's good, and so's the little stream wriggling around in the bottom of it all. And down in that little stream there are waterfall pitches between rock walls, and not all of the waterfalls are easy though all can be walked round. You can walk round it if you want, you're just doing it for fun, and because you're just doing it for fun, fun is what you get. There's an overhanging wall above a pool, but lo! under the heather-stalks, a line of magnificent handholds. There's a bit of leg-on-each-side. And there's the emergence below the beech-branches to the lay-by where Tim and Pete are waiting with hot coffee in a flask.

2: Buttermere to Ennerdale

The path through the tunnel's unsafe and blocked off with plywood. Don't they know it's unroped scrambling that's the most dangerous of mountaineering practices? And the newly permitted path around the lake foot's been unpermitted again, lest the dog we haven't got with us should frighten the lambs. But the Landrover's still there, where the National Trust tells you all you need to know. Well, it's very good on where to find more leaflets, but not on where's this Breast Path that's their 50th birthday Erosion Reduction Proposition. Now if more people took to the rocks there wouldn't be all this trouble with the paths...

But in fact up in Burtness Combe the people are taking to the rocks; and since they're rock climbers, and this bit of scrambling is actually a very very easy rock climb, why not? Well, why not is that we're going to have to wait at the bottom while two ropes go up; each rope with a caribiner-dangling young man at the top end and a young woman who hasn't done it before on the other.

Unless we do it the way we really should, as an unroped scrambling practice in exposed situation. Unroped, we can go up between the two parties in an unobjectionable bit of queue-jumping. But, but... this scramble Grade 3(S) is a rock climb grade Moderate, indeed in the latest guidebook it's a rock climb grade Diff.

But truly the holds do look rather huge, and we do have to get over Pillar Rock as well today. So we do it, and the awkward step out of the top of the groove isn't awkward at all, and according to the Book this was the hardest part of the whole route. Well, this and Chockstone Ridge.

So on we go to Chockstone Ridge.

Now on Harrow Buttress the holds were clearly well-handled, and many of the handlers will not have been hillrunners and so probably heavier than us who are. Thus, on Harrow Buttress, we could hang onto the handhold happy that the handhold was going to hang on to the mountain. But Chockstone is no proper rock climb but a pile of tottering towers, and when one of the towers has a hole right through and sky the other side, we decide we're going to put on the rope.

Yes, Moderate is the easiest rock climbing grade: there are eleven grades above Moderate (though six of these grades, the E numbers, weren't even invented when I last rock climbed 24 yrs ago.) But we're not rock climbers, we're scramblers, and 3(S) is the most high and fearsome scrambling you can scramble, and anyway the rope's such a gay shade of pink for the pictures.

"Steel krabs," says Keith, examining with interest my historic equipment. "It's a long time since I saw steel krabs."

There's a couple of pitches tht wouldn't have been such jolly fun without the rope. But we coil it away below the summit, in case the walkers should mistake us for something serious.

High Stile to High Crag's not really what the Scramble Circuit's about. It's a popular ridgewalk all covered with popular ridgewalkers. But there's fine exciting views of the crag we just came up, fine exciting views of Buttermere down sudden gullies, fine and ... well, unsettling views of Pillar Rock. Since all those popular ridgewalkers can't be wrong, we ridgewalk down to Scarth Gap, and take the scree-slant path to Ennerdale.

Chockstone Ridge

3: Ennerdale to Wasdale

The dusty forest road up Ennerdale constitutes one of the less wonderful passages of Wainwright's Coast-to-Coast walk. Pillar Rock hangs dreadful overhead but all you see is fir trees; or if you do see the Rock it just looks, face-on, like a patch of crag, part of a broken hillside.

117

All this changes as we come out of the trees onto the lower slopes of Pillar Mountain. There's a whole lot of rock up there, and you can tell by the way your neck has to bend to look at it that it's not just a flat slab or two and a grassy path round the side.

Pillar Rock is the only summit outside the Isle of Skye to have been, within the period of written records, an Unclimbed Peak. Its first ascent took place in 1826 – 39 years later than that of Mont Blanc. Later in the century, when print-makers wanted to exploit the market for thrilling scenes established by the early Alpine explorers, they found they could do so most quickly and cheaply by sending their engravers up to Pillar Rock.

But you do have to go up there. From Pillar Mountain, the thing lies unsuspected below the curve of the hill. From Ennerdale you can see it in outline, but only from the shores of Ennerdale Water, and from there it's just a wiggle in a distant ridge.

For walkers, the best approach is by the High Level Path from Looking Stead. A good approach it is, going over crags, under crags, and in and out of grassy coves until it gets to Robinson's Cairn and the Rock itself leaps out from around the corner and hits it over the head. For climbers, the best approach is the New West route.

The New West is absurdly easy - not only in terms of its technical grade of Difficult, which is five grades lower than the lowest of the contemporary E numbers - but in terms of the face it goes up. The face is a steep one, with lots of overhangs. A third of the way up the face and most rock climbs would give up in despair. The New West finds a surprising line of holds out from under the overhang on the right that happens to end up on top of the overhang on the left. Pretending to be scared by all the over-hangs, the route scurries into the bottom of an open chimney or groove. The chimney steepens, the walls on either side are just about vertical, and there's another overhang so what now?

What now is a line of large holds leading sideways across the wall on the right, above one overhang, below another overhang, and with plenty of empty space in all directions. Once again things become impossible, but now what guidebooks call an 'airy traverse' leads round a corner onto steep but hold-rich slabs, and these lead to the very summit of the Rock itself.

All right, we're scramblers and we're not going to do that. We're going to do the Old West, the original route of that very brave shepherd John Atkinson in 1829. (Some sources deny that Atkinson was a very brave shepherd. They describe him as a very brave cooper, or barrel-maker.) But first, just to get to the foot of the Rock, there's the West Waterfall.

Now the West Waterfall's not in Evans but it is, very briefly, in my ancestral rock climbing guide. We can go up the left side, on a polished rock climb graded Moderate. Or we can go up the right side, where a difficult chimney low down is followed by mere scrambling.

That's it. The rock climbing guide offers that exploration of the unknown that partly compensates the miserable scrambler for the extreme easiness of his terrain. But how difficult is a difficult chimney? We decide to go up on the left.

There's easy scrambling, and then everything steepens and a well-walked-on ledge wanders round right to the brink of the gully. It's been a long exciting day and we decide to put on the rope again now.

Rather steep grooves and cracks lead upwards. On the right are quite big drops into the waterfall. Still it's only a Moderate so it must be absurdly easy really, and we know

118

it's the right way because generations of ancestral climbers in nails have indeed well-scratched it. Each groove is a bit steeper than the one below, and the holds are a bit smaller and a bit more awkward. Keith is the more recent ex-rock climber and Keith's leading this stuff and Keith starts to go a bit quiet. There's a necessary handhold that's nothing but a tiny crack you can just squeeze your fingertips into, and then lean out on it as the footholds are the sloping frictional sort... and when I reach Keith he says "I've done Difficults that weren't as difficult as this Moderate; but I think this may be it now." So I climb past him and across onto screes at the top of the waterfall gully and yes, that was it, and where's this Old West got to?

Well when you've been doing one of those Moderates that turn out to be more difficult than some Difficults you just want to walk uphill briskly for a while to use up that excess of heartbeat and rest the thinking brain. So we do that, and in no time at all we're at the neck behind High Man. Which is a fine and scenic spot, but not where we meant to be, so we go back down and look again for the Old West Route which was in fact right there at the top of the Waterfall.

I did go on a bit about the New West, which is a real climb. The Old West is a mere scramble, but as mere scrambles go it's pretty absolute. It's grassy ledges, and big comfortable handholds, but it's above several hundred feet of vertical rock and below a couple of hundred more. It's lovely; but it doesn't go all the way.

It goes to the summit of Low Man. Low Man is a little grassy picnic spot with its own little cairn 500m above Ennerdale. But with the difficulties of High Man still to be confronted, it's difficult to generate the tranquil meditative state for a proper bit of indolence and lingering. Anyway, we haven't any strawberries, and we don't know if the Wasdale Head serves strawberries or not but it probably doesn't serve anything at all after 9:00 pm.

So we clamber onwards and ever more steeply. The line's a witty one, that goes sideways and even downwards on its way up. But then it gives up being clever and just says 'Up that steep crack there, go on with you.'

The steep crack has a great big handhold that's been in continuous use since 1826. But it's just a boulder in earth, so I call down for an end of the rope, why not, it's been a long and exciting day.

High Man is an even higher and even better picnic point than Low Man. But still, no lingering on the little lawn (it'd make a fine golf green) in states of contemplation or Wordsworthian rapture. For there's still The Descent.

The Descent is Slab and Notch: not discovered until 1863, this is in fact the shortest and easiest way to High Man. (There used to be something called the Steep Grass, but these days it's the Steep Rubble and not recommended at all.) We walk a few yards towards Ennerdale and lower ourselves into a hole in the lawn that's the top of the Great Chimney.

Slab and Notch has big comfy handholds, and since you're inside the Great Chimney, it almost feels as if the huge drops below aren't actually there at all. Slab and Notch, even in descent, is easier than what we romped up at lunchtime. But the state of the nerves goes steadily downwards, and so would someone who fell off the Slab and Notch. And our pink rope does look nice against the grey.

The early climbers had little or no protection technique and lots of courage. The distance the leader fell was the length of the leader's rope, multiplied by two. This length, accordingly, is given in the ancestral guidebook: for Slab & Notch the leader requires just 35 ft of rope. And we climb down it that way, in little pitches, and running belays on the spiky handholds. This makes it very slow and very safe. Through the notch; down the very steep wall where it requires some ingenuity to use even half of the spiky handholds available; across the Slab and then up it, and out onto the hillside.

And up to the neck behind High Man, the place we visited accidentally just two hours ago.

The Rock has one last summit. Pisgah is a scramble Grade 1*, which really is easy; and on Pisgah you can at last relax and have that picnic. But we still don't have any strawberries. So I relax and coil the rope. The rope doesn't need coiling: it's too short to tangle and just gets stuffed in the bag. But the resonance of the moment demands rope-coiling, a ritual akin to the rolling of the fat cigarette, the business with the silver paper and the candle... rope-coiling is what you do as the adrenaline drains away and the endorphine-tingle hits the ends of the capillaries.

Pisgah is where Moses stood and gazed over Jordan at the Promised Land. Here, Jordan is represented by a deep boulder-choked gully, and the Promised Land isn't the green coastal plain out in the west under its evening sun, nor the deep hollow of Ennerdale, but that slightly higher lump of bare rock just the other side. Early adventurers tried to drop a ladder across. Jordan Gap is narrow, but, fortunately, not narrow enough for that.

So now it's time to leave the Rock - everyone else left hours ago, so we can't take any of those pictures of them silhouetted in the Notch. There's no need to climb Pillar Mountain when you've climbed its Rock, and we leave by the High Level Path. And so down quiet Mosedale under a cloudless evening sky and the sun already gone behind Yewbarrow, but still shining sideways on the crags of Scafell. May it may be, but in the gullies of Scafell that sun is shining on snow. Well, well; we'll think about that tomorrow.

I stand in the campsite with a tentpeg in one hand and a silly grin. Tomorrow's quite long but we've done all the really frightening bits and even included that West Waterfall. We should be able to achieve tomorrow, whatever the weather. And then, remembering that weather forecasts aren't always wrong, I take out the single peg I've managed to place so far and turn the tent with its toe to the gentle breeze. There's not a cloud in the sky, certainly none of those high whispy ones meaning here comes weather, but Keith knows better than to protest such irrationality at the end of days over Pillar Rock. He'd only got two pegs in at his end anyway.

We find a dim corner of the Wasdale Head bar and sit to mix our sophisticated cocktail of mind-altering drugs; adrenaline, endorphine and alcohol. The alcohol is John Smith, the endorphine is Pillar Rock - a potent combination. Tim entertains us with the various things he's put into his microwave to dry them out. A lady at the next table had intended a quiet evening with a mountaineering book but gets swept into our post-Rock jollity. She tells a sad sad story of a cat in a tumble drier. A cat with rigor mortis in a tumble drier.

4: Wasdale to Eskdale

In the night, weather arrives. Lying below wet flapping nylon we postpone our early start from six to seven, giving the weather at least a chance to go away again. It doesn't; but at least there's fun to be had in emerging to see the tents that weren't pitched toe

On Pisgah

to the breeze and are now bent into various strange shapes. Even in the camp site the wind's quite hard to stand up in and we wonder about the top of Scafell.

We'll find out soon enough.

Rainbows arch over Wastwater and at the lake foot it may even be a nice sunny day. In Hollow Stones, though, the cloud's down and down thick and it's snowing. And Lord's Rake, which is usually a fairly nasty scree gully, is full of quite hard snow with big steps in. What a treat! A bit of Scottish Winter Climbing in the Lake District, in May, when we'd come intending something quite different.

Keith kicks up the gully and misses the turnoff to the slightly more interesting variant of the West Wall Taverse but I don't call him back. For today, Lord's Rake will do just nicely. Mist blows around the various pinnacles. We're in the middle of Scafell's great northern crags and even though visibility's limited to twenty yards, those twenty yards are impressive ones.

Lord's Rake dumps us out onto the summit ridge. It's windy, but actually no windier than the camp site. And it's hardly snowing at all. However, Keith is wearing one layer too few, and this is no place to stand while adjusting one's dress. So we hurry down to Foxes Tarn. Foxes Tarn is a puddle in a hollow, but even its tiny waters are being whipped into furious ripples.

There's a gully of wet boulders, but at least it's out of the wind. And then there's a long dropping path between crags. We descend into Lakeland's empty valley of Eskdale.

5 Eskdale to Langdale

What Eskdale's empty of, even when it isn't half past nine of a fairly nasty morning, is

people. You can stand alone in Eskdale while two miles away and two thousand feet above they're queuing to get onto the cairn of Scafell Pike. But in terms of crags and cliff faces Eskdale's full – even overcrowded.

We wander downriver while Keith gradually warms up. Being no longer rock climbers, we can look at all these crags without anxiety. Then the path teeters along the brink of a nice gorge with a waterfall.

It's only afterwards we realise that, since this is a Scramble Circuit, we should be down in the gorge getting splashed by the waterfall. But it's already clear this is no one-off walk; the route is one to come back to. We'll get splashed by the waterfall next time.

Next we wander up Lingcove, which adds up to quite a lot of wandering but why not when the cloud's on the tops and the bottoms have nice rocky streams to wander along. The diversion is for the sake of the famous 'Bad Step' on the Crinkle Crags.

Here you have to get down a short vertical wall into a gully. I haven't done the Langdale Race, but the Langdale Race does the Bad Step and when I come this way with people who have done the Langdale Race they stop here and look worried and go: "Now, I came down to that foothold there and then jumped onto the scree there. Or did I come down to that one... and then jump to that rock? No, no, surely not."

After Crinkle Crag comes the less-interesting section of the Scramble Circuit. It's a wide stony popular path down to Red Tarn. The people on the popular path look happy enough, but we know better, and as soon as we can, lower ourselves into a hole that's the top of the next gill scramble.

Browney Gill gets only grade one, and a single star, for beauty. The trouble with Browney is that some of its little waterfalls are too difficult altogether, and it's necessary to take ignoble bypasses up the side. Still, there are several that you can climb down, and a little pool that you leap across from an insubstantial foothold. The crags bounding the gill have a special attraction for suicidal sheep, and white bones lie among the boulders.

At the bottom we walk left to drink from the neighbouring Crinkle Gill. Oxygen in splashy gills kills bacteria, but still it's nicer not to know exactly how many suicidal sheep are lying in your drinking water. Langdale is Great and also grey: the weather's stopped being romantic and turned to ordinary Lakeland drizzle.

6: Langdale to Langstrath

We look at our watches. Keith has to be back at Borrowdale at six; it's now 1:30; and we've two more valleys to do. This can't be done. But when it comes to can't-be-done, that also covers the leaving out of Cam Crag, the seven hundred feet, three stars and two-grade scramble out of Langstrath. Two impossibilities are reconciled by agreeing that we now double our speed.

Doubling speed means halving map reading, so we cross the bottom of Dungeon Gill on a little footbridge and suddenly realise we've done quite a bit of Stickle Gill by mistake. We should have guessed when we overtook the crocodile of primary-school types in their blue helmets and blue waterproof coats-on. Dungeon Gill has a nice gothic spelling-mistake ('Ghyll') and a nice gothic chockstone-crossing pitch ('rope advised for security') but Stickle's quicker. It's not a gill at all, just a strip of bedrock with the stones washed off it, but more fun than the path.

And it does lead to Stickle Tarn, and Stickle Tarn's the not-quite-deep-enough pool under the high diving board of Jack's Rake.

When I was young and innocent I believed the Lake District would be full of places like Jack's Rake. Thus in later life I suffered grave disappointment at Billy Bland's Rake, Fisher Wife Rake, and even Lord's Rake: all of which are scree bits between crags. Jack's Rake isn't between, but on, a crag: an astonishing ledge, bottom right to top left, up the face of Pavey Ark. It's got a sort of parapet so it doesn't feel as exposed as it is and that's a shame; for it really is very exposed indeed. Still, it's an easy route, and a popular route, and even Wainwright takes his life into his hands and goes up it 'by a series of convulsions unrelated to normal walking'.

It's only Grade 1, so of course we're not meaning it when we relax on the summit and say 'gosh that was a bit frightening.' But the people who went up just in

Climbing Jack's Rake. This steep little pitch is the hardest point, but, comfortingly, feels less exposed than it actually is.

front seem pleased we said it first, and quickly agree it was. Still no time for map reading, so we follow the people in front and let them lead us into a knee deep summit swamp.

The front of Pavey Ark's a fierce mountain, but the back side isn't even a hill. When you get up there it's only a corner of a moor, and not even a highest corner. We jog gently across the moor, and down some grassy slopes into Langstrath.

7: Langstrath to Borrowdale

Of the Seven Valleys, Langstrath and Eskdale are the ones without roads in.

Keith on Cam Crag

Langstrath's not as craggy and glamourous as Eskdale, but it does live up to its name by being, at least, long. And it's not altogether cragless, for across the footbridge is Cam Crag Grade 2***.

This once tried to be a rock climb, but failed. It keeps on having these grass ledges leading off to the left. Also, a rock climb's supposed to be a route and on Cam Crag you go up wherever you feel like.

Now we know about nasty rock. Nasty rock is loose, and mossy, and it goes all greasy with a little rain. Nasty rock's got bad strata so the holds slope wrong. You'd think that nice rock was simply rock that lacked these nasty qualities, but that's before you find Cam Crag.

Cam Crag goes out of its way to be nice. Cam Crag's not simply polite: Cam Crag's effusive. Put your foot on Cam Crag and Cam Crag goes 'all right all right I've got you.' Land on a ledge and it's 'are you sure this ledge is flat enough for you? We had the sheep over it last week but if you would like the grass a bit neater just say.' At one place there's a wall to climb up that consists entirely of handholds, with no spaces between at all.

So it's most ungrateful of Keith when he says 'it's getting a bit steep, can't quite see what happens up here. Think I'll come down and rope up.' Because when he gets back up again, the reason he couldn't see what happened was because it got all anxious about being too steep for us and suddenly sloped back at a gentler angle.

But the rope doesn't stay on for long, and soon we're back looking for ways to keep off the grass and get a bit more friendly rock. And soon after that is the top, a rock knoll with a view. Keith's a bit embarrassed about the rope. But it is the end of two long days, and it does also happen to be raining - and most crags (not Cam Crag, though) use a bit of rain as an excuse to go all slippery on you.

The view's probably got Bowfell and all sorts of other places in it, but for now grey cloud and grey-green moor and the odd Langdale Pike do nicely. And turning to leave, we find our rock knoll just the first of many leading across Rosthwaite Fell to the little hidden Tarn at Leaves and the biggest and final rock knoll of them all which is called Bessyboot. Now Bessyboot derives from the Norse, Beiz-y-Bjellt, which signifies - no, I give up. It must just be called Bessyboot because that's so obviously what it is.

We drop into Borrowdale between rain-bright birches, and the woodpeckers that woke us up two days ago are still at work, making a noise like a submachine-gun if submachine-guns were made of wood.

The camera looks ahead down the length of Borrowdale to a gleam of Derwentwater and isn't interested: 'that's just grey cloud, dead bracken and rain.'

Which just goes to show that cameras don't know everything. (Or perhaps that I should get a more expensive camera.)

Now comes some riverbank of the Derwent, with overhanging oaks and smooth grey stones below still water. It's delightfully different from anything yet on this walk, but we aren't all that delighted as we're still going at double-speed and our feet are rather sore. It turns out that Keith's 'back at six' actually means 'phone home before seven', and at five to seven we reach the payphone at Longthwaite Youth Hostel. So that's all right.

Do we go up the back of Castle Crag for the second-best view in Europe? We don't. We go back to the cars, where Tim has left our rather damp tent and a whole flask of nice hot coffee. The campsite's empty: the weekend's over. We listen to the rain on the leaves, we drink the coffee, and then, very reluctantly, we get into our cars and switch on the windscreen wipers.

Route Description

1: Borrowdale to Buttermere
Start: Hollows Farm camp site, Grange

To reach Hollows Farm, cross the Derwent over the double humpback bridge, into Grange, and turn left onto a road that's unsurfaced for first few yards.

The route starts through the camping field on the right. Above the washblock is a stile onto open fell.

NITTING HAWS (grade 1): the lowest rocks are just above on the right. Go up easy rocks to the first steep section. This is climbed by a traverse left and then back up right. Holds are marked by the passage of previous scramblers.

The ridge flattens over rocky hummocks. Where the ground steepens again, the rocks form three ribs divided by scree. Push through junipers to gain the bottom of the left-hand rib and climb its first step. The continuation up this rib is used but is a bit difficult: cross scree on the right and continue up the middle rib to the terrace below the next steep wall.

Walk right to a recess and climb up the steep wall. At the grass terrace above, walk up left to start the final steep section just left of a rowan tree growing out of the rock. (Note that such trees tend to die and fall off; although, unlike unroped scramblers, they die first and do the falling off afterwards. The hawthorn mentioned by Evans lower down is now dead branches in the heather.)

Continue over the hardest rocks you can find to the little summit.

Strike up across the moor to a little rocky turret at GR 237165, which offers a few more feet of scrambling. (On the large-scale map this is "Minum Crag". The name will be a contraction of 'minimum', indicating that this is not a very small crag – it's even smaller than that.) Continue to the slate cairn of High Spy.

A path leads down towards Dalehead Tarn, but in the hollow just before the tarn turn sharp right to descend a path on the right bank of Newlands Beck. Once you can see the waterfall (300m contour) turn left to cross below it and traverse to Far Tongue Gill without gaining height. The lower section of Far Tongue Gill is a narrow, shallow

On Chockstone Ridge

stream gully. Simple scrambling can be found in the bed of the stream and on rock slabs to its right. Two little cascades give good sport, and then the miners track from Newlands crosses at the 400m contour.

The rest of the gill is a simple boulder walk between high walls, until it trickles out onto open grassy slopes. Traverse right, to where slabs on the face of Hindscarth offer more scrambling.

HINDSCARTH SLABS: The shaly eastern slope of Hindscarth has areas of cleaner-looking whitish rock. The first (leftmost) runs up to steeper rocks above – further to the right is a second whiter section. This is a wide, gently-angled slab going to the top of the face. This angle is easy but the rock is loose. For reasons given in the main section, no route will be described. The rocks can be by-passed by going straight uphill from the stream top.

Walk right for 200yds to the summit of Hindscarth if you want it, then return. Drop down the western slopes with scree on the right to find a small path contouring into the col on Littledale Edge east of Robinson. This is, after all the dodging about, a bit of ordinary ridge. It has a view down into Buttermere and a big path. As well as a path, a fence guides along Littledale Edge and up Robinson; at its corner strike off right on the wide path to Robinson summit.

Descend the well trodden path towards the three little tarns on High Snockrigg, but turn off left at the col before them (Buttermere Moss). Of the various streams feeding the Hassness Gill, you want the northernmost.

HASSNESS GILL: grade 2 in descent by route described if lower waterfalls are included. The stream drops into a deep hollow with trees. Follow the stream bed down through a rocky entrance onto the upper slopes of this hollow. Descend shaly slopes, first to right and then to left of the stream, to the bottom of the hollow. Here other streams join from the left.

Continue down the stream bed. Several small waterfalls provide interesting pitches on clean sound rock. All can be avoided on the left. The difficulties end at a small reservoir. Continue down the stream bed to join the path from Robinson. Go down under beeches to reach the road at a small lay-by.

Cross the road onto a permissive path signed "Lakeside". Turn right, along the lakeside. The entertaining tunnel section has alas been closed off, with a diversion through the woods above (but is to be restored). At the lake's north corner, a permissive path continues along the shore to bypass Buttermere village (this path is closed during lambing April - May). Or continue ahead to Buttermere village, which has a cafe but no shop.

2: Buttermere to Ennerdale

A bridleway past public toilets is signed for Scales Force and Red Pike: its left fork leads to the west corner of Buttermere. Don't take the Red Pike path steeply up half-left but turn left along lake shore, to take a broad path gently up right after a few yards. After 750yds this starts to slant back downhill. Take a less-used broad path on the right, gently uphill to a stile out of the woods.

The path, not clearly defined, traverses left and climbs gradually to a stile between two sections of stone wall. Turn uphill along the far side of the stone wall to a ladder stile. Continue beside the stream into the rock-surrounded Burtness (or Birkness) Comb.

GREY CRAG (grade 3S): The most striking feature of the combe is the overhanging formidable Eagle Crag in its back left corner. Opposite, in the back right corner, is the cluster of small crags collectively called Grey. Go up scree to the lowest point of the lowest crag, which is Harrow Buttress.

Harrow Buttress is an easy and popular rock climb. It is steep and becomes quite exposed. However the holds are good, and the way is clearly marked by the passage of climbers.

From the lowest point of the buttress climb an open corner and a chimney above (awkward in rucksack). At the top of chimney traverse left for 10ft (3m), then strike back rightwards up a groove towards an overhang.

Pass round to the left of the overhang to the summit of the lower buttress. Scramble on along the easy-angled ridge to a perched boulder. Stop here to compare the route up the next buttress with the diagram in Evans' book. Then descend right, beyond the boulder, to walk right, across scree, to the foot of Chockstone Ridge.

CHOCKSTONE RIDGE (grade 3S): Climb the rock-strewn crest to the base of a steep little tower. Traverse into the little gully on left. You now see that the little tower is detached from the ridge, with a flake stone lying across the top of the gap. Climb up onto the flake stone.

The rock here is not so reassuringly climbed-over, and the adhesion of handhold to crag is not to be relied on 100%. The next move is slightly awkward and considerably exposed. We used our rope here. From the top of the flake step right, above a large drop. Climb the groove above to return to the crest.

Above is a crack with large handholds. At its top the large handholds are vertical rather than horizontal so that this has been described as 'awkward'. However, on sloping footholds vertical handholds are the best sort. Leave the top of the crack leftwards to the top of the buttress.

FINAL WALL (grade 1): the final short but steep wall ahead has a jumble of rocks lying against its front. Walk left, to pass up right, behind these boulders. Now an open gully gives easy scrambling to emerge a few yards short of the summit of High Stile.

From High Stile descend, south at first, on the well-used path along the top of Burtness Comb. There are fine views back to the crags just climbed. After High Crag descend the new pitched path on the steep eroded slopes of Gamin End, and cross over Seat to Scarth Gap.

Take the large path down right towards Ennerdale, but as it steepens after 200yds, turn right, below the lowest outcrops, onto a small path that slopes gently down westwards above the forest. It enters the clear-felled area at a large stile, another stile leads out onto scree, then a third leads into trees. Slant down westwards to join the forest road at sign "Scarth Gap".

Turn right along the forest road for a few yards, and left (marked "Footpath") to the Fell and Rock Club's memorial footbridge over the Liza (GR 176132).

3: Ennerdale to Wasdale

From the footbridge over the Liza, walk forward to the forest road, turn right, and take the left fork uphill. In 100yds a sign points uphill: the side of it you can't see says "Path". Turn up the forest ride to the top. A rough path continues uphill to right of a stream.

Pillar Rock appears overhead, bounded on the left by the black crack of Walkers Gully, on the right by the West Waterfall. The path wanders off to the right to gain, eventually, the cove above the West Waterfall. But go directly uphill to the bottom of the West Waterfall.

WEST WATERFALL CLIMB: Rock climb graded Moderate, not in Evans' Book, grade 3S. The route to West Cove goes up the rocks on the east (Pillar Rock, left-hand looking uphill) side of the waterfall gully. Note that at the level where Green Ledge comes in from the left, you can cross to the right-hand side of the gully for an easier scramble route.

Scramble up the gully, passing a waterfall by a small buttress on the right. At the level of Green Ledge, further progress up the gully becomes impossible due to two overhanging waterfalls. Here it is easy to break out onto the left-hand buttress.

Scramble up beside the gully until the buttress ahead steepens. Here a narrow ledge leading right, above the gully, leads to the bottom of a series of cracks and grooves. These grooves lead up, always with the sheer drop into the gully on the right. The rock is clean and firm, well-marked by the passage of the hobnaily boots of a previous century. The rock is well-supplied with holds, but steep. There is plenty of protection if you have nuts.

After about four pitches you can traverse easily right, above the top of the gully, onto the lowest screes of the West Cove. Go up the screes for a few yards, with the steep rock of Pillar Low Man on your left. A tongue of rocky ground comes down on the right so that the scree you're on becomes the floor of a wide gully. Opposite the foot of this tongue, stop and look left.

PILLAR ROCK Old West Route: grade 2 to Low Man, grade 3S continuation to High Man. See Evans' "More Scrambles". The line of weakness is an obvious series of ledges leading up and leftwards across the sheer rockface. The holds are large and well-used: this is the climbers' descent from the routes on Low Man. The scrambling is technically easy, grade 2 only because of the exposure and because, unless you continue on the harder scramble to High Man, you'll have to do it downwards as well as up.

Two thirds of the way up, a short traverse left and slightly down gives the easier line. You reach the gap between Low Man and the main rock, and walk left to Low Man's little cairn. If you have a strategic friend at the top of the Shamrock Traverse, they can take a fine photo of you at the cairn.

PILLAR ROCK FROM LOW MAN: grade 3S. A small path leads to the bottom of the onward route. This slants leftwards across the face of High Man, ascends an easy groove, and then traverses left. Now you can climb up and rightwards to the bottom of a very steep crack. The crack has large holds, but is exposed.

Walk forward to the summit of Pillar Rock.

PILLAR ROCK: SLAB & NOTCH DESCENT: grade 3S, see Evans' "More Scrambles".

Directions 'left' and 'right' apply to a scrambler facing outwards. Retrace steps for a few yards. A deep chimney (Great Chimney) leads right, down the east side of the rock. Descend the floor of the chimney for a short pitch, then climb down large well-used holds on the chimney's right (facing out) side. A short traverse

The west face of Pillar Rock. The Old West Route runs up the left hand edge of the picture, then right along the skyline

to the right leads into a notch but looking through it and down you realise that it's not The Notch which is still a few metres below.

Don't go through the wrong notch, but descend on the left, Great Chimney, side until a second short traverse right leads into the Notch.

Go through the Notch and descend steeply on good holds to the Slab below. Two good spikes for runners on this descent allow the last man down to be well protected on the rope. Cross the bottom of the Slab and ascend its further edge. Now a short easy wall leads down onto the rocky slopes of Pillar Mountain.

Traverse below the gully coming out of Jordan Gap and walk up to the col where Pillar Rock joins the main mountain.

PISGAH (grade 1): The lower rock-summit, between the col and High Man, is Pisgah. Climb up a few feet from the col, and walk across flat rock. The final short wall is easiest by the groove on the right, though the easier descent is by the wall a few feet further left (looking up).

The summit of Pisgah has superb views of Jordan Gap, the Rock and out to Ennerdale and the sea. It's a place to relax, let the pounding heartbeat slow, and with no difficulties left ahead to absorb the craggy atmosphere of the Rock.

From the col between Pisgah and the main mountain, a path descends left (eastwards) with splendid views of the Notch nicely in silhouette and the sky-hung cairn of Low Man. The path slants eastwards and down across the top of the Shamrock Buttress. Here the former grassy covering has been eroded away to leave a stony, sloping shelf.

Having passed along the top of the Shamrock Buttress, descend a short scree slope into Pillar Cove. The path traverses across the floor of the cove to the large Robinson's Cairn. Stop here and admire the retrospective views of Pillar Rock.

The path runs around the hillside eastwards with crags above and below – this is the Pillar High-level Route. It emerges on the east ridge of Pillar Mountain at the 770m contour, just above Looking Stead.

Descend the almost horizontal ridge. The path drops right to contour below Looking Stead. Here a smaller path branches downwards, turns suddenly and heads back across the screes to join the main path from Black Sail just before the Gatherstone Beck. Follow the large path down Mosedale to Wasdale Head.

4: Wasdale to Ennerdale

From Wasdale Head Hotel follow the tarred road south for 300yds. Where the road turns right, a footpath signpost points left. Follow the footpath (not the bridleway) across a field to a footbridge, and then rising around the flank of Lingmoor. There are fine views along Wastwater. The path joins the large one up Lingmoor Gill just before a gate.

Follow the track uphill. Most of it has been rebuilt by the path people. Where the gill divides, the path on the right crosses the stream and heads up to Hollow Stones below the crags of Scafell.

After Wastwater has gone out of sight the path steepens. As the angle eases at the top of the steep section, the path passes a five-metre boulder. At this point a scree fan is descending out of the crags on the right. Stay on the path for another 50yds, then turn up right to ascend the left edge of the scree. It narrows into a rightward slanting gully – here a path joining from the left is the line of Lord's Rake.

Clamber up the deep, loose, gloomy gully to its top: a narrow col with a pinnacle on the right. A few feet below the col a groove back left is the line of the West Wall Traverse. For Lord's Rake, go through the col to descend a few metres along the bottom of a cliff, then slant up to the notch behind a second rock pinnacle.

Descend again about 20m in a loose gully, then traverse forward below cliffs onto an open slope. Do not ascend, but keep horizontally forward to a scree before the next rocks. Go up the left

Scafell Pinnacle and Pisgah seen across Deep Gill

edge of the scree to emerge onto the west ridge of Scafell at the 850m contour.

Go up the ridge to the shallow col between the top of Scafell Crag and Scafell itself. Walk right (south) for 400yds following cairns to the summit.

Return to the shallow col, and turn sharp right to descend a constructed path down nasty rocky ground to Foxes Tarn GR 208064. Follow the outlet stream, then move a few yards left into the top of a rocky gully. This runs down into the green valley between the Scafells. A small path beside the stream takes to bare rock beside waterfalls as it reaches Eskdale.

5: Eskdale to Langdale

Cross the Esk River and walk down its east bank along the top of the Esk Gorge until the path starts to drop to Throstle Garth. Cross bracken and grass eastwards to join the path up Lingcove Beck. The path climbs away from the stream to cross a low col and round the first spur of Crinkle Crag to Rest Gill.

REST GILL: the stream has carved itself a shallow bed. The industrious will dig out a little scrambling from among the boulders. There is a 5ft cave pitch if you want it.

Where the stream emerges onto open fellside strike up south-east to the top of Crinkle Crags.

The path off the summit runs south-east past a cairn, then turns south along the top of the Langdale face.

CRINKLE CRAGS BAD STEP: the path eastwards off Crinkle Crag has a notorious "Bad" step where you must drop into a gully on the right below a chockstone cave.

The thin can do this, without their rucksacks, by a hole above the chockstone. Otherwise the low but overhanging gully wall must be descended on large well-scratched holds. The line of holds furthest down the gully is the easiest, to reach the floor some 20ft (5m) below the cave.

Follow the path over Stonesty Pike, with drops on the left and Langdale at the bottom of the drops. The path becomes broad and boring as it descends around the flank of Cold Pike to Red Tarn. The tarn's outflow stream becomes...

BROWNEY GILL (grade 1). Note that in Evans' book the various waterfalls seem to have become confused. In the following, right and left are when facing downhill.

Where the descending Oxendale path turns away from the stream is the point where the stream drops into the hill and starts to be a gill. Go down 10yds from the waterfall on the right bank and traverse back in towards the fall on a small gritty ledge.

Below this uppermost hollow the stream runs narrow between rock walls. A variety of small falls are descended close to the water.

Now the gill widens and becomes a boulder-walk. Just above the stream junction (400m contour) a sudden waterfall can be avoided by crossing a narrow rib on the left and descending the earthy groove beyond.

After more boulder walking, a two-stage fall announces the beginning of a further interesting section. The upper half is undescendable. Two routes present themselves:
1   (easier) go back a few feet to a traverse path out left. Descend a groove with small incut rock holds sticking out of the loose earth. This leads to the bottom of the fall.
2   Leave the gill on the right, to descend a small path through trees to the fall's halfway pool. Cross the water, traverse left and descend the stream-side slope of the bounding rock rib.

Again the stream narrows between rock walls; at first descending short waterfalls, whose bottom pools offer the choice of deep paddling, ticklish traverses or dodgy leaps off poor footholds. Lower down, a horizontal passage can be straddled with a foot on each wall. All too soon the walls open out and you walk down below trees, threading a way between boulders and the carcasses of foolhardy sheep.

If the water has been low enough for you to achieve this descent, then you'll be able to cross the Hell Gill stream and won't need the footbridge 100yds upstream. Cross to the paths on the further bank and follow the lower of the two down Oxendale, passing along the riverbank to Stool End Farm. Go through the farm to the Langdale road. Turn left over the old bridge to the Old Dungeon Ghyll Hotel.

6: Langdale to Langstrath

Pass round to left of the ODG Hotel to the track running east along the bottom of the fellside. This broad stony path crosses the Dungeon Gill Beck on a footbridge and arrives above the New Dungeon Ghyll Hotel.

STICKLE GILL (Also known as Mill Gill): grade 1. The stream running up to Stickle Tarn is not a true gill as no high rock walls enclose it. However, the cleaned rock on either side of the stream offers a number of short wall-climbs on the way up. In between, boulder-hopping in the stream bed is surely preferable to the overused path alongside.

Such boulder-hopping continues all the way to Stickle Tarn.

Walk round the right hand side of the tarn, admiring the high wall of Pavey Ark ahead.

JACK'S RAKE (grade 1): the obvious bottom-right to top-left diagonal ledge up the large crag of Pavey Ark is the line of this celebrated scramble.

Castle Crag, Borrowdale

The rake is formed by a sort of trough, so that a parapet on the left conceals the empty spaces beyond. The route feels less exposed than it actually is.

The crag is bounded on the right by a wide gully. Go up the right hand edge of the scree fan below the gully and cross to the foot of the rake.

You can ascend the long diagonal rake in the groove, which tends to be damp and a bit muddy but feels nice and enclosed. Or you can take the parapet on the left where the rock is cleaner. Either way, the holds are large and plentiful.

After a horizontal few yards, a steep little pitch with a rowan tree outside it is the hardest part and if a rope is used anywhere it'll be here.

The rake ends at a small platform. Go up a small gully for about 20ft(5m), and then across leftwards and up a couple of short walls. Now an

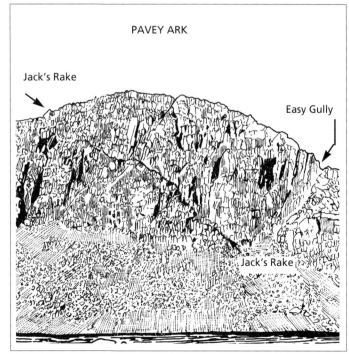

easy groove leads onto the flat rocky fellside above. You see a stone wall ahead. Turning right before the wall allows more easy (and unexposed!) scrambling to the very summit of Pavey Ark.

Strike across wet moorland to the higher but incomparably inferior summit of Thunacar Knott. Descend grassy slopes north-west to join the Stake Pass path as it steepens at the foot of the upper valley. Descend in zigzags beside the Stake Beck, cross it by a footbridge, and strike down to a clump of trees beside the main Langstrath Beck. Here is another footbridge (GR 264100).

7: Langstrath to Borrowdale

From the footbridge walk down the west bank for a kilometre. Cam Crag is the gently-angled rock-ridge rising on the left. It is recognised by the whitish rock along its crest, and by the jumble of boulders lying against its foot.

CAM CRAG (grade 2): Evans recommends the scrambling of the knoll below the foot of the ridge proper. But this is overgrown, unused, and compared to the ridge above quite unattractive. So strike up to the jumbled boulders at the foot of the ridge.

A small path leads left round the jumbled boulders till you can scramble rightwards to their top. Now a short wall on the left is climbed on good holds. Follow the crest up and slightly to the right.

The first of many grassy terraces would allow an escape to the left. Follow footsteps through the grass. The next rocks are climbed diagonally rightwards up an easy crack. A steep crack above is rather fierce: a traverse left allows an easier ascent.

The next steepening offers a second diagonally-rightward crack. A third diagonal-right crack starts to feel a bit tricky, but immediately turns left onto gentle ground. This is the top of the steep lower buttress.

The ridge continues with short easy walls interspersed with grass. After the first grass, you can move right to a steep rather exposed wall with many handholds. Above this, it's a matter of seeking out what difficulties you can to the ridge's knolly top.

Wander northwards along the flank of the knolly ridge to where Tarn at Leaves nestles in its col. From the tarn go north-west through the col to left of Bessyboot (GR 257124, not the col further left marked on maps as right-of-way). A small path descends north-west to a stream. Descend grassy slopes to left of the stream to the combe floor. A descending path is just across the main stream (Combe Gill).

The descent through the birch trees offers views along the length of Borrowdale. Turn right on a track at the bottom. Go straight across the Borrowdale road onto a field footpath. It leads to the stone Folly Bridge. Slant up right to join a broad stony path that runs downstream and into the bottom of Johnny Wood. Where this path rejoins the river, it takes to the rocks for a brief scramble to avoid being tipped into the water. Walk along the front of the youth hostel and down its entrance track.

Just before the bridge over the Derwent, turn left to a narrow gate onto the river-side path. Follow this past the tree-hung pools of the river. Stepping-stones (GR 253148) lead across to Rosthwaite if you want Rosthwaite and its shop. If the water is too high, there's a stone arch bridge 200yds downstream. Otherwise continue down the left bank into the woods under Castle Crag. The path veers away from the river and climbs to visit an abandoned slate mine. Where it forks take the right branch to descend and rejoin the river. Soon after this the wide path becomes the track through Hollows Farm camp site.

Turn left past the wash block to a stile onto the open hill... No, no! No need to go all the way round the circuit a second time. You can stop now.

Fact File

Suggested break-points are:
> 5-day: Borrowdale, Buttermere, Ennerdale, Wasdale, Langdale
> 4-day: Borrowdale, Buttermere, Wasdale, Langdale
> 3-day: Langdale, Buttermere, Wasdale
> 2-day: Borrowdale, Wasdale

The one-day can start anywhere: but the Borrowdale - Buttermere section makes a good warmup, and the serious Buttermere - Wasdale section is best fairly early on. So again Borrowdale is the recommended start-point.

Accommodation:
> Borrowdale: Camp sites (Hollows Farm, Seathwaite). B&Bs (Grange, Rosthwaite). Camping Barn (Rosthwaite). Shop (Rosthwaite). Buses to Keswick.
> Buttermere: Cafe, camp site, hotel, camping barn. Buses to Keswick.
> Ennerdale: Youth hostel (Black Sail)
> Wasdale: Hotel, camp site
> Eskdale: running water (Esk Gorge)
> Langdale: hotels, camp site, shop (camp site), B&Bs. Buses to Ambleside
> Langstrath: nil.

Map:
Harvey's Western Lakeland, or else Outdoor Leisures 4 & 6

Guides:
R Brian Evans: *Scrambles in the Lake District* (Cicerone 0-902363-39-5) and *More Scrambles in the Lake District* (Cicerone 1-85284-042-0). Most, but not all, of the scrambles are described, with diagrams, in Evans' first, excellent, book. The descriptions are, of course, uphill. The Old West route on Pillar is in Evans' sequel *More Scrambles in the Lake District* (just as good); this also describes Slab & Notch in descent. The West Waterfall is described in rock climbing guides only, and only briefly. The Hindscarth Slabs route is original to this book.

Close study of Evans' two books, the rock climbing guides, larger-scale maps and of course the country itself will suggest various ways of making this route even more complicated and interesting. Go for it!

You can trace the changing geography of Ennerdale in old etchings. Two hundred years ago, the valley sides were steeper, so that you walked in silence lest rocks and avalanches be set in motion by an incautious shout or sneeze. Bowness Knott was higher then, and much more frightening.

By the mid-nineteenth century, Ennerdale had got slightly smaller: it was now merely Alpine, rather than Himalayan. Picture editors had realised that, when you needed something for a nice article on the Matterhorn disaster, it was cheaper and more convenient to send the artist off to Pillar Rock.

Today Ennerdale has shrunk still further, into something green and pleasant. Its former Alpine terrors have withdrawn, like the local Britons in the face of the tourist Viking. They are now to be found in a single high cove on the side of Pillar.

Many who do the Pillar High-Level Path, do it from Wasdale. (And the descent by Scoat Tarn and Nether Beck is a good one, described in Chapter 2.) I like Ennerdale even better. Ennerdale is a busy, civilised valley, that manages to be busy and civilised without having a road. Ennerdale is encouraging, with its two youth hostels, its passers-by who are on their way to Robin Hood's Bay, or carrying their bikes over seven high passes.

That's political. But the real-life reason for doing it this way is Steeple, and its Long Crag. This is a ridge that's sharp, grassy, and unwalked: unwalked because it doesn't lead down to Wasdale or the Old Dungeon Ghyll.

You can do this one from either of the youth hostels. You can do it from Ennerdale Water Foot, and get that Ennerdale waterside walk twice over. I've been conventional, and described it from the nearest car park. But this is Ennerdale, and the nearest car park is not near.

Start/Finish: car park at Bowness Knott GR 110153
Distance & Climb: 14 miles/3300 ft (22km/1000m)
by way of: Black Sail, Pillar High-Level Path, Steeple
Map: OS Outdoor Leisure 4 (NW) or OS Landranger 89

An unsurfaced road leads along the lakeside, with a path alongside on the right some of the way. After the head of Ennerdale Water, a side-track leads right, across the river, to enter plantation at a double gate. Turn left, to cross the Woundell Beck. After another 200yds the track bends right, and a path with green waymarks leads ahead.

This is the Liza Beck Path, and it follows the edge of the unplanted valley ground, and then the river. After two miles it reaches a forest road beside its bridge over the Liza (GR 165135). The Liza Beck Path should eventually continue up the south bank, but until it does, turn left on the road across the river, and right at the tee-junction beyond.

The dusty road up Ennerdale gives glimpses only of Pillar Rock between the branches. When the road bends right, a rough track runs forward out of the trees to the Black Sail hut (youth hostel). Cross the footbridge beyond, and climb the steep path to the pass of Black Sail.

The path up Pillar skirts Looking Stead on the left-hand (Wasdale) side. After the following flat section, the ridge steepens and becomes rocky. At the foot of this steep

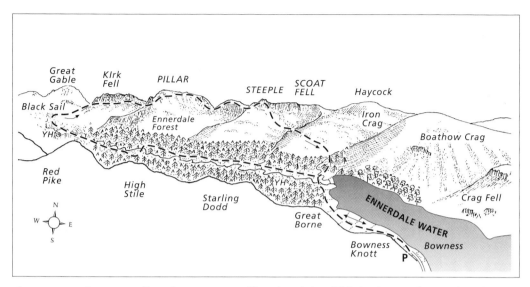

slope, at a cairn, a small path contours off to the right. This is the High-Level Path.

Immediately it drops to avoid a crag above, then climbs to avoid another crag below. The path is narrow, and there are vertical views down into Ennerdale. It crosses the floor of a high green coomb, to reach Robinson's Cairn. This can be recognised by a memorial plaque just below, but more immediately by the huge crag hanging in the sky above: Pillar Rock.

You can see the three tops: Pisgah, High Man and Low Man. But the main part of the Rock is obscured by a lesser but nearer crag, the Shamrock. Our way goes up to the left of the Shamrock on scree, then turns right to traverse along the top of it. This, the 'Shamrock Traverse', is a rocky ledge with loose stones.

At its end you look down into the Amphitheatre, a hollow of scree and rock under the east face of Pillar Rock. Cross the top of this to the col between Pillar Rock and the main mountain. From here the nearest top, Pisgah, is a short but exciting scramble (Grade 1). (The top of High Man is real rock climbing, described in the main chapter.)

From the col beside Pisgah, scramblers will simply set off up the slope of Pillar Mountain. There is a path that avoids rock-adventures: it slants up left, then back right to the crest of a small rib. It continues to the right, then up a short, easy rock groove to the summit plateau.

Pillar from Ennerdale

In mist, the descent direction off Pillar is not obvious. Follow the cairns south-west, not the path north-west. Soon you're descending steeply over eroded jammed boulders: the rocky crest is easier than the eroded boulder path. From Wind Gap, a broad path leads up the ridge towards Great Scoat Fell. Do not try to circumvent the preliminary top, unless you like sideways boulderfields. A wall appears, and you pass through a gap in it. The ground beside the wall is grassy, but there are sudden drops on the right. A slight bend in the wall, and a small cairn, mark the summit of Great Scoat Fell. As Scafell Pike is a higher outlier of Scafell, so Great Scoat is a large lump attached to the side of Steeple.

Small cairns lead north-west towards the brink: just over the edge is the narrow arete to Steeple. The summit is a delightfully narrow one, and a grassy ridge descends beyond. The crags that are the ridge's right-hand slope are what climbers call 'rotten rock', which is the nicest sort to look down onto: not just the feeling of glad-I'm-not-involved-with-that-lot, but perched blocks and drooping vegetation.

As the ridge runs out into ordinary hillside, bear off left to cross the Low Beck at the 400m contour. A path runs west around Lingmell, above the forest-top fence. It drops into the unplanted strip leading down the north-western spur of Lingmell.

Go down beside the trees on the left, to a waymarked path that contours left into the trees. This crosses a minor track, then the Woundell Beck by two footbridges, and drops to the forest road at GR 131138.

You have rejoined the outward route. Go through the double gate ahead to the track that crosses the valley floor. Once across the river turn left on the main track back to Bowness Knott.

Many will prefer a high-level return to their car: either by way of Iron Crag or, after a night in a youth hostel, by the long straight ridge to the north of Ennerdale. Iron Craggers should know that the path from Boathow Crag to Angler's Crag no longer exists, and that this is a most awkward slope. However, there is a nice descent line from Crag Fell towards Crag Farm House, crossing Ben Gill at the 300m contour. North-siders may enjoy a path off Great Borne south-west, immediately to left of the Rake Beck. There is no access off Herdus to the Floutern Tarn bridleway.

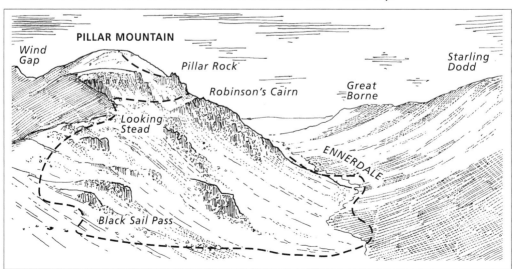

Borrowdale Rain

It's not just that Borrowdale has more of it than anywhere else. Borrowdale's rain is real rain. It comes in lumps off the trees, and off the leaves of the grey houses. It comes sideways on the wind. It bounces up off the rocky ground. It has no trouble getting in under your umbrella.

Borrowdale's rain makes the rest of Britain's rainfall merely drizzle.

Ice made Borrowdale; two glaciers, one out of Langstrath, one from the year-round snowfields of Scafell and Gable, joined at Rosthwaite and rose in a crevassed hump over the tough rocks at Hollows Farm. But rain made the detail. Rain fell mercilessly on dirty brown ice, turned it to saturated slush, washed it away a spoonful at a time to leave the Bowder Stone perched on one corner half-way up the valley wall. Rain carved it into noisy hollows, surged through it in grey rivers loaded with gravel and rocks. Water spilled round the back of Castle Crag, crashed down through holes in the ice, and emerged as a spate torrent, loaded with boulders, that broke through the Jaws of Borrowdale and spread in a lake from Grange to the suburbs of Cockermouth.

The rain didn't stop when the ice went – you could say it hasn't stopped yet. Rain made lakes, four altogether, in the upper valley – lakes whose flat floors are now part of the shape of Borrowdale. Rain makes green pasture, and even greener woodlands. Rain splashes down in waterfalls, then wanders in slow golden curves across that lake-bottom floor.

Across the Stonethwaite Beck, the tents of the campsite had that grim concave look they get when thoroughly wet through. Beneath them, folk were wondering whether to lie longer, getting gradually damp and miserable, or to get completely damp and miserable straight away – and for some the decision would be made for them as the wind tweaked their tent-pegs out of the softening ground.

The first brown leaves had been ripped off the trees and clung wetly to the path. Rowan berries were brilliant against the grey sky. The beck was a white waterfall from top to bottom, and Lining Crag gleamed like a battleship. I stopped in a hollow to put on more clothes, and the wind cleverly came around the corner and caught me with head in sleeve and knocked me over. The stream bed is nice clean rock, and the pitched path is nice clean rock, and there was so much water coming down the path I started up the stream by mistake...

Ullscarf is not very high, it's not very steep, it's peaty on top and would be quite at home in the Pennines. Ullscarf in the sun would be a dull day. I made my way up Ullscarf in a series of leaps, as the wind plucked me off the tops of tussocks and dropped me into soft peat-holes beyond. The tussocks were nowhere green, but shades of orange and purple and Autumn brown. An inch or two of water ran around between the tussocks: on flat-topped Ullscarf the water has nowhere to go. Except back into the sky. A mist of rebounded rain lay across Ullscarf. It lay thickest in the hollows, bringing out the shapes of everything in shades of grey. Autumn rain is warm, and the best thing is to get altogether wet as quickly as possible and then stop worrying. Borrowdale rain does this for you both quickly and efficiently. But even quicker is to step onto a peaty place on the path and find it turned to a sort of soup, into which you sink suddenly like a surprised crouton.

The Norsemen called the tarn up here "Blea" or blue - this could be Viking irony, we can't really know. (Judging from the Njal Saga, their idea of a joke was someone, at a moment when they didn't expect it, getting suddenly killed.) Blea Tarn lies in a wide grass bowl, with nothing to see but sky. Today though the sky is dark, fast-moving cloud; the tarn takes up the grey colour, wrinkles it into small waves and embellishes it, discreetly, with a few white caps.

A kestrel leapt out suddenly from among wet boulders – in the racket of wind I must have approached it undetected. It gave me a glimpse of its brown back and then the wind snatched it away over the tarn towards Armboth. I hoped it didn't need to return to this particular boulder, as it wasn't going to be able to.

A slate signboard warns not to go on down Bleatarn Gill, one might become the victim of a Viking joke. So the path squelches uphill from the tarn foot, onto the aptly named Shivery Man, back up into the full wind. Now the ground becomes slightly rocky. And all at once - Watendlath.

For these Armboth Fells are a Lakeland joke. Just as it's managed to persuade you that Lakeland is a grim and peaty place, and you've settled into the wet-foot plod, and aren't bothering to look at the view because the view's entirely brown and rounded, it says "ha! Just pretending!" and drops away suddenly.

A beck leaps out from where it had been hiding under the bog, and scampers away between high pines and lumpy grey rocks. And at the bottom are green pastures, and a bright tarn; a grey huddle of houses, and a jolly orange slurry-spreader. Even from the fell top you can tell that Watendlath is going to have geese around the tarn, and one of those stone arch bridges for pack-ponies.

Beside the pony bridge, the man from the National Trust has his Landrover and his damp leaflets. The Landrover Man does some entirely justified boasting about the path they've just rebuilt on Gable – the one you used to be able to see from the moon. It's a warm sunny day in London, apparently. We find this fact amusing, the Landrover Man and I. Poor people in London, who aren't at Watendlath in the rain.

The Rosthwaite path starts off under the surface of the tarn, then rises as a small river. Why go on holiday to the seaside, when there's such fine paddling on the Rosthwaite path? The birches bend under the wind, then lift again, flinging water. The noise is from the treetops, from the whitewater beck, and no longer the rattling of the nylon hood in my very ears; it's cosy under the birches. Down in Borrowdale, it's a different sort of day. In stead of flying sideways, rain comes straight down between the houses and spreads slowly across the valley floor. This isn't rain in a hurry, this is rain that's got all the time in the world, and who says Lake Rosthwaite has really gone for good? It's rather dark down in the valley. You can feel the extra weight in the air due to all the water falling through it, and you can hear the shapes of things from the water trickling down over them. There's a water-board man in the car park, happy as a duck in his yellow waterproofs, and making water-board jokes about hosepipe bans.

But really, it's the same joke as at Watendlath. It's a joke that maybe even the grim Norsemen enjoyed; and it's the Lakeland joke, certainly. It's the joke of having fun, in Borrowdale, in the rain.

A slate sign on a slate wall says: 'Home of Judith Paris' – with no indication that Judith Paris is a fictional character, a heroine of the Herries novels of Hugh Walpole. And why should it? Lakeland is also an invented landscape, a place that we see through the eyes of others who've seen it before us. Here is Hugh Walpole on Borrowdale's rainfall:

It is rain that has little connection with either earth or sky, but rather has a life of its own, stern, remorseless and kindly. It falls in sheets of steely straightness, and through it is the rhythm of the beating hammer. It is made of opposites, impersonal and yet greatly personal, strong and gentle, ironical and understanding. The one thing that it is not is sentimental.

The newcomer is greatly alarmed by it, and says: "Oh, Lord! Lord! How can I live under this!"; the citizen of five years' habitation is deprecating to strangers but proud in his heart; the true native swears there is no rain like it in the world and will change it for none other.

Beside the pony-bridge, the man from the National Trust... Poor people in London, who aren't at Watendlath in Walpole's unsentimental rain.

6: Events

A Fell Race

The first thing to understand about fell runners is that we don't actually run up the fells. Walking up the fells is less trouble. It's also quicker. An experienced fellrunner will walk up fells fast enough to overtake an inexperienced fellrunner who is running. And on the way down he (or she) will overtake the rest of the inexperienced fellrunners who ran up the fell and got exhausted.

The idea of fell-running is to get exhausted in due course, but not exhausted on the very first fell. Running 13.1 miles along a road is very bad for the feet and knees. It's also tiring. Running the same distance up and down some fells is less tiring because of the restful effect of the uphill bits. It's also gentler on the feet and knees because of the cushioning of all that scree and squishy mud. Then there's the views, for even thick mist is prettier than your average roadside. Add to that the very real pleasure of frolicking around in all the wind and rain with hardly any clothes on, and you won't need to wonder why 300 people arrive at Kentmere on a chilly March morning to run up High Street.

Superman wears his underpants outside his trousers and so do fellrunners, except that fellrunners don't bother with the trousers underneath. So it's pretty chilly standing around in the March breeze. Like emperor penguins on the Antarctic ice we take it in turns to be the one on the outside of the pack. Then someone says "all right, off you go then;" and we do that, up the stony Garburn Road.

The track veers off towards Windermere, and strings of bright fellrunners stretch away uphill through the dead bracken. Good: it's time for hands on knees and some relaxing walking. Experience tells me that it's not worth doing quick little sprints through the bracken to move up a few places in the string; but I do it anyway.

Three little pointy summits along this ridge are Yoke, Ill Bell and Froswick. Yoke, Ill Bell and Froswick are probably the best little pointy summits in the Eastern Fells. But fellrunners care only for those summits that have a tent, a CB radio and a very cold man with a clipboard. So we run along the side-slopes of Yoke, Ill Bell and Froswick on little muddy paths. The little muddy paths are interesting at speed as the sides-slopes are steep ones with long views down towards Troutbeck and streaks of hard old snow. (Does a fellrunner carry an ice-axe? Come off it. A fellrunner carries some flimsy waterproofs of ripstop nylon, a fun-size Mars bar, a whistle, a compass and a few square inches of map. Ah, for the carefree days before BAF safety rules imposed all this cumbersome baggage...)

Between the summits are eroded Lakeland descents, and these are the places to give whoops of delight and leap down like a young gazelle on its way to the disco - or in my case like a getting-on-a-bit gazelle that's trying to stay groovy. I cut off my frivolous cries as I realise I'm overtaking someone I know. It's Peter T, a runner of very moderate

On High Snab Bank. This long gentle ridge of Robinson makes a reasonably comfortable finish to the Bob Graham Round.

pace who's rather pleased to find that he's been in front of me. My excuse is that I'm running tired after a 30-mile Bob Graham recce the day before. Given the excuse, you might wonder: why race at all?

Running tired allows moderately paced runners who usually come behind you to come in front, and it's good to give pleasure to others. But it's a social thing as well. Fellrunning's a lonely game, just you and the odd sheep in the mist, and that's the point, of course; but just sometimes, it's nice to run in a huge sweaty crowd. At races you run 20% faster than you usually would and thus have 20% more fun. Then there's the camaraderie of the car park, the orange juice at the finish, and the van from Pete Bland Sports with all those bargain Lycra tights in colours so horrible even fellrunners won't buy them...

The bog on High Street's a flat bog, which means you have to run not walk, say a brief hello to the frozen man with the clipboard, and then run back again. Nan Bield is somewhere at the edge of this plateau. Who needs a compass when you can navigate through the mist by the eerie glow of the man in front's fluorescent shorts?

See him come, the fellrunner. He wears a ragged vest in the pink-and-purple of Penge Athletic. No amount of mud can cover the nylon brightness of his discordant green shorts. On his knee he wears an elastic support bandage. Mingled sweat of his brow and snot of his nose trickle down his contorted visage and from time to time he spits, disgustingly. One of the words that does not spring to mind is 'godlike'.

Yet godlike is how it feels. To run unencumbered along this grassy ridge; to cope with the tussocks and know your compass is the master of the mist, and not worry

about getting your feet wet because they already are, and feel the wind in your hair and the rain on your face – it's an odd form of fun, certainly. Odd, but also godlike.

Those who aspire to be as gods must, occasionally, pay with their lives. Fellrunning isn't a particularly dangerous sport but it isn't a particularly safe one either. During twenty years, four people have died on fell races. The most recent of these, Judith Taylor, lost her life on this Kentmere Race the year after I did it. It was a day of wind, low cloud and driving sleet. She left the race route at High Street, heading north for the shelter of Hayeswater; she wore a thermal layer as well as windproofs, which is more than the safety rules require, but not enough to keep her alive for more than three hours after she stopped running. Her body was found at the Knott, just at the turnoff for lower ground.

Hill runners rely on our exertions to keep us warm and our speed to get us off the hill. Clearly we'd be safer with a big rucksack, two spare jerseys, a bivvy bag and a little stove. Safer - but also slower.

Speed is the thrill. Those stony descents give all the excitement of a ski-run at Tignes at a fraction of the cost. The uphills are slightly harder to enjoy and a lady in the colours of Kendal is getting a bit annoyed. This is the fourth time she's overtaken me going up uphills. I explain about being a terribly fast person suffering from 30-mile lassitude but still managing to keep slightly gazelle-like downhill.

Downhill is what every race must end with and off Kentmere Pike it's steep grass and mud. Steep grass and mud are what fell-running shoes are best at. Provided you lean forward, hit ground infrequently but hard, and retain your sense of humour, you probably won't get hurt. None of that weary end-of-day plod for us runners. I come below the mist and see Kentmere a long, long way down and a few minutes later, with trembling knees and fresh blood running down a shin, I'm there. It's stopped raining so a few people are hanging around at the finish and I even hear a bit of hand-clapping. Actually, it was meant for the Kendal lady.

Afterwards we sit around in a damp village hall enjoying the fatigue poisons. It's a straightforward pharmacology: morphine and heroin are laboratory copies of this stuff. Such is our drug-induced stupor that we actually enjoy the orange squash in plastic cups and the waiting for the prize giving. Anyway it's the traditional entertainment, the fellrunners' equivalent of purple lampshades, joss-sticks and the Velvet Underground.

Fellrunners are not consumers, except of our own bodies. We don't discuss the latest expensive gear; we discuss our leg injuries. Then we get into our cars and drive home.

Spring In Lakeland

It's not a race. It's a long distance walk organised by the Long Distance Walkers' Association (Westmorland Branch), who offer you tea and well-buttered fruit cake all the way round. How mean it'd be not to stop and enjoy the fruit cake, as well as wasteful. And we fellrunners are nothing if not mean. The faster start after, and there's a cat's-cradle of loops and short-cuts. Thus you get to pass everybody sooner or later, or sooner and later – and they get to pass you. It's an event for conversation not competition. It *isn't* a race. This means that, supposing you wanted to, it wouldn't be all

Opposite top: Windermere and Coniston Water from Fairfield (daywalk 4; bottom: Windermere seen in evening light from Dow Bank above Elterwater; Overleaf: Frost in May: Keith in Lord's Rake (chapter 5)

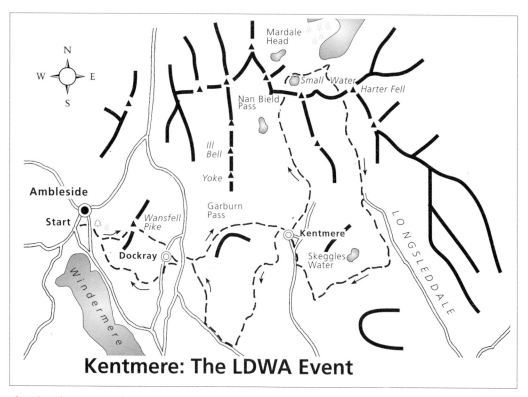

Kentmere: The LDWA Event

that hard to come first.

Well, thirty four miles means plenty of space for thinking about that. Is anyone else serious enough to be worth coming in front of, while at the same time slow enough to make coming in front reasonably possible? What sort of a day is it? And what sort of a course?

It's a running sort of day, cool and grey. And it's a running sort of course on tracks and valley bottoms and well-known passes. So what about the competition - or rather, as this is a non-competitive event, the non-competition? About thirty humans and a dog called Charlie. They look lean and fit, some of them have coloured tights with calf-exaggerator stripes on. Best hang back then, enjoy the bright beech-leaves in Skelghyll Wood, enjoy the backwards view along the long length of Windermere. Windermere looks best in the grey, all folded shapes and inlets with the flick of a white sail and no boring postcard blue.

A couple of runners overtake me on the run off Wansfell – but we're not being competitive - and anyway I catch them again on the rough river of stones that's Gardale Pass.

Now it's the long trot up the Kentmere valley, where little streams splash across the track. The trees here are still bare and brown, with only the odd blob of sunlight to liven up the scene. There's a runner in a blue rucksack ahead, a runner who's on the lower path. Is he going the wrong way then?

Well, not really. I'm going this way because it's the way I came down two months ago on my 'Lakes of Lakeland' circuit. But the bottom track may well be quicker, specially if you're good on track: the path we're on, now I think about it, has a few feet of

145

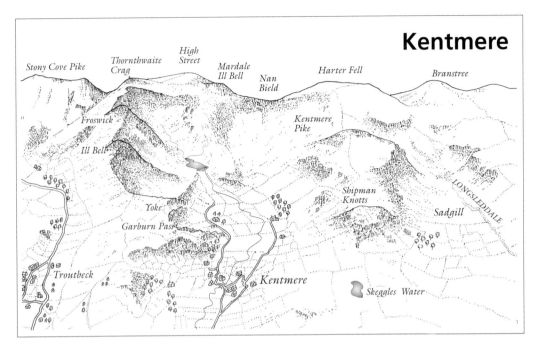

unnecessary descent above Tongue Scar.

But the man in blue looses his cool. Glancing back he sees us on the different path and makes an awkward climbing traverse. Once he's in front of us on the same path, we accelerate slightly and overtake him. Out in front; wrong path (even if it was, in fact, the right one); and then overtaken – the man in blue rucksack is now, in competitive terms, a spent force. Were we being cruel? No; for this is not a competitive event.

Now Charlie the dog, Charlie's human and I lead the group up the Nan Bield. The Nan Bield is serious stuff: a high steep slope to a notch in an impeccably jagged skyline. Charlie's human is also serious stuff, with a nearly-did-it Winter Bob Graham Round to his credit.

Charlie and his human leap away down the steep grass and rocks at the back of Nan Bield. Deliciously gloomy is Small Water, hung round with rocks and sunless when it isn't cloudy. The two in front are moving beautifully, specially Charlie, and soon out of sight. No point in racing against them – I can relax, and chat with the early-started walkers. Our event's walkers can be distinguished from walkers of any other sort: every walker on an LDWA event has a plastic mug dangling from the rucksack.

But Charlie and his man are lingering in the car park as I emerge with two hands full of hastily, but I hope politely, snatched fruit cake. Now in a race that'd be simply a matter of more fool them, but this isn't a race and more sophisticated rules apply. Perhaps they're simply slow eaters, but no, let's be mannerly and accept the conventions of companionship. Comradeship accepted, if only by implication, it becomes churlish for either of us to dash off in front. This removes anxiety – the one in front struggling to get out of sight so as not to do the one behind's navigating. Also, I would like to find out about that Winter Bob Graham.

We walk strongly up Gatesgarth, telling each other how tired we are, how we aren't properly fit, how we're just about to blow up and flake out. The top of Gatesgarth's horrible, like trench warfare. It's the four-wheel-drives that do it: fun, certainly, but an even more destructive fun that us in our boots or little running shoes. We're passing plenty of walkers with their dangling mugs but: "I don't think there's any runners left in front. Do you?" Imperceptibly our joint velocity increases, and we're pounding down to Sadgill at a thrusting 5 mph.

And chatting ethics, at a previous event, Charlie's man entered as a walker – "not properly fit, you know." But most of the walkers were joggers, and one particularly determined one wanted to know: "are you a walker or a runner?" "Well, a walker." The jogging walker said nothing, but speeded up.

"Well I waited for a gate, to catch up while he was fiddling with the latch, but no! He went over the gate, crash, like an SAS man in a sack." This is non-competition of the sternest sort. "So I kept him in sight until the last mile and then overtook. Burnt him up."

But then – how embarrassing – there was a prize for the fastest walker. Well, it's unfriendly to refuse a prize. And anyway, that'd just have let the other fellow get it, and he wasn't a walker either, plus he obviously really wanted it. Tricky business, ethics.

Now we're on forgotten grassy bridleways in the far south-east. Skeggles Water – whoever's heard of Skeggles Water? A pool among peat hags, it has no business masquerading as one of the Tarns of Lakeland. And so back to Kentmere for more fruit cake. And here are friends from further back who've taken the shorter cut just so's to say hello once more.

But this is the final fruitcake, and on the uphill bit of road Charlie's man said "I've been going too fast for a 30-miler. You go ahead if you want to." And thus absolved from the ethics of companionship I decide to get all competitive again. And, as I leave the village hall, there on the step is the man in the blue rucksack! Now probably he's done the short cut, but possibly not, and to stop and ask would be overtly to compete. So, eating fruitcake with both hands, I jog on and catch up with a woman in go-faster tights and a distressingly vigorous 60-year old. And a dog: "Hey, that dog's called Charlie, and he's not my dog, Charlie's man's still back in the checkpoint."

"I know. Charlie's my dog and that man's my brother. He came into that checkpoint with you looking the way I look when I've been out running with him – somewhat run down. So let's see if we can finish this thing in front of him."

Now those go-faster tights aren't just for show: this is a serious woman who's contemplating the 50-peak extension of the Bob Graham, and with all the freshness of 18.6 miles as against 22.3. (Yes, fell-running brings a completely new meaning to the phrase 'good-time girl'.) And as for Charlie, he just keeps glancing back to see if I've taken to running holding fruit-cake again. But one can but try.

Why do comparatively few women complete the Bob Graham? Is it that they're too busy looking after the children to do the hours and hours of training required? Or, more simply, just insufficiently obsessive? Churn over such topics in a well-shaken brain and the miles fly by. Here's Windermere still gleaming grey, and here's a walker who says there aren't any runners in front of us, and here are the stones and gleaming beeches of Skelghyll, and here's Ambleside.

It's not a race, but a search of the Raynet time sheet reveals that Charlie and I are first runners on the longer route. And Charlie, at any rate, wasn't being competitive at all. And Charlie's man? Well, he kept us in sight for four miles but then he came up with a walker from the earlier start, and the walker turned out to have the same kind of motorbike as himself.

Next year they're thinking of running it the other way – over to Wetherlam and back by the Langdale Pikes. There'll be no need to get competitive, or even to talk about motorbikes, to enjoy that one. Competition? Pah! The results roll out in their own good time and two weeks later it turns out that someone called Speight was twenty minutes ahead of us all along.

Conversations are as recollected in tranquillity and must be regarded as fictional: names, other than my own and Charlie's, are therefore omitted. Only the LDWA support structure is real.

Hunting High And Low But Mostly High

If you were on Haystacks or Great Gable over the Whitsun weekend, you noticed some strange activity. Down in Ennerdale people were running up and down steep hillsides, crouching behind boulders, or setting off suddenly to cross horrible screes. You may even have met in the mist a soaking wet man wearing a red sash and carrying a hunting horn. Perhaps he asked you to carry a message to someone you would find lurking in Windy Gap...

The sport of rock-climbing had its birth on the slopes of Great Gable and so, not many years later, did the Lakes Hunt. Since 1898 it has taken place over the ground between Wasdale Head and Honister; these nine hills and the wide grassy valley they surround are probably the best Hunting ground in the western world. The rules have varied over the decades, but since World War II, have settled into a form close to the children's game of tag.

Out of the 30-odd hunters, four of the younger and faster are chosen as hares. These are the ones with the red sashes and the horns: the same sashes have been in use for over 50 years. Hares have a half-hour to position themselves before the hunters burst onto the hill at 9:00. A hare once caught is 'dead' and may take a half-hour to rest and to reposition himself. He signifies his ghostly status by removing the red sash. Play finishes at 5:00 and the hare gets first use of the bath water.

It is easy enough to disappear into mist, boulderfield or the bar at Wasdale Head; a hare who remains uncaught is an unsuccessful hare. He must expose himself recklessly, attracting the hunt with blasts of the horn and leading it into uncomfortable situations - boulderfields, stormy summits, rivers, rock faces and ravines. He'll try to keep them in close contact for hours on end without getting caught, and if they fall behind, will go to ground among outcrops and burst out again from under their very noses. He will creep up on them and disturb their lunches.

Meanwhile the hunters will be lurking and stalking; arranging an encirclement from a high path or simply wandering in the mist hoping for a chance encounter and a sudden dash.

The hare in the opening paragraph has been chased down to Sty Head and now seeks to return to the game by Windy Gap, the pass between Green and Great Gables. Other routes across the Gable Range are too slow, therefore unsporting; the hounds above know this; so the hounds will be lurking in Windy Gap. The path enters thick mist as it eases towards the Gap. The hare mingles with some fell-walkers. "You'll find a person called Conrad lurking in Windy. Take him a message from the guy in the red sash."

The message is simple and age-old: "Nyaa nyaa na nyaa nyaa!" Under cover of the conversation the hare circles onto Gable, and sounds his horn. A hound leaps in pursuit.

He leads the hound all the way up Gable. He hides behind the cairn. He leads the hound all the way back down to Windy Gap. Again he sounds his horn. A hound below and a hound above, boulderfields and mist: here are the ingredients for a miserable half-hour for everyone.

But alas! The man in the Gap is Conrad himself. Inflamed by the derisive message he leaps forward and runs down the hare before he can reach the slippery slopes. And yes; that hare was me.

There are places around Ennerdale and Honister that fellwalkers simply don't get to: the steep screes above the Black Sail Hut, the interesting Ennerdale face of Kirk Fell, and the bed of the Derwent River. (And yes, the hound was quite prepared to follow me into the Derwent River.) The tarns and knolls of Haystacks are fascinating, but they're even more fascinating when incorporated into the predator-prey relationship. Even the drab pines of Ennerdale are attractive when they're somewhere safe to eat your lunch among.

There has not so far been any fatality on the Hunt, and injuries requiring a visit to Keswick Cottage Hospital occur to only about 1% of hunters. (It's surprising how many somersaults you can turn down a scree-slope without really hurting yourself.) Only once in two hundred and fifty hunting days has the Hunt been moved downhill because of bad weather.

To take part in the Lakes Hunt you have to be descended from a certain early Alpine pioneer, to belong to a certain Cambridge college, or be invited. However, there is no reason why any mountaineering club should not organise its own. The requirements are
• A stretch of hill ground of up to 1 square km (one grid square) per hunter, and containing
• at least one wide grassy valley
• some intricate knolly ground, preferably with rocks on
• obstructions, such as crags, lakes, wide rivers
• screes and boulderfields
• a wood
• paths or roads around the boundaries for evacuation of the injured
• An accommodation centre, preferably on the edge of the playing area. Beer, bath and a big meal are essential at the end of the day
• A set of hunters not too varied in ability. A single hill-runner won't have much fun among a crowd of Sunday walkers

Hares should practice beforehand to ensure a sufficiently loud and taunting noise from the horn. Oh, and do tell the Mountain Rescue what you're up to. Your behaviour on the hill will be such that innocent hillwalkers may take you for dangerous maniacs in distress.

And, you know... they may well be right.

"If it's east of the Kirkstone it doesn't count." So says the Ancestral Fell-and-Rock Member: and it doesn't do to argue with ancestors.

And it's true that there are lakes prettier than Haweswater; specially at those times when the inhabitants of Manchester have flushed most of it away down their toilets. Lakeland has sharp and exciting summits, but their names aren't High Street: the edge of High Street's flat plateau cuts off half the view.

As a respectful descendant, I shouldn't mention the ridge that connects these two slightly-less-wonderful points. Because it's a ridge that's pleasure from bottom to top. It's called Long Stile, but it's longer than that; by the time you get to the bottom the original name's been forgotten and it's The Rigg. It rises from the waters of the reservoir in one continuous two-mile crest to the summit plateau two thousand feet above. From over on Harter Fell, the crest looks like the blade of a worn-out saw.

Start/finish: Mardale Head car park GR 470107
Distance/climb: 7 miles/2500ft or 11 km/800 m)
By way of: High Street, Nan Bield Pass (Extended walk over Harter Fell and Selside Pike adds 4 miles/1200 ft or 7km/350m)
Map: OS Outdoor Leisure 5 (NE) or OS Landranger 90

From the car park walk 50yds upstream. Turn right at a sign, "Public Footpath Bampton". After the footbridge over the Blea Water Beck, a footpath turns left for Blea Water itself; but we turn right. Our path rambles along above the reservoir, looking down onto where Haweswater was before the Mancunians drank it. Above is one of those Lake District slopes of bracken, rock and tree.

The path rises up the hillside along the top of a small plantation. The ascent of the long ridge starts where the stone wall runs into the plantation at GR 474115.

The ridge path runs up the south side of the wall, which is itself slightly south of the crest. Better views are seen from the crest itself, and you'll also find a few rocks to clamber over. The ridge ascends by knob and wiggle. The path is bigger than I'd expected to find on this route that starts nowhere and runs all the way up to nowhere else. The mystery was solved when I met descending parties who believed themselves to have just crossed Kidsty Pike. It's formed by the feet of those who think they're doing Wainwright's Coast-to-Coast.

An airy little top at 628m just asks to be stopped at and sat on. Drop into the grassy pass of Caspel Gate, and then climb to where the ridge runs out suddenly onto High Street's plateau. Here is a large cairn to tell descenders where to go over the edge.

Linger here over lunch, not on High Street's summit which is a place to pass through fast on the speedy Roman road. Look down... down... down into Blea Water, the Lakes' deepest tarn. Tarns aren't snobbish about their addresses – one of the best of them, Bowscale, lives on a grassy lump at the back of Skiddaw – and Blea Water doesn't worry at all about being the wrong side of the Kirkstone. In Blea Water, they say, you can see the stars reflected at noon. That's optical nonsense. The only stars you'll see are if you fall over the edge and hit your head on the way down.

A faint path runs south-west to join the path and wall 200yds short of High Street's trig point. This is a place of dark peat and yellow grass, half-melted snow and freezing wind. Hurry past, descending into a gentle col and turning west, still on the wide path,

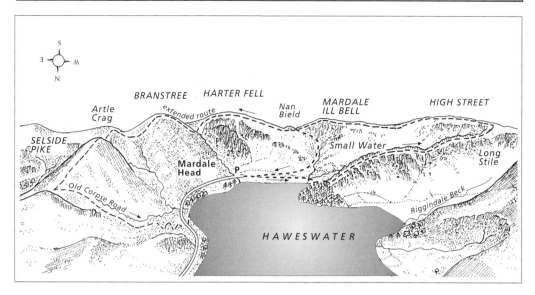

to Thornthwaite Crag.

This has a splendid tall summit cairn but isn't by any means a splendid tall summit – however, it does look out in a completely new direction, all the way down Trout Beck to distant Windermere.

Return across the col. Where a stone wall runs up to the path, leave it for a much smaller path on the right, running east. This is peaty in parts, but your eyes gain as your feet suffer: the view now is to Kentmere.

The path contours below Mardale Ill Bell. At a stony knoll of the ridge, the path turns suddenly left. A large cairn just out of sight down the back marks the start of the slanting descent to Nan Bield Pass. This descent is rough to start with. The Pass itself is marked by a large wall-like cairn.

You could continue now over Harter Fell. Harter Fell isn't one of the 17 Lakeland Peaks; the drop to Nan Bield is one metre short of the full 150. More seriously, Harter Fell's a rubbish summit – quite literally. Its cairn is made of rusty fencing.

On the other hand, the Nan Bield Pass is another of those bits that have no business on this side of the Kirkstone. A pass is more than a gap between hills. A pass should be rocky, and an achievement. Nan Bield is such a pass: a sharp edge dividing two valleys. So turn downhill at Nan Bield (and if there's time left at the end of the day, use it to visit Blea Water). The path descends in stony zig-zags, and spirals round the rocky slope above Small Water. Having enjoyed this tarn from three directions, cross its outflow. The path continues to right of the beck, then bears off right to Mardale Head.

Extended Walk: The whole point of this walk is the single ridge of Long Stile. Those whose ethics are flexible rather than – oh dear – ridgid – will spoil it all by going on from Nan Bield over Harter Fell, Branstree and Selside Pike. They will gain pleasures of a gentler, grassier sort; pleasures that have nothing at all to do with that long ridge from Haweswater to High Street.

A well-used path leads up out of Nan Bield onto Harter Fell: not itself a striking summit, but with a good stony ridge for the descent. Path and fence lead down gently

151

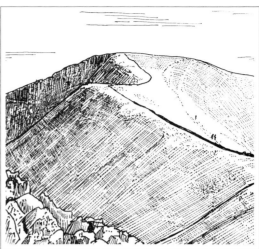

Above left: the Pillar near Artle Crag; Above right: High Street from the Straits of Riggindale

north-east, then steeply south-east, to Gatescarth Pass. The path divides to go down the two sides of the pass, but the fence continues onto Branstree. The summit, marked with a few piled stones, is to left of the fence.

Two high cairns decorate Artle Crag, but you'll have to leave the guiding fence, heading out right into the col, to visit the fine double-headed one marked as 'Pillar'. Haweswater has dropped away into its hole, and views now are into a new valley unfolding on the other side.

Our Harter Fell was the wrong one – the real one's in Eskdale – but what are we to say of this Mosedale? 'Moss Dale' is the name the surveyors gave when they wanted something appropriate but hadn't actually been there. Not going to Mosedale, Wastwater was sheer laziness, but this Mosedale has in common with Mosedale-under-Crinkle-Crag, Mosedale-under-Mellbreak and Mosedale-back-of-Blencathra a deep green remoteness, a silence and forgotten quality.

Rejoin the fence for the gentle climb to Selside Pike. The men of the Bronze Age clearly didn't know the first thing about piling stones, and the infrequent modern visitors have improved their cairn into the shape hopefully known as 'shelter'. The fence leaves us, and we proceed alone down the grassy ridge of Selside End. This is pleasant walking, remarkably dry (if, at this end of the day, we still care about such things) and grassy. Keep to the right-hand edge for views into Swindale with its crags and waterfalls. At the ridge-end head north-west across a flat col to the path, which is marked with poles.

Life's getting better. But when it comes to death, the journey in the long black car to the crematorium is nothing special. I'd far rather be carried in a box down the slanting zig-zag path that drops to Mardale Common. The path is marked with little cairns, and there are waterfalls alongside. The church it leads to is now underwater – so perhaps it's better, these days, to do this path while still alive.

A permissive path below the road leads northwards back to the car park.

Ice Is Nice

It's a fine white powder that brings ecstasy - and also death. Addicts sell up their houses, abandon their families and chase their habit half-way round the World. A bad trip - and most trips are bad ones - causes numbness in the hands and feet, leg-aches and uncontrollable shivering. A good trip lifts you into a biting blue sky and hangs you there like a booted angel.

They call it, 'snow'. But this isn't the sort you buy in little plastic bags and sniff through an empty biro. This is the original, old-fashioned snow. Sprinkle it on English hills and walk around on it.

It is in the nature of scarred and hardened addicts to corrupt the young. We want to seduce you onto the slippery slope. You won't feel a thing as the chip of ice enters your heart...

The first thing you need is an ice-axe, and straight away we run into confusion. An ice-axe isn't an ice pick. An ice-pick was formerly used by Americans for making frozen water small enough to go in their cocktails. Ice-axes are for climbing mountains, though one was also used to murder Leon Trotsky in Mexico in 1922. As yet, nobody particularly famous has been murdered with an ice-pick.

Ice-axe technique has been explained in words and pictures in many useful books. But don't just read about it: find a safe slope and practice falling down it.

Falling down safe slopes is fun. But it's even more fun to turn and walk up them to where white ridges and black rock stand against a washed-out Winter sky and the morning air's crisp as cornflakes.

If the snow's boring soft stuff, then just plod up it. Gradually the views get more interesting and so does the snow.

It's just like walking upstairs, but more exciting. After all, only the first 5cm of your foot is actually touching the slope. It doesn't take long to kick your way up two or three hundred metres of firm snow; that leaves a lot of air below the bootsoles.

It's odd. A slope of 30° – when it's covered with snow and you look down it... and down it... over the little cliff to the frozen tarn at the bottom - that 30° slope is vertical. Ullswater's a blue hazy pit, ranges of sparkly Pennines have climbed out from somewhere, and you can tell who practised their ice-axe braking. They're the ones who're looking at all this and going 'Oh, Wow!' The ones who didn't are looking at all this and going green.

The slope steepens towards the top – they always do – and also hardens. Possibly it gets so hard that you can no longer kick steps. This is when you wish you were wearing crampons.

Funny thing about crampons. When I started climbing in the snow, you got shouted at if you were seen in crampons. Crampons were what foreign people wore in the Alps. In England crampons were unnecessary and spoilt the fun.

Worse: they were dangerous, leading to a false sense of security. The climber who relies on his crampons will neglect the noble art of step cutting with the adze.

Nowadays, you get shouted at if you're seen not in crampons.

Myself, I carry my axe whenever I see snow, but for normal hillwalking leave the crampons at home. If I come to somewhere too hard to kick steps in, I turn back, or practise the noble art and long-forgotten art of step cutting. But plenty of people disagree: and when they see me, they shout at me...

In crampons, on hard snow, you walk like a fruitfly up a banana, with the whole of your foot flat against the surface. (On real ice you kick in the front two spikes; but if you're doing that you're an ice climber, not a hillwalker.)

Hillwalking is a low-risk sport but it certainly isn't a no-risk sport. Winter hillwalking is somewhat worse. In Summer, the main danger of your day's walking is the drive home afterwards. In Winter, the risks of the hill and the risks of the road are probably roughly the same. Can I make my personal plea for mountain safety? At the end of a long day, a half-hour's snooze is better than a half-pint of beer as preparation for snowy roads in the dark.

Leaving aside crashing your car, the extra dangers of Winter are: avalanche, benightment, cornices (falling off from underneath you), cornices (falling on top of you from above), hypothermia, involuntary glissades, storms and white-out. It's a tempting catalogue.

If you never run any risk at all, then you're having less fun than you could. On the other hand, if you never get sensible and turn back, then you're a bad hillwalker. OK, you're tough: you can walk out of Eskdale through two feet of fresh snow. But two metres?

Have the courage to be a wimp. There are days when the best you can do is go to the Pencil Museum in Keswick, and even that's not much fun. There are days when the view's mist, the snow's porridge, and you're too cold to eat your sandwiches.

Winter is more unpleasant than Summer can ever be. But conversely – take some dismal gully, full of mossed rock and scree, its walls black and dripping; take Lord's Rake on Scafell, whose ascent is a penance even without the people above dropping pebbles on your head; fill Lord's Rake with firm snow, and you have a whole new wonderful way up Scafell. Easy, but exciting; spectacular, but sheltered; and those drips off the walls have turned into elegant icicles.

You can't see much sky, but what you can see is an interesting yellow colour with fluffy pink clouds. (Pink? Well, dusk is at three o' clock. Still, there's a good moon, and I'm sure one of us remembered the spare batteries for the torch...)

Behind, the long ribbon of snow winds away between black walls: and that ribbon of snow has your footprints up it. Ahead, the little patch of sky never gets any closer, until suddenly your head's above the col and you stand in a freezing wind and look across five white ranges to the sunset sea.

Who wants Summer? Come out and play in the snow.

7: Sharp and Icy

The Edge in Winter

Winter arrives in the Lake District like one of those rich but inattentive uncles who take you to the most expensive eating-house in town. The uncle will pay but has little patience. You have just one brief teatime to choose, and then eat, the seven most absolutely delicious cream cakes; and if you get it wrong, there's a whole year of regrets before you get another chance.

That Siberian air-mass descends heavily from its taxi, lifts out its parcels from the back seat and peers around, blinking, at the strange southern landscape; then settles down among our silly little hills for its brief Christmas visit. The presents are traditional rather than surprising, but none the worse for that: breathing-air in chilled and sparkling gusts, snow-cornices in exotic Hansel-and-Gretel shapes (not at all English), pale chunks of sunlight and delicate hand-crafted frost crystals to hang on your tree. So run your finger down the cake-shop menu, rejecting the ordinary and wholesome. Reject the walk along the Dodds and the path to Goatswater. It's Christmas; go on, spoil yourself!

The finger lingers on the section marked 'ices'. There's crisp sugar-ice with streams underneath, and yellow lump-ice on frozen paths. Seriously tempting is the blue dangling ice in the gullies of Scafell...

"Is that what you want, then? The West Wall Traverse, and a helping of Lord's Rake with snow in stead of scree?"

"Wait... I'm still thinking." It says they do summit plateau glazed in grey striated hoar: whatever the first course, we'll have a bit of that for afters.

But below the ices come the rocks, and here the greedy eye is drawn to Blencathra, and the most crunchy, creamy, sugar-sprinkled, cherry-on-top treat in all Lakeland. Sharp Edge: with snow on. Then some of that plateau-ice, and on top of that... well, there's only so much one can ask for.

"Speak up, there's something else you're after. I can tell by the greedy look on your face."

"Well, Uncle... winter conditions on Halls Fell for the descent? But no, forget I said it. Halls Fell faces south, after all."

The Siberian Uncle whips out his charge card: a strange, magical card where all the credit balances are sub-zero. "It's Christmas, Child. Everything is possible."

We parked at the bottom of Mousthwaite Comb on a bit of gravel verge that in Summer's always full up. I prefer this path in the Comb to the higher one that starts from the White Horse Inn. The Comb is more sheltered and enclosed, and its grass and stones frame the outward view. We'd hardly started up before we met the first people coming down: two adults with ski poles descending the iced-over path. They trod carefully – their luggage included a small person in a backpack. They reported high winds and icy footing no further above us than the top of the Comb. The luggage was wide-eyed, clearly thrilled by the perils of winter travel. The luggage spoke. "You have to be careful," it told us.

Soon we began to feel like characters in one of those unsettling fairy tales by Grimm. Two tall young men came down the path towards us bearing ice-axes. "Sharp Edge? We didn't fancy it. We didn't fancy the frozen footholds and we didn't fancy the wind." The path traverses above the sheltered slot of the Glenderamackin River and clambers up beside a frozen stream. We met an old man, white-haired, in tweeds. "Sharp Edge? We had a look and then we came back down."

Sharp Edge was high and icy overhead, but icier by far was Scales Tarn, frozen grey all over and dotted with black rocks. There descended a maid and her man in matching Goretex. They'd avoided Sharp Edge altogether and reached the beginning of the summit plateau itself before turning back. "Frozen icy ground," they said: "and icy winds."

We stopped for a freezing but scenic snack of turkey sandwiches. Whatever the practical difficulties, Sharp Edge is a fine spectator sport. We watched the party that didn't turn back as it dithered among the pinnacles. "You need to get your feet lower down," shouted the leader, who was getting cold waiting for his friend. "And keep your hands high." We were enjoying the contradictory instructions more than the poor man trying to obey them.

Two climbers came past us, climbers in purple rucksacks and smart gaiters. They clambered around the bottom bit of Sharp Edge and came back down again.

"Wind?" we suggested knowingly.

"Wind," they confirmed. "Plus a bit of ice."

We decided to go for it.

We climbed onto the beginning of the ridge. With every upward step the wind got higher and the drops on either side got lower. This didn't matter; we were on clean grey rock, and wherever we placed a hand was a handhold. To make things more exciting for my friend, the McLean, I told him of the last time I was on Blencathra in Winter. From across the corrie I'd watched a helicopter lift a casualty out of the gully now below us. They hadn't put a helmet on the casualty; he hadn't survived his fall from Sharp Edge.

Two ravens wheeled among the snow-flurries. They were enjoying the updraughts: enjoying, also, the prospect of pecking over our broken bodies once we'd fallen off. The ridge narrowed. There's the rocky windswept crest, or the little path down the side all covered in frozen snow.

Fiddling with crampon straps in the gale isn't really an option. Anyway, firm rock's always safer than any gritty little path. We clambered along the crest, and where the ridge flattens were not ashamed to crawl. Fabric-covered knees grip well the odd icy patch.

Now the ridge becomes jagged, with downs as well as ups. Sharp Edge is real ridge, unique in England (Striding Edge has a path round the side). Sharp Edge would be quite at home on the Isle of Skye. Sharp Edge with snow on, and a sufficiently brisk wind, was making me think of the Nordgrat of the Zinal Rothorn.

The Rothorn has higher drops, and an edge of such sharpness you have to be careful not to tear your trousers. The Rothorn has the Matterhorn to look at. But Rothorn and Saddleback share the sudden downward view of rocks, the same friendly handholds

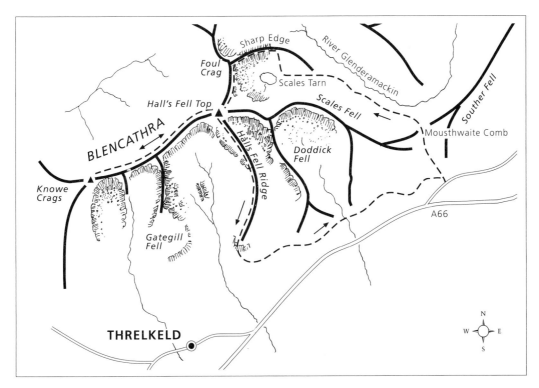

smoothed by a century of mountaineers.

We came to where the party ahead had lingered. The final pinnacle is passed by a simple rock ledge on the right. But the simple rock ledge was wearing an inch of ice and we weren't wearing crampons.

We looked round to the left. Footholds crossed the top of a rock wall which dropped in a single swoop to the frozen tarn 400ft below. The footholds were large and friendly: the rim of the pinnacle offered handholds big enough for wind-chilled fingers. The final block is round on top and the camera-bulge under anorak makes it awkward to sidle. The solution is to sit on the thing like a gargoyle in the wind, then slide down behind.

Now we were on the face of the mountain itself. This is climbed by a rocky groove except that the rocky groove was an icy groove so we took to the face on its left. This has plenty of bits to hang on to even when a mischievous handicapper had filled every third foothold with ice. Tussocks appeared with snow between, axes were deployed, and as the slope eased the wind started to blow properly, revealing that what we had before was only a playful breeze.

The cairn at Atkinson Pike is the first one to visit but something's wrong here... my feet were moving uphill but the cairn wasn't getting closer. Then I fell over. There's quite a drop beyond the top so the most comfortable way to get there was to stay down and crawl. (The other comfortable way would be to put on the crampons and walk. "It was so windy and icy I had to put on my crampons"? No, no. "It was so windy and icy I had to crawl.")

The wind was blowing away from the big drops with the cornices, so we enjoyed being buffeted around and waving our ice-axes for balance. We walked, staggered and

Sharp Edge, Blencathra in wintry conditions

Photo: Graham Thompson

leapt to the final top above Gategill Fell. From here we could inspect the ice on Derwent Water. Returning, I found a spot below a summit that was so sheltered that when a glove blew away I actually managed to catch it before it vanished into the Back o' Skiddaw. Here I finally did put on the crampons. Frozen plateau's less fun in crampons, but they do make lovely crunching noises when you leap about.

Others on the mountaintop were clad in gleaming Goretex, but few seemed to have asked Santa for an ice-axe. In considering the balance between safety, timidity and fun, you may not want advice from someone who climbs Sharp Edge in a gale unroped... that person's advice would be that crampons make things easier, if you want to make things easier, but an axe is what you require to stop you sliding to your death off the plateau.

"Is this going to be difficult, this Halls Fell?" wondered the MacLean.

"Twenty-two minutes in running shoes," I reassured him.

"Hmmm - I think I'll put my crampons on too."

Halls Fell is a blunt edge of bare rock and turf that drops in a steep straight line to the A66 two thousand feet below. In our crampons we trotted merrily down the frozen turf. On the bare rock we rediscovered the ancient truth: crampons grip rock a whole lot better than boots grip ice. Sharp Edge would have been better with the spikes on. We caught up with a party that'd turned back off Halls Fell: no crampons, and an unhappy dog.

What's wrong with today's walkers? Better equipped than ever, they fail to understand that a simple plod up the path is a hundred times better when your fingers are freezing off, whereas proper rock climbers with their muscle-bound fingertips and sticky shoes consider such places as Sharp Edge too easy to bother with. For me, the in-between ground - the place that's frightening without being dangerous, or dangerous without being frightening - is the best place of all.

Though I also enjoy the evening stroll along the bottom of Blencathra, between the bracken and the trees. The path runs along the top of the stone wall, through various gates marked 'Please Shut the Gate'. At Scaley Beck it surprises us with a little rock climbing.

Behind us, the sun goes down behind Cat Bells and the lights come on in a dozen scattered farmhouses.

"The Caldbeck Fells are worth all England else." Wainwright quotes this slogan approvingly. Few hillwalkers will agree with him. The northern fells have very little rock, only two tarns and an awful lot of heather and grass. Skiddaw has its size to recommend it. Skiddaw also has its scree.

The top of Skiddaw is a conical heap of small flat stones. The approach from Bassenthwaite village lets you enjoy the scree-heap from below, and then from the side – from, indeed, the Long Side. Finally, you enjoy the screes under your very bootsoles, on the penitential trudge from Carlside Tarn.

The Bassenthwaite route has other benefits. Here is Skiddaw's only section of real ridge, with long drops and short crags. On the way down is a waterfall. And the struggle with the scree is of just 180m: long enough to stir the spirit, too short to demoralise.

In Winter, the scree-struggle holds its snow, and it crosses a high and steep slope. At any time, Skiddaw's high and separated summit is even more exposed to wind and weather than all the others.

Start/Finish: Bassenthwaite (car park opposite the Sun Inn in the village centre). Parking at Peter House Farm (GR 249323) or near High Side (GR 236310)
Distance/climb: 9miles/3000ft (14km/900m)
by way of: Longside Edge, Bakestall
Map: OS Outdoor Leisure 4 (NW – new double-sided version) or Landranger 89 (West Cumbria) or 90 (Penrith)

The first advantage of the Bassenthwaite start is a pleasant and unfrequented field path. From the corner of the village green, follow the road south and fork left onto a very minor road. Where this bends left after 300yds, there are two stone stiles on the right. Take the left-hand one.

The field-path is not well-trodden, but is equipped with all necessary stiles and waymarks. Straight away it crosses the Chapel Beck at a footbridge, then turns left, upstream. After 50yds it slants up right, through a strip of woodland to a stile at its top edge.

Bassenthwaite Lake starts to appear beyond the nearer hedges, and this gives something interesting to look at apart from the grey screes overhead. In Spring the way is scented with hawthorn flowers, or, alternatively, by that other April messenger the muck-spreader.

The way follows fences south-east. After two more stiles a gatepost has a waymark pointing left. Head up beside the fence without going through the gate. A track joins from the right. After 50yds, look out for a stile and footbridge down right, and slant up across a field to the hill road.

Turn right for a quarter of a mile, passing High Side house, to a small car park (GR 236310). A bridleway sign points back left. The wide green path slants up a field. After 200yds, and before the end of the field, waymark arrows mark a path junction. Turn directly uphill, beside the remains of a hedge.

After climbing for five minutes, turn left, across the slope, to a ladder stile. Continue around the hillside onto a clear track running into the Southerndale valley.

Opposite: Hard Tarn, Helvellyn, swum in on the Ten Tarns Tour (chapter 8); overleaf top: Swirl How disappointingly snowless on the Slow Route to Scafell (chapter 9); bottom: The Ullswater sunset seen in Chapter 2

After a gate and stile, turn right, off the track, onto the ridge crest above.

A clear path runs up the crest. Nearly 500m must now be climbed to reach the high point of Ullock Pike. Effort invested finds here a generous payoff: not just a sudden view of Grasmoor, Derwent Water and the Central Fells, but also a mile of fine high ridge over Long Side.

The landscape here is half Lakeland, half slag heap. Little Man rises as a perfect cone. Skiddaw throws down long, straight slopes of scree. The composition is clean, uncluttered by the crags and rocky lumps we find in the Central Fells.

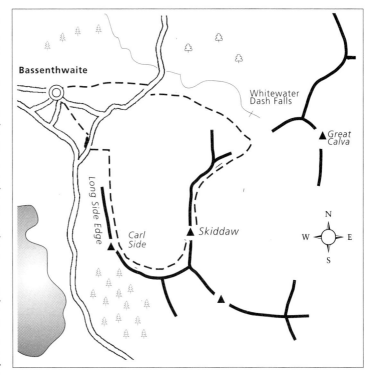

The ridge turns east and broadens to the flat top of Carl Side. This is counted by Wainwright as a separate summit (as indeed were Ullock Pike and Long Side). For the less acquisitive, the path alongside the drops into Southerndale will be found more rewarding.

The steep path now slants left, diagonally up the screes of Skiddaw. The slope it crosses drops steep and long into Southerndale. We can divert ourselves in commiserations with our fellow-sufferers: walkers out of Millbeck have joined us on the penitential treadmill. The path reaches the ridge-top at a sprawling shelter-cairn. Skiddaw's final trig is 100yds north, beyond a small col.

Continue north, down slopes that are stony but not particularly steep, then flatten to a small plateau. Now descend slightly east of north, with a fence on the right, on a small path or grassy slopes. A slight rise and cairn indicate the summit of Bakestall, which is yet another of Wainwright's peaks.

Retrace steps from the cairn for 50yds to rejoin the fence, which now descends north-east. Go down beside the fence; or 50yds left of it, for the sake of the view over the top of a loose and unexpected crag, and along the valley of Dash Beck. At the slope's foot join a stony track beside the Dash Beck.

The Whitewater Dash is just below the path. It can be peered into, adventurously, from various perches. Or you can wander down the track and enjoy the waterfall from a distance, while finishing up the sandwiches. The track leads out along the deep-scooped valley to the tarred trackway of Dash Farm, and here, quite suddenly, it leaves the Lake

161

District. The mountains are behind, the green fields are all around, and an odd-looking crag opposite is made of limestone and not proper rock at all.

Turn left along the tarred track, or on the short grass alongside, to reach the public road and a small car park after a mile. The bridleway continues directly opposite: it is signed 'Bassenthwaite 2miles', purely to discourage those who don't look at maps – the distance is actually a mile. Follow the track for 30yds only, then bear left, following white paint-spots.

This bridleway is little-used, but is marked with white-topped poles at every stile. And because it is a bridleway, and not a footpath, each of those stiles has a gate alongside. Remorseful knees may appreciate this subtlety. The final mile is gently downhill, and grassy; and this is the second advantage of the Bassenthwaite beginning.

The bridleway crosses open field and passes a single plane tree to a stile. Keep ahead at a 4-way signpost, crossing stiles with a fence on the left. At a line of five oaks, white paint-spots indicate that you should head out for 50yds into the field, then turn down the field's middle towards the village. A gate leads onto a track that drops to the village green.

How satisfying it is to walk straight off the hill into the pub. Here is the Sun Inn, for sitting on the benches in the sun and looking back at your mountain – or else for forgetting about your mountain and getting in out of the rain.

And that ending is the final advantage of the Bassenthwaite start.

Top Left: Whitewater Dash Falls, seen on the way down; Top right: snow scene of Longside Edge from Ullock Pike

Unhappy Formations and Natural Melancholy

There are three types of tarn: the valley tarn, the corrie tarn, and the tarn lying out on a ridge. Wordsworth didn't like any of them.

The valley sort of tarn "implies, for the most part, that the bed of the Vale is not happily formed... accordingly, Tarns are often surrounded by an unsightly tract of boggy ground."

Where are they today, these bog-edged unhappy puddles? Have the bogs been built over for the foundations of post-card shops and car parks – or was Wordsworth simply wrong?

A valley-floor tarn is, technically, a very small lake. Trees dangle into it and drop their leaves to make autumn patterns. There are wide easy paths, and benches, and people with push chairs who look on you in your big boots with something approaching awe. After a windswept day along the Coniston ridges, come down along the side of Tarn Hows. Shelter under the branches, finish up the sandwiches, and listen to the rain falling into the water.

Tarn Hows is a fake lake, for Tarn Hows is a reservoir, built simply to improve the scenery. So let's come off Wetherlam the other way, down Wet Side Edge to Little Langdale, and enjoy Little Langdale Tarn instead. Little Langdale Tarn has trees too, but not so many of them as to block the reflections of Bowfell and Pike of Blisco. Little Langdale Tarn has lilies, and the evening sun rolls gently down the Wrynose Pass and lies across the water.

Mountain tarns, says Wordsworth, are even worse. "The prospect of a body of pure water, unable to give furtherance to the meagre vegetation around it – excites a sense of some repulsive power strongly put forth, and thus deepens the melancholy natural to such scenes."

It's true that the mountain tarn has no trees. It's true that no shepherds in smocks play croquet on the surrounding lawn because the lawn is actually boulders and the croquet ball would quickly vanish down a hole, the smocked shepherd break his ankle. Wordsworth's right that the blue sky reflected in the water is actually black or grey, because half of that sky is crag, and the rest of it is raining. A "not unpleasing sadness" is indeed induced by the fallen rocks. His error is in thinking of all these features as disadvantages.

The Lake District is a lump of three different sorts of rock, rough-shaped by ice and rain and worked over by sheep, charcoal-burners and the Brasher boot. Yet is also a created thing, a sort of artwork. And like the 'Fate' motif in the operas of Wagner, like the little upside-down bird in the paintings of Paul Klee, Lakeland keeps repeating the crag-hung corrie tarn. Each tarn has different rocks, but all of them do the same thing – being jagged still shapes on a moving splashy surface. Screes plunge in, and keep going below the waterline.

There's a flat place to sit by the outflow, and the stream below has a waterfall. It's what art critics call a 'rhythmic element' – and that's the function of the corrie tarn.

Glaciers leave piles of rubble in all sorts of places. The third type of tarn lies out, suspended in glacier-rubble, on the open ridge. For the ridge-top tarn we'll leave Wordsworth and turn to the painter Heaton Cooper. For Heaton, these tarns are the 'eyes of the mountain'. They are a lump of earth-fallen sky. He painted all of the tarns – even some of the reservoirs – and you can see his book at the gallery in Grasmere.

Wainwright's favourite was Innominate – and I'm not going to argue with Wordsworth and Wainwright both on the same page. Blea Water Mardale is the deepest, and there are three other Blea Tarns to collect. Devoke Water is the biggest and Foxes Tarn on Scafell is the smallest.

How many are there? Timothy Tyson and Colin Dodgson of Grasmere used to jump into them; they only counted if they were chest-deep. Their list extended to over four hundred. The runner Mike Cudahy led a trip past his personal 'Top Twenty Tarns'. They were all above 500m, and even when he'd settled that the Three Tarns were to count as only one he was foxed by Dry Tarn (GR 215098 on Great Gable) which lived up to its name and wasn't there at all. Members of the Rucksack Club completed the 60-mile, 20,000-foot trip in thirty hours.

"It is wise to give your tarns time," says Heaton Cooper, "rather than try to bag as many as possible." But for those who wish to ignore this advice, his list of 106 is the definitive one to bag from. The book is called *The Tarns of Lakeland*.

Easedale Tarn

8: The Ten Tarns Tour

Tarn-bagging is hard, even when one of the tarns you plan to bag isn't Hard Tarn which in the case of this walk it is. Tarns aren't placed conveniently at the tops of paths. Tarns are in unfrequented combs, or behind knolls at the ends of long flat ridges. Tarns delight in making you cross rough country to get at them. In return they offer you, not a pile of stones or a trig point in the mist, but a little circle of sky trapped in a bog and decorated with small flowers.

Tarn bagging takes time: not just time to get there, but time to sit and appreciate there when you've got. And it takes even more time if you mean to swim in each one. Each tarn is different to swim in. The small ones will coat you in peat-flecks. The large will freeze you deeply, and the middling ones will tip you over with their loose stones. Some are in passes with paths through, and for them you'll need a bathing suit. For Grisedale Tarn you'll need a wet suit, and Scuba, and metal detector - for in the depths of Grisedale Tarn lies the crown of Cumbria. On hot, sweaty days, take time to let the heart slow down. Leaping straight into freezing tarns can be bad for it.

From Glenridding: 22miles/9000ft or 35km/2800m over one or two days on Harvey's Eastern Lakeland map
Lanty's Tarn, Red Tarn, Hard Tarn, Grisedale Tarn, Scandale Tarn, Red Screes Tarn, Caudale Moor Tarn, Small Water, Blea Water, Angle Tarn.

Take the track just left of Glenridding Bridge, and bear left on a path that zig-zags up to Lanty's Tarn.

LANTY'S TARN
Lanty's Tarn is green and soupy, seasoned with a century of leafmould. This is odd, as it's a hilltop tarn: and if it weren't for the trees it would have a view of most of Ullswater. You get the view anyway as you arrive; and then blink as you plunge into brown shadows.

Go down past the tarn to a wide path and head up-valley. Where the path branches take the higher one, which climbs the flank of Grisedale; it's one of the main ways to Striding Edge. Once on the ridge, do not turn left towards Striding Edge, but keep ahead to contour round to Red Tarn.

RED TARN, HELVELLYN
The tarn comes suddenly, big and not red at all but often very green. Eagles used to soar here. Striding Edge provides a jagged skyline, rendered still more jagged by the

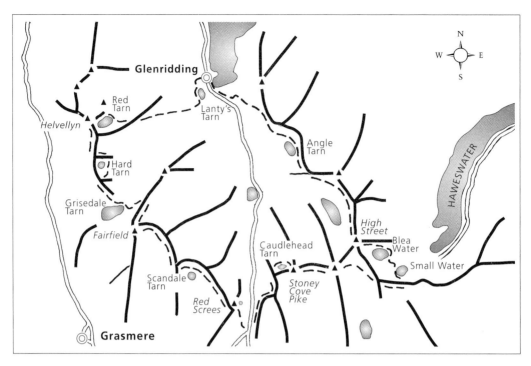

dozens or even hundreds of projecting people. It's a stony place rather than a craggy one, and harsh rather than romantic.

From the tarn foot, a path slants up onto Swirral Edge. This Edge is shorter than Striding, and isn't quite so exposed. The path avoids the difficulties, not that the difficulties are very difficult. It's a fine ridge with slaty spikes in all directions, and reaches the plateau a few steps from Helvellyn's summit.

Walk down the grassy flats next to the eastward drop, to Nethermost Pike. Enjoy the easy ground, for it does not last. The tarn hunt takes you into wild country, even if tarns unlike foxes stay still when you chase them. (And however hot and tired you get, you can't go for a swim in a fox. Any more than you can go for a swim in Foxes Tarn. But that's another walk, for another day).

Walk out on Nethermost's plateau to its eastern point and look over. A little rocky ridge presents itself. For every thousand people striding up Striding, just one or none at all scramble this little arete. Sweet it is, but short, and soon gives way to a harsh little path zigzagging down scree. At the foot of this steep ground a small peatpool is just below. Traverse out right along the foot of the screes. Here is some boulderfield, with the sharp green of parsley fern frothing out from the gaps. A large split boulder with a cairn on marks the way. Just beyond, Hard Tarn sprawls sunbathing on its rock shelf.

HARD TARN

Though tiny, Hard is a true tarn and no peatpool. Ice formed it and rock contains it. Lying up to your neck in Hard Tarn – sadly you can't stand up to your neck in Hard Tarn, not unless you're someone very low like a Lakeland terrier – but lying up to your neck in Hard Tarn, you can gaze out across that rock ledge to the other side of

166

Ullswater and perhaps the Pennines. The other way to look is upwards at the great split crag of Ruthwaite. The twiglike figures along the skyline, part of the year-long Helvellyn Picnic Party, are getting a good view of you if their binoculars are the really expensive ones. But they're not getting any view at all of the Ruthwaite Crag.

Incidentally, bathe in Hard Tarn but please don't wash in it. You're a form of natural occurrence like frogspawn or dead sheep, but soap and shampoo are pollution.

Cross the floor of Ruthwaite Cove northwards, loosing a little height to pass below some scree and small crags. Rise again to the top of a grassy spur projecting from the east ridge of Dollywaggon Pike. (This east ridge is the Tongue; the preliminary spur top, level with Hard Tarn, is at GR 348133.)

From the top of the spur, go up boulders for 100ft (30m vertical) to below a small crag. Traverse left on grass. Soon you reach the ridgeline of the Tongue, and can go up easily, with splendid views down the sides. It doesn't take long to reach the small cairn of Dollywaggon Pike – and there you are back among the picnickers.

Turn left on one of the most popular paths on Britain's most popular mountain. So it must be good, no? No. It's steep, and it's stony, and it goes down grass. However, it does lead to Grisedale Tarn.

GRISEDALE TARN

Grisedale Hause isn't one of those low strategic passes for fighting battles in; it's one of the high narrow ones for escaping through afterwards. The battle was in Dunmail Raise: and Dunmail himself was the king escaping with an embarrassing great crown tied to his saddle. Is that crown in this tarn? The water's 115ft (38m) deep, and silt builds up in tarn bottoms at approximately 5mm per year...

Take the slanting path from Grisedale Tarn's outflow to the pass called Deepdale Hause. It's a teasing path, that takes you most of the way there and then traverses across under the col, showing you this interesting steep slope with little crags on. Indulge it, it's not just being tiresome....

Cofa's a silly sort of name, sounding like a G o v e r n m e n t Committee or else some sort of South American foodstuff. And it's a silly sort of hill, if you want to look at it that way: about ten metres high and half a metre wide, stuck on the side of Fairfield. And it has this silly little knobble on its ridge, as if it tried to be like the Alps but got the scale

Grisedale Tarn and St Sunday Crag

wrong. On the Weisshorn they call it the Grand Gendarme, which is a policeman, and we recall that on the Continent the policemen carry guns and kill you if you get it wrong... What Cofa Pike has is no policeman, more of a primary school guinea-pig monitor; and if you get it wrong you have to go back and do it again because your friends are in the col with the camera, and you really do look rather bold on the blocky bit with the corner of Ullswater in the background.

And so to Fairfield. It's a busy place, because people do like to do that Fairfield Horseshoe, and it does have splendid views but then where in the Lake District doesn't? That's a debating topic for the wide unexciting ridge over Hart Crag and Dove Crag. Leaving aside the Back o' Skiddaw, my choice for the least spectacular view in Lakeland would be Burnmoor Tarn under Scafell. Then again, there's Skeggles Water. Talking of tarns, the map shows a puddle at the head of Houndshope (GR 374111). There's some route description in Chapter 1 about working round below Dove Crag. However, once you start arguing about the least lovely viewpoint in Lakeland you don't want to stop, and up along the top there's plenty of folk to argue it with. The trees of Ennerdale? Grike? Loadpot Hill? This quickly becomes a game of onedownmanship: I've been to a less lovely bit of Lakeland than you've been to... 200yds after the summit of Dove Crag, turn left away from the wall and follow a broken fence down past Little Hart Crag to pass above the next tarn.

SCANDALE TARN
The thing about Scandale Tarn is the wet perspective. You look over the small pool to Windermere, and you look over Windermere to the sea. I like this best under a wet sky, when the effect comes out in silver and grey.

A ridge-path with a wall leads up Red Screes.

RED SCREES TARN
Like Cofa Pike, Red Screes Tarn is a funny little place. If a tarn is a little bit of sky come down onto the hill, on Red Screes the hill's trying to put the tarn back up into the sky again. This is something unique: a true summit tarn. It sees a lot of sky, a little bit of Helvellyn, a fringe of grass and a summit cairn.

Behind that Red Screes summit cairn is the big hole leading down to the Kirkstone. The Kirkstone's half way. If you want you can stop here, drink some beer and go to bed.

A path leads up to left of the Inn, to join a wall on the ridge of St Raven's Edge. The wall leads up onto a wide grassy col just before the summit of Stony Cove Pike.

Mark Atkinson's monument, Caudale Moor

CAUDLEHEAD TARN
There's one more small grass tarn to knock off, and dawn's a good time to do it, though the pool on Stony Cove Pike feels like dawn all day with its whispering grasses and solitude. It's a clump of puddles, divided by grass isthmuses. Or

Small Water from Harter Fell

else it's a small grass archipelago separated by narrow strips of tarn.

But we'll press on. For after three tarns that've been rather troublesome to get to and rather puddlesome once arrived at, we now head for three classic wet bits. A rocky drop leads to the pass of Threshthwaite Mouth, and a scree climb to the high cairn on Thornthwaite Crag. Keep on eastwards, walking the rim of the Kentmere Valley and contouring just to right of Mardale Ill Bell. Cross the ridgeline to find the path slanting down to Nan Bield Pass. Turn left at the pass to descend onto Small Water.

SMALL WATER
This tarn is at its best when we use it, as in Chapter 2, as part of a high pass between Mardale and Kentmere. Rocky slopes enclose it on three sides. It's sheltered but grim, and the upward traveller must think here of bandits, avalanche and hurricane in the pass above.

As the path reaches the northwest corner of the tarn, slant up away from it onto the ridge of Piot Crag. Cross the ridge, and drop down grassy slopes to Blea Water.

BLEA WATER
Old snow now builds up on northern and eastern slopes, and here the glaciers form. Once it reaches a certain weight the ice starts to dig its own hole, and this is your

169

Above: Blea Water from Mardale Ill Bell. Below: Caudale Moor (L) and Threshthwaite Mouth from Ill Bell

corrie: but how does it dig it so deep? Blea Water goes down 200ft (70m) below the corrie floor. It's a mystery. One answer may be that, with water trickling down the back and freezing in the winter, the whole ice-mass starts, very very slowly, to rotate. It's a climate-powered seasonal brace and bit.

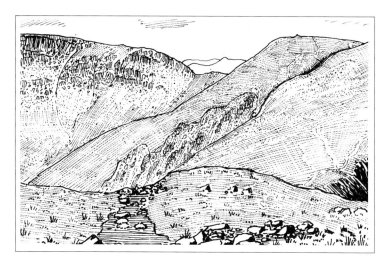

From the outflow, a path slants up steep grass to the col of Caspel Gate. A rocky ridge, with some loose scree, leads up onto High Street's plateau. Turn right, and follow the wall along the ridge. After the narrows at Straits of Riggindale, the wall runs to left of the crest. Where the wall turns up left, keep ahead on

170

a stony path. Just before the path drops over the steep edge towards Hayeswater, turn off right on a less large path.

For its next three miles, the path is a pleasantly gentle descent. It follows fence and wall over Satura Crag, then crosses just above the final tarn.

ANGLE TARN, PATTERDALE

Glaciers fill the valleys on either side, and deposit their moraine rubble along the ridge crest. And so, when glaciers melt, there forms the ridge-top tarn. Angle Tarn has an island, and rock-buttresses that drop into the water. Out in the open, it's a tarn of evening, gathering light from the fading sky.

The path crosses the steep slope of Dubhow Brow, and dives into a little hollow at the back of Rake Crag. After Boardale Hause it steepens, and becomes uncomfortable. A tarred track crosses the valley floor to Patterdale, and roadside paths return you to Glenridding in the dusk.

Helvellyn, Fairfield and High Street: you have visited three of Lakeland's principal summits. Those summits were high and also dry – unless it happened to be raining. It's the shining waters of the ten tarns that colour the memory silver and blue.

Angle Tarn

Goatswater is in my upbringing. Its stony shores were where we sat and looked up at Dow Crag and wondered which bit of lovely firm easy rock to do today. My mother climbed Lazarus on her honeymoon in a woolly bonnet and a ragged jacket. My grandfather could never get up Intermediate Gully, and neither could I. And on one splendid day, the wind hit us like a wall, and bits of Goatswater were blowing up the screes as far as the rescue box at the bottom of B Buttress.

On the 'Lakes of Lakeland' I came upon Levers Water; and Levers Water was so fine and frightful that whenever I was on the Coniston Fells I arranged to come upon Levers Water again. And so for several years I missed out on Low Water. Low Water is right beside the main way up the Old Man, but I always avoid the main way up anything. When I finally got up to Low Water, late on a midsummer evening, the cloud was blowing across the ridge and Low Water was a mysterious shining green, like corroded statues. It certainly went well with the pink sunset.

And then there's Blind Tarn...

Start/Finish: Little Langdale
Distance/climb: 16 miles/6500ft or 26km/2000m (mostly pathless)
by way of Greenburn Tarn, Levers Water, Low Water, Goatswater, Blind Tarn, Seathwaite Tarn
Map: Outdoor Leisure 6 (Lakes SW)

From the Little Langdale Inn, take the road up-valley for 200yds to the entrance track of High Birk Howe. This becomes the path that has the wonderful view of Little Langdale Tarn, and leads to Slater's Bridge. Slater's is every bit as good a footbridge as Little Langdale Tarn is a tarn. The track beyond leads up the Greenburn Beck to Greenburn Tarn. This tarn is less wonderful, being a reservoir, but it is in a little-visited valley below huge hill-slopes. These slopes are now climbed, on bracken and then rough grass, to Swirl Hause – the pass between Swirl How and Wetherlam. Go straight through the pass and down a grassy slope, onto a path leading to Levers Water.

Go round to right of the tarn, below the rocky slopes of Swirl Band, to enjoy the narrow path under Gill Cove Crag. At the tarn's southern corner the path divides. Take the right fork, turning away from the water. Boulder Valley is a gently-slanting hollow in a mountain face that's mostly pretty fierce. Across the Low Water Beck you join the wide and well-used path towards Coniston Old Man.

The path zig-zags up through mine tailings, passing abandoned machinery that's like monumental sculpture of the more modern sort. At Low Water turn off across the tarn's outflow, and head north up the slope beyond. This is grass and rocks, and leads to the eastern spur of Brim Fell, and up to that summit. Wait for a gap in the traffic that passes along the busy ridge, and go straight across to the pass of Goats Hause. A very large path leads down to Goatswater.

Follow the stream down onto the wide, wet, flat place that is The Cove, and slant up right to find Blind Tarn nestling on its little shelf. Coniston Water is stretched out below: beyond it are bits of Windermere: and Morecambe Bay should gleam along the southern horizon.

A steep and rough path leads straight up to Brown Pike – or an easier one, southwards and gently descending, to the Walna Scar track. After so much lurking on the

eastern flanks, the sudden view west at the Walna Scar pass is thrilling. It takes a while to work out that the mysterious hills behind Harter Fell are simply Pillar and Kirk Fell seen from behind.

Four miles south-west now is Dunnerdale's Stickle Tarn: four miles of low but rocky mountain, and a bridleway track through outcrops to go down on. What's that you say: tarns must take their turns, and for today seven is plenty? Quite right. So follow the track down into the Duddon Valley, and turn left on the signed path to Turner Hall campsite.

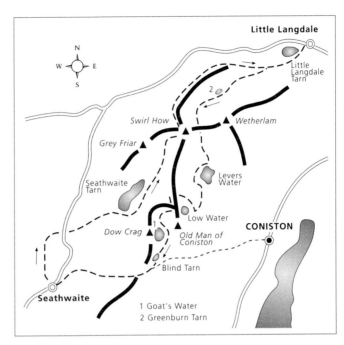

Seathwaite and its inn are just down the road.

A footpath opposite the church leads to a wooden footbridge, and left, around the base of Pen, to a high stone one. Head upstream, through the Wallowbarrow Gorge. After another, smaller, footbridge, the river itself is recrossed on stepping stones. Go straight across the road above, onto a small footpath that bends left and drops through a wood to cross the Tarn Beck upstream from Tongue House. Turn left through a gate, and head uphill across fields to a track leading to the dam of Seathwaite Tarn.

Each side of the tarn has a path: the one on the right is drier, but rockier. The damp valley of the Tarn Head Beck leads up to the broad col between Grey Friar and Great Carr. Near the top of the slope to Great Carr is a memorial cairn including parts of a Halifax bomber that crashed here in 1944.

The long green ridge of Wet Side Edge is just right for coming down at the end of a tiring day. It runs north, with fine drops on the right, over the minor summit of Little Carrs, then bends round north-east. At its foot a wall crosses ahead. Turn right, alongside the wall, to cross the Greenburn Beck and rejoin the track of the outward route.

Goats Water from Dow Crag

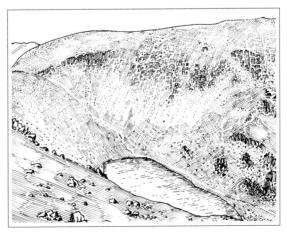

Starlight

The modern tent is a wonderful bit of kit. It weighs very little, you can put it up in half a gale, and it stays up even when that half-gale increases to a full one. It doesn't leak and you don't need to leap out in the night and slacken off the guys. It's your home from home in the middle of the wilderness.

A bit of a shame, really. Half the pleasure of a nice night in the wilderness is knowing it could have been a really nasty one.

The bivvy bag is lighter than the tent: it is also cheaper than the tent. But that's not really the point. In the bag, no night out is ordinary. You're never at home in six feet of green plastic.

There are only 215 hills in Lakeland, and you can do half-a-dozen at a time. This could mean nothing left to do, and half a lifetime left to do it in. A longer project is to sleep, in the green bag, on each of the 215. I'm not a fanatical bagger: so far, I've done just ten.

On a summer evening, after the pubs have opened, there's no problem finding a space in the big Langdale car park. The people coming down the path warn that it's going to get dark – you don't look like a hill sleeper: hill sleepers are supposed to suffer under heavy baggage with a bedroll tied on top. But in fact the summer evening's in no hurry to become a summer night; you've time to walk across five summits and be alone on them all. And on the sixth you open up the bag. Nearly every hill has a grassy place somewhere within 50yds of the summit; or better still, a heathery place. Lights come on in the valley, the moon shines down onto the sea. Great Gable turns into an interesting purple shape.

If you want to see the stars, and you're in a tent, that means two lots of zips and getting sworn at by your companion. In a bivvy bag, it just means opening one eye. In fact, that eye was probably open anyway: bivvybag sleep tends to be intermittent. The sun has left a green glow behind High Stile: the glow moves round, Skiddaw gets the coloured background, and lo! the sun's coming up again beside Helvellyn. We don't normally feel the Earth rotate: but in the green bag, looking up, perspective shifts. The world turns below the stars, and the horizon drops to reveal the Sun.

Or else it doesn't. You've actually been asleep, and that's because it's less freezing cold than it should be, and that's because you're in the cloud. It's pretty sheltered in this hollow below the big rock, but still, the night air blows across your face, and the rain, when it comes, patters an inch away from your ear.

In the morning it's a quick damp sandwich, and within ten minutes everything's back in the sack. Soon you're 500ft downhill and warming up nicely. It'll be two hours, and four more hills, before you meet another fellwalker.

And that's one more Wainwright summit – in the bag.

9: Scafell Slowly

You can do Scafell Pike the short way – or you can do it the silly way. On any sunny Sunday, about two hundred people will walk up onto that stony, boulder-hoppy route from Angle Tarn to Esk Hause and do Scafell Pike. Why should they do this if it wasn't fun? What's not fun is to walk through Lakeland with a tent, where a tent is never necessary; and to pitch that tent in a place without a pub, in the middle of January, and then go to sleep in it.

A realist sees those two hundred having fun on the sideslope of Great End, and goes up there and joins them. A romantic sees the two hundred having fun, and goes somewhere else. A realist does Scafell Pike the short way, from Borrowdale. Now it's perverse to apply reason to romance, but we romantics are nothing if not perverse, and we say: if you enjoy Scafell Pike, why not enjoy it at length rather than shortly?

Thus we arrive at the logical, the self-indulgent start-point for Scafell Pike. We arrive at Coniston village.

We arrive at Coniston village at nine o'clock on a January Saturday, and adorn the windscreen with double parking-tickets. Nine is not the best of times: lemon-coloured January sunlight is playing over the crags of Wetherlam, and if we were already up on Wetherlam that lemon sun would be playing all over us.

We take the lane beside the Black Bull, and head up under the crags that guard the entrance to the inner mysteries.

The lane becomes a patchy track, the crags draw in closer and try to look fierce. However the gay red bracken at bottom, like the red neckerchief below the fierce face of a pirate, slightly spoils the effect.

Grimness retreats in the upper valley, where a dusty track leads through gravel heaps to the youth hostel.

"And look," says David, "we aren't really late, there's people just in front of us on the track."

When other people are on the track is what I call late.

But most of the other people head off towards Low Water, as their idea is the short route up the Old Man rather than the long one up Scafell Pike. For us, a wooden foot-bridge leads to the foot of the Levers Water Beck. Waterfalls are below, crags above, and the wide wastes of the copper mines behind.

Such surroundings take the effort out of the thousand feet to Levers Water, but a further thousand steepening feet, with our two-day packs on, might be a less enjoyable sort of fun. So, where the rocks on the left come closest to the Cove Beck, we go over and start climbing them.

It's supposed to be a Grade 2 scramble: but really the grade's whatever we care to make it. The rocks have a thin coating of dried slime, as they face north-east and never see the sun. By keeping well left, it's possible to dangle above the tarn on sweeps of

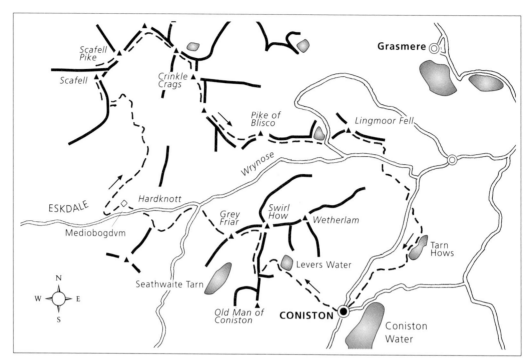

sound, clean, albeit slightly green crag face. However, with our two-day packs on we're happy to do a fair bit of our rock climbing on grass. We gain height, and enjoy ourselves, even if we don't manage to get particularly terrified in the process.

Near the top, our path is crossed by dogs. In the patches of rocky steepness between the trodden paths, the Lakeland hounds are still attempting to pursue, it would seem, the fox. Embarrassing it must be for them, though, as the bright red-and-yellow windproofed procession along the ridge cannot but observe that half the hounds head excitedly down towards Low Water while the rest seem to think the action's at Goat's Hause. Meanwhile the associated humans stump along half an hour behind, muttering into their CB sets. If those humans wore red Goretex instead of green tweed, and pointy fleece caps instead of flat ones, then when they got embarrassingly far behind their dogs they could put their CB sets away and pretend to be doing the same silly sport as the rest of us...

The dogs, though: the dogs are impressive, the way they're here one minute and a thousand feet down the hill at Low Water the next.

Half a mile away, the outline of the Old Man is becoming fuzzy as the first dozen walkers sit down on him to eat their sandwiches. On the steep ridge below, more are outlined against the sunstruck mud of distant Morecambe Bay. Here on the hill, though, the cloud's coming down and a brisk north-easterly's coming up, and it might be going to snow. The forecast has promised snow in gullies and eastern faces above 800m, so we look round the back of the cairn on 802m Swirl How. Disappointment – no snow.

Great Carrs is less disappointing. Frost has whitened the rocks, and snowflakes sweep up out of the chasms alongside, do a brief somersault above the cairn, and disappear into the mist. We stroll on along the plateau towards Grey Friar, and what

176

View of the Scafells from Coniston Old Man

exceedingly comfortable strolling this is, with the wind behind, Dow Crag looking edgy against the golden estuary, and crisp frozen grass under foot. Gradually, the crisp declines to bog on the long drop to Dunnerdale; finally sinking into farmyard mud.

A ladder stile with waymarks is the start of a muddy bypass round to left of Black Hall. A sheep-feeder generates an intense zone of mixed mud and slurry, and can be applied as a precision brown bomb to decrease the enjoyability of a path: here, the sheep feeder has been placed not on the right-of-way, but on the exact intersection of two different rights-of-way. Farm dogs bark at our heels across the field, then sit at the gate and rest their tongues ready to bark at the heels of the next lot of walkers coming back the other way. Duddon is a lovely valley, but this farm at its head makes back on the hill seem the better place to be. A sloping bog leads up to Hardknott, a wonderful view down Eskdale to the sea, and the Roman fort.

The Roman fort at Hardknott has been carefully positioned to catch the best of the Eskdale view. We potter around in the afternoon light, looking over the crag tops, appreciating the stonework and thinking about how far it is from Rome, how unlike are the cloud-topped slopes of Scafell and Hardknott to the vineyards of the Sabine hills, how long and hard and high is the way to the next safe place at Penrith.

On the road below a cyclist sits mending his chain – quite annoyed at having this honourable reason for a rest before he was even half-exhausted enough to need it. He means to do the Hardknott Pass (a thousand feet of one in four) and then the Wrynose one as well. It's always reassuring to meet those prepared to enjoy sports I wouldn't even attempt to find fun in: this man makes January camping seem positively self-indulgent.

The day is fading into evening as we take the long path into Lakeland's only roadless valley. The brisk north-easterly means we're not going to camp on top of Scafell. The Great Moss of Eskdale is lower in altitude, and also in romance, than the top of Scafell; but it is about as far from anywhere else as you can get in the Lake District, with big spiky mountains all around.

Behind us, the sun is doing one of those nondescript mauve sunsets: around us the ground is fading to brown, the Esk River is reflecting the mauve, and the waterfalls are the unlikely white of toothpaste advertisements. And then, far above us, the final sunbeam wriggles through a gap in the clouds and turns the Crinkle Crags all pink.

A man comes down the path. This is not, in the Lake District, an unusual thing to have happen. However, a man at dusk in Eskdale is, perforce, a romantic. And so it

177

proves – but this is a romantic of the Wertherian, the sad, sort. "My wife divorced me," he tells us under the purple sunset in Eskdale, "and then I lost my house."

This sounds like carelessness. How do you lose a house? "It's a long story..." and we look at the descending darkness: there's no time for long sad stories. "Stress," he summarised. "Stress, and depression. So I called in sick from my work, and came out here." "You don't look sick." Indeed, he looked impressively fit. "Ah," he explained. "I came up from Langdale, and then I slept the night on Ill Crag. So then I felt much better."

Naturally: one would feel much better. So then I started to babble about how in Summer you can do the same thing in a bivvy-bag, and let the stars shine straight down onto your nose, and he explained that indeed a bivvy-bag was what he'd used for his January sleep-out at 3000ft. Bivvy-bag in January: really, there's no need to be quite so romantic as all that...

We went up alongside the gorge, and found a flat bit under a crag, just before it got too dark to see the tent-pegs. I'd brought various domestic pleasures like a stove, and a tea-bag, and some dehydrated curry. "Damn," said David, "We didn't bring the scrabble."

Scrabbleless, we lay and looked at stars, and watched the moon slide out from behind the crag and reflect in the Esk River.

Dawn in Eskdale consists of hopping across dark streams below a sky of pink and yellow. Dawn is topmost crags gleaming golden like castles in heaven. Dawn is the first sun-rays hitting a crag of icicles. And we're on a way up Scafell that's a perfectly easy, grassy way that yet, whenever we feel like it, can become a perfectly easy rocky way; and that way winds up around the top of a perfectly enormous precipice. David, lacking Scrabble, has spent the night chasing the alphabet from Ambleside to Yewdale, and now wants a place in the Lakes beginning with J. But I'm very happy with the place in the Lakes we've already got: for now comes a narrow ridge that dangles sunlit above dark Eskdale, that leads onto England's finest mountain, and that has no path.

There's a dusting of snow on the summit stonefield: below the snow, Autumn brown extends down to Burnmoor, and Spring green is all the low country of the coast.

Sellafield is looking particularly lambent in the early light. The Screes of Wastwater are quite big hills, but we're looking down on them, through crisp air, from way, way above. This godlike view impels David to start telling me about various interesting deaths and murders that have happened on the Wastwater Screes.

We go down towards Wastwater, and while the nuclear power station twinkles merrily in the sunlit view behind us, we stare into the shadows and consider Lord's Rake. We're looking for some of that snow in northern gullies above 800m, and there is indeed a very small patch. But mostly, it's ice-hard rigid shale.

Rigid shale is not a nice surface. However, we do have our crampons. Crampons are the way to deal with rigid shale, even if it does feel a bit silly. But you can't feel silly for long below the high cold wall of Central Buttress, looking up at the famous Flake Crack. They went up that in nailed boots, the second man clinging to the chockstone and the first man climbing over his head. And here's us thinking we're a bit tough taking a tent up Eskdale, and worrying about frozen shale.

Grim are the thought processes under Central Buttress in January. Even where all outside is golden, the shadow of Central Buttress lies blue across the hill opposite, with a deep slash for Mickledore, and Scafell Pinnacle a distinct bump at the top.

We work our way between the famous rock climbs, our crampons scratching the frozen scree. Up at Mickledore we stop in the sunlight, and hide the crampons in the sack. Let's not show the crampons to the two hundred sensible people on the path to Esk Hause.

Dusted snow makes the boulder-hopping

Scafell Pike summit

even more annoying, while making the boulders themselves quite beautiful. The lichen glows like amber in the low sun, and beyond the lichen the mountains crowd close in the chilled clear air. What seems from the eye-corner to be Great Gable is, when you stop hopping and take a look, actually Skiddaw.

They say that if you sit long enough at Esk Hause you'll see everybody in England. Well, I'm not keen on Esk Hause so I usually hurry through. Today, though, with the big romantic rucksack, I'm a bit slower – and yes! Someone who was at school with my wife, now heading for Scafell Pike from a sensible car at the Old Dungeon Ghyll. So where's our car? When we say Coniston, she laughs.

For Coniston is not close: and the sun, never high, is already thinking of calling it a day. On Bowfell they're looking down thirstily onto the Old Dungeon Ghyll and wondering how much they're going to suffer getting down the Band – but we have a torch, and spare batteries, and don't need to start thinking valley thoughts. And the Crinkle Crags are never crinklier than when the sun slides in over Eskdale and the Langdale side's all shadow-dark. Black fold follows gold fold, with the late walker on the crest lit up all heroically like a socialist poster.

David's never been on the famous Bad Step. I nip down quickly in front and squeeze into the little cave, waiting to take his picture as he comes down the slightly overhanging wall on the big footholds. A foot appears in the viewfinder, waggles around for a while and then withdraws. A voice wants to know where I've got to.

"I'm waiting to take your picture as you come down the slightly overhanging wall on the great big footholds."

"I don't see any great big footholds. Come round here and show me them." So the photo of the Bad Step is a posed one.

Another late walker appears overhead, stops, and looks surprised at finding a rock climb at the bottom of the path. "It's the Bad Step," David tells him. "Don't worry, it's perfectly OK."

The Coniston hills are turning red, and Red Tarn is sinking into brown shadow. Two hundred metres above, on the top rocks of Pike of Blisco, the sunset is in full

179

swing. Do we chase the last rays up the two hundred metres, or do we retire meekly to the Wrynose road?

We chase it – slowly.

Two more late sun chasers pass us on the path. The first one surges uphill like a fell-runner. The second, like a slightly tired fellrunner, hesitates and says: "I bet you'll get up in time for it anyway, and we'll be lying there half-dead."

I reassure him. "We're half-dead too."

We rise slowly up the side of Pike of Blisco, but the sun sinks even more slowly into the gap at the end of the Crinkles. We reach the cairn, still well over 50% alive. We sit and gaze around the circumference of a two-day circuit dyed pink.

For us romantics, there's always discomforts you haven't thought of. The other sunset-chasers are interested in our rather large rucksacks, and we want to know about their length of rope. They've been doing Bowfell Buttress – "not windy at all, cold fingers though. Plus a bit of ice in the cracks." Bowfell Buttress is a Winter Grade Five – they do all the rock climbs in winter nowadays.

"What, like Scafell Central Buttress?" Ah – apparently people cheat on Central Buttress by doing it when it isn't properly iced up all over. Alas for the frailty of the mere human confronted with the North Face of Scafell.

Like a hillwalker sinking stiffly into the fireside seat at the Old Dungeon Ghyll, the sun sinks into the orange notch at the end of the Crinkles. Scafell rises black over the rim of Langdale, Windermere gleams in the east, and in every direction Lakeland is fading to the end of a short but happy winter's day. And even though we're seven miles from closing the end of our circuit, everything comes together. You can never finish Lakeland – there's no Z and of course no X – but: "Jenkin Hill! The place in the Lakes beginning with J!"

We walk down the grassy back of Blisco and hitch a lift in Little Langdale.

The Route

START/FINISH: Coniston (bus service to Ambleside: pay-and-display car park)
DISTANCE & CLIMB:
**   Day 1: Coniston - Eskdale 14 miles 5000ft (22km 1500m)**
**   Day 2: Eskdale - Coniston 16 miles 5500ft (25km 1700m)**
MAP: Outdoor Leisure 6 (SW Lakes)

The description that follows gives route detail only when that is not apparent from the map. The map should be the Outdoor Leisure (or Harvey's), as the route is off-path on steep broken ground, and good contour detail is needed, especially in mist. The Eskdale-Scafell part of the route is detailed in Daywalk 3.

The route crosses the Coniston range by Levers Water and the scramble of Gill Cove Crag. The scramble is started by following the Cove Beck up to the 480m contour, then taking to the rocks on the left at their lowest point. On the left, along the top of steep drops, the scrambling is Grade 2, but can be made as easy as required by taking a line further right. From Brim Fell, the route follows the ridge north to Swirl How, then west to Grey Friar.

A few small cairns indicate the small path north-westward off Grey Friar. It joins a broken wall (on the left), to reach a crossing fence with gate and stile at GR 256008.

The stile has a hydraulic action, tilting with a slurp as you transfer weight. Below, descend grass to left of the rock hummock of Copthorne Howe, and find the track just below it. This leads down by the stream side to enter a field above Cockley Beck. In the back right corner of the field is the stile leading to the roadside at a white cottage and road bridge (phone box: no other facilities).

The footpath of the former Roman Road leads past Black Hall farm to the top of Hardknott Pass. Divert to the Roman fort, before rejoining the road above Brotherilkeld.

Summit cairn on Broad Crag

The route up Eskdale to Scafell Pike is described in detail in Daywalk 3 (Eskdale). Going up Eskdale to the Great Moss, the path on the west of the Esk River is interesting but difficult: the path on the east is easier. Go up the How Beck to the 500m contour, then beside Cam Spout Crag to Long Green and Scafell. Gain Mickledore by way of Lord's Rake, and follow ridges and paths over Scafell Pike to Esk Hause, and then across Esk Pike, Bowfell, and the Crinkle Crags. On the descent from the final Crinkle Crag, there comes the short rock pitch: it can be avoided by leaving the summit south-west.

A path climbs among little outcrops onto Pike of Blisco.

The path off Blisco descends eastwards among outcrops to a plateau at 530m altitude. Here it drops off left towards Langdale, but we leave it to cross this plateau. It's a place of rocks, grass, and tiny tarns – I passed eight plateau pools, in each of which either Swirl How or the Langdale Pikes reflected themselves. It's a fine wild empty place, just 2km up from one of Lakeland's busiest car parks.

Head east to the cairn on Blake Rigg (Bleaberry Knott also has a cairn. This ground will be very difficult in mist.) Go down the rocky, grassy spur south-east. The spur flattens and turns east at the 430m contour (Miller Stands). Here a look over the left edge will reveal a stream descending to the outflow of Blea Tarn. This will be our line of descent, but the top is steep and stony, and it's easier to continue east, steeply down the ridge, for 100ft (30m vertical), then slant back left on a grassy rake to the stream.

The descent is brackenny, but ground above is crag and juniper. From the tarn corner, a gravel track, wheelchair flat, leads across to the car park.

Turn right, down the road, to cross a cattle grid and follow a wall up to Lingmoor Fell's summit. Go down to right of the wall to its corner (GR305044) and drop right, to the ruined quarry buildings. A green track runs east, through a small col, and eventually descends in zig-zags into Little Langdale just east of Dale Head farm (hotel nearby).

Just downstream from Little Langdale Tarn is the delightful Slater Bridge. A track then a minor road runs east, to become the Cumbria Way at High Park (B&B). This follows a tarred lane, then a field-edge footpath beside the A593. Its rough track leaves the Outdoor Leisure Map at GR 330011: keep ahead for another 500yds, and where the track bends hard left, keep ahead on a wide path signed 'Tarn Hows'.

After the Tarn, the Cumbria Way takes, briefly, to the road. Paths lead by Tarn Hows Cottages and Low Yewdale, to enter Coniston by Shepherd's Bridge.

The Styhead path up Great Gable used to be an eroded road. It was one of three human artifacts visible by daylight from Outer Space. (It's better now. The National Trust have rebuilt it into a harsh stony staircase.) The direct route from Burnthwaite isn't quite so ugly; it is merely steep, loose and very long. The way from Windy Gap is short, but equally unpleasant.

But why climb Gable at all? By not doing so you gain a quiet hollow in the crowded heart of Lakeland; an exciting path for goats and rock climbers through serious crag-scenery; and a hidden smugglers' track round the back.

Start/Finish: Honister car park GR 226135
by way of: Green Gable, Nape's Needle, Moses Trod
Distance/climb: 6 miles/11 km or 2200 ft/700 m
Map: OS Outdoor Leisure 4 (NW) or Harveys W. Lakes or OS Landranger 89 or 90

From Honister, climb south-east on grassy slopes away to the left of the Grey Knotts path. At the top turn south and drop gently into the grassy hollow. Gillercomb hangs above the world like a suspended bowl. Various other places peep in over its edges, and the wind blows straight across the top without coming in. It's a secluded spot in a noisy world, and its crags are little friendly ones (there's a short rock climb and good scrambling on Gillercomb Buttress).

Don't take the tempting turn left, towards the so-close-looking Styhead path. This 'short-cut' loses you your temper, skin off your ankles and, if you were a runner in the 1996 Lake District Mountain Trial, many minutes by the race clock. Take the good path up the comb to the col behind Base Brown (GR 222111). A grassy slope leads down to the footbridge and so by the gill and tarn to Styhead itself.

Five arterial paths meet at Styhead. Take none of them, but a slightly rising traverse westwards. (The big path descending to Wasdale should be below on your left). In a few minutes you pass below the small but famous climbing crag of Kern Knotts. Continue on a narrow path which is clearly-trodden over grass, clearly-scratched where it crosses rock as it does more and more. Carefully follow these signs on the ground, rather than any written attempt at describing the 'right' route. If you're on unmarked ground you're wrong.

Soon the Napes Buttress soars overhead, and so does the famous Needle, oddly foreshortened. Aim to pass between the Needle and its parent rock – a manoeuvre called 'threading the Needle' and a Grade 2 scramble. There's no question of where you should be going: early members of the Fell & Rock Club have marked the way with their hobnails. The walls lean in reassuringly on either side, so that it all feels nice and safe even though it isn't particularly.

If you don't fancy Grade 2, then pass below the Needle on the path, and head up a small scree to its left. Either way you reach a viewpoint called the Dress Circle level with its top two blocks.

Lunch here, and watch the rock climbers. This was the first rock in Britain to be climbed from motives of pure sport rather than sheep-rescue or the persecution of eagles. Large cracks lead up to the shoulder below the final two blocks: a confident scrambler can reach this point provided it's not too crowded. The next step is off the edge of the platform to perform a mantelshelf move above the empty space on the

Kern Knotts

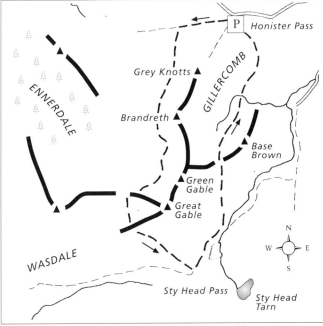

Needle's eastern side. Confident scramblers will look at this move in fascinated horror.

Sphinx Rock

Theatregoers in the Dress Circle cannot see the mantelshelf move, but you'll watch the climbers as they shuffle back with their toes in the crack between the two blocks; and hear their appreciative comments as they discover the foothold called the 'Baby's Bottom' on which they must make their final step to the summit.

Continue to scramble interestingly along the base of the cliffs. All this section takes twice the time you expect – three times, with a camera. Cross a scree gully and a new odd rock breaks the horizon: the Sphinx. Passing between it and its crag above gives more white-fingertip work (Grade 1). Cross a wider scree-shoot towards the broken buttress of the White Napes.

This scree is Little Hell Gate. I mentioned some unpleasant routes to Gable summit, but if you want one that's really very nasty indeed, use Little Hell Gate.

If you really must climb Gable, you can do so up the White Napes (Grade 1, scrappy). Otherwise traverse onwards and somewhat downwards without path or difficulty onto the spur

183

called Gavel Neese. The name is not so mysterious as it sounds: Gavel is the old name of Gable (used, for instance, by Wordsworth) and Neese is not what's half-way down your legs but rather what's half-way up your face.

Great Gable, as seen from Scafell Pike

Half-way up the face of Gable, now, you cross an awkward scree to the col called Beck Head. Take the scree path up Gable for its first 50yds. Our path, Moses Trod, now descends at first before traversing below crag and scree across the north slopes of Gable. The smugglers chose their route more cleverly than those runners in the Mountain Trial. Starting in Wasdale, the path ends ambiguously in either Borrowdale or Buttermere; but is overlooked only by watchers in Ennerdale.

By now the sun will be low in the sky, and the long shadow of Pillar doing its best to hide the ugly trees in Ennerdale. The path passes like a whisper in the night below the screes and outcrops of Gable, and then of Green Gable. Hillwalkers may choose to cross the boulders of Gable's summit but smugglers have more sense!

Follow it round to the tarn at Gillercomb Head. On the open slopes of Brandreth you can at last take your attention off the interesting stuff underfoot (and underhand) to look at the interesting stuff in the distance. Night has already slid into Buttermere and Borrowdale; sunset flares behind Pillar Rock.

From Grey Knotts it's tempting to make a beeline for the car park. This route is great for those who like steep grass in the dark. The rest of us will descend north-east for five minutes, then north to pick up the old tramway.

"Been on Gable then?" they ask in the car park as you stumble off the tramway under your head torch.

"Oh... I suppose we just about climbed Brandreth. We certainly didn't do Gable."

To Hardknott Or
Not To Hardknott

You go to the Lakes for the walking. You go to the Lakes for the rock-climbing. You could even go to the Lakes for the caving. But judging by the amount of traffic at times when all good hillwalkers are up on their hills, good cavers down in their holes, there are people who go to the Lakes for the driving around in cars. The most challenging and exciting driving-around-in-cars is on the Hardknott Pass.

The ancestral member of the Fell and Rock witnessed a hill climb at Hardknott in 1927. And yes, the hill climb was in cars. The contest was not to see which of the bull-nosed Morrisses and Model T Fords could get to the top quickest. The contest was to see which of then could get to the top. It was a memorable sight: "stones flying everywhere!"

The Hardknott Pass starts with deceptive gentleness. Stone walls with roses growing over conceal nothing more demanding than a sudden tractor or a badly parked hillwalker. But then you pass the Warning Notices, and start to wonder about places to turn round, and realise there aren't any. And then you look up, and see a little strip of grey among the clouds at the top edge of the windscreen, and realise that's where you've got to go.
The slope's one in three, which is 20°. In skiing terms that's a red run, and you go up it like the skier comes down, in zigzags all the way. All your CDs fall out of the rack and slide past your ankles. Half way up you realise you should have been in first gear all along, and you attempt to double declutch but it's too late and you're rolling backwards with your engine stalled.

Now we'll suppose you've got a handbrake that works. So you pull that up a notch futher than it usually goes and do your hill start and stall the engine again. And now there's two cars coming down waiting for you to get out of the way, so naturally you stall the engine for the third time.

And then it transpires that the two cars have to go uphill backwards to get out of your way, and one of them doesn't have a handbrake that works, and while the driver's perfectly capable of doing heel-and-toe on the brake and throttle simultaneously, perhaps the rock under the front wheel is simplest, after all. The rock, when you pick it from the roadside, looks to have been under quite a few front wheels already...

At the top there's a flat bit that's very short indeed, and then you're going down the back, and it's still one in three, and it's still remarkably like skiing with those dreadful moments where you're pointing straight downhill, down, down, into the valley below, and wondering what happens if you fail to complete the turn. The CDs come back out from under the seat and get tangled in the pedals. After that there's the Wrynose Pass, which is an anticlimax as a lot of it is only one in four; but you do notice that you've finally found a use for the red bit at the top of the temperature guage.

The Hardknott Pass is not a sensible way to get from the coast to Ambleside. If you need to get from the coast to Ambleside (which you don't), almost any other route is quicker, cheaper, and you don't have to put your CDs back afterwards. The Hardknott was tarred for the first time just before the second war, and one has to wonder why. Was it any more than the simple conviction that hard, flat and black is the way a road's supposed to be?

A car-free Cumbria would have park-and-ride all the way up the M6, boats every ten minutes along the main lakes, cycle hire at every station from Staveley to Seascale and dining cars between Ravenglass & Eskdale. The last to come, Hardknott could be the first road to go. It wouldn't need bollarding off. Just stop mending the thing and let the winter frosts do the rest. For the first few years it'd be a fine demanding bike ride; then a fine demanding mountain bike ride; and finally, like a snake that sheds its skin, out from under the tarmac emerges a fine demanding long walk.

Ambleside to Ravenglass is 21 miles. This is the Lakes equivalent of the Lairig Ghru, although Boot has pub lunches, which you don't find on the slopes of Ben Macdui. And it's the walk the Romans used.

The Romans came along the summit of High Street, which was a good way of getting above the swamps of Patterdale, and built their fort at Hardknott on the way to the sea. Ambleside to Hardknott was a good day's walk for the legionary, who marched in hobnailed sandals and invented for his own long-distance comfort the exotic garment called 'soccus' or sock.

Twelve miles a day may not seem much to the modern-day backpacker. But the legionary carried the equivalent of three modern-day backpacks. Cooking pot, weapons (sword, shield, two javelins) entrenching tool and a stake for the overnight palisade came to around 90 lb. With that lot on his shoulders he marched from Rome to Ravenglass; and with that lot on his shoulders he could, when necessary, cover not twelve but thirty miles a day.

Replace the palisade stake with an aluminium tentpole, and walk with the Romans along the green valleys and over the two short but savage passes. And then turn the map round and look at it the other way. Remove the Hardknott road, and you have continuous hill from Walna Scar to Walla Crag, from Keswick just about to Duddon Sands... a mountain hut at Cockley Beck, supplied by ponies with special refrigerated panniers, and selling icecream at a fiver a cone... upper Duddon, with the Christmas trees run wild, infested by wolf and wild boar... and then, as civilisation retreats towards the natural boundaries of the M6 and the Cumbria Cycleway, there come the first reports of bandits at the Three Shire Stone.

But what of the poor motorist, who's lost the last exciting drive in all England? Must the primitive pleasures of double declutch and boiling over engine be forgotten for all time?

NOTE: I may have let my imagination run away with me here. Under the European Union's Habitat and Species Directive of 1992, Britain is not actually committed to the reintroduction of the Bandit.

Transport, Accommodation and Ethics

1   **Transport**
2   **Accommodation**
3   **Tourist Information**
4   **Ethics and Environmentalism**

1   Transport

Trains

Virgin West Coast runs a fast and fairly efficient service connecting Penrith and Carlisle with the rest of the world. A branch line, fiercely objected to by Wordsworth, runs in from Oxenholme to Windermere.

The Cumbria Coast line is one of Britain's prettier routes. From any of its stations, a bus or a half-day of fairly pleasant walking will bring you into the less familiar edge of the mountains.

"L'il Ratty", the Ravenglass-Eskdale railway, is a slow but utterly delightful way to get into the heart of the hills.

RAIL ENQUIRIES: 0345 484950
RAVENGLASS & ESKDALE RAILWAY: 01229 717171

Buses

Long-distance coaches link Carlisle with Keswick, Grasmere, Ambleside, Windermere, Kendal and cities of the south (such as Leeds). Within the Lake District, the bus service is steadily improving year after year. Top of the list is the Borrowdale Bus, with several services daily linking Keswick, Derwentwater, Seatoller, Honister Hause and Buttermere.

The following have two or more buses a day during the Summer:
Keswick - Mungrisedale - Caldbeck - Carlisle
Keswick - Dockray - Patterdale
Penrith - Patterdale
Penrith - Haweswater
Keswick - Watendlath
Ambleside - Langdale
Bowness - Ambleside - Hawkshead - Coniston
Workington - Ennerdale Water - Buttermere
Broughton-in-Furness - Dunnerdale
Kendal - Kentmere
Kendal - Langsleddale

A very useful free bus timetable *Lakeland Explorer* is published annually by Stagecoach Cumbria, and can be had from them or from Tourist Information Centres.

STAGECOACH CUMBERLAND TIMETABLE INFORMATION: 01946 63222
CUMBRIA COUNTY COUNCIL TRAVEL INFORMATION: 01228 606000

Public transport comments and suggestions:
Economy and Environment, Cumbria CC
Citadel Chambers, Carlisle CA3 8SG

Boats

Times of first and last sailings are for Summer season, and approximate.
Windermere chain ferry (Bowness - Sawrey) 0600 - 2100
Windermere Lake Cruises (Bowness - Ambleside) 0900 - 1800:
015395 31188 or 015394 43360
Coniston Launch (Coniston - Brantwood) 1030 - 1800:015394 36216
Coniston Gondola (Coniston - Brantwood - Park-a-Moor, in Victorian splendour) 1100 - 1600: National Trust 015394 41288
Derwentwater Keswick Launch (Keswick - Lodore - Butterhow) 1000 - 2000: 017687 72263
Ullswater Steamer (Pooley Bridge - Howtown - Glenridding) 1000 - 1900: 01539 721626

2   Accommodation

Camping: At the time of writing, high camping in lightweight tents is tolerated generally within the National Park. In Chapter 8 I camped under Scar Lathing and wondered: did anyone else ever camp here? This is Lakeland, of course they did; the very next time I passed there was a yellow dome where our green ridge had been. All credit to those previous for leaving no sign. Discreet camping includes such fussy behaviour as putting stones back, lichen side up, in the holes they came from.

Low camp sites are abundant, though often full at weekends. Particularly congenial are the high-on-scenery, low-on-facilities basic sites run by farmers. Two of my favourites are at Hollows Farm Borrowdale (woodpeckers) and Turner Hall Farm Duddon (great glaciated boulders). Another is at Loughrigg Tarn.

Camping barns - 'your stone tent' - offer a roof, a sleeping platform, and cooking facilities. They are cheap but chilly, not as well-used as they deserve to be. They are currently to be found at:

Hesket Newmarket: Hutton Moor End (nr Blencathra): Skelgill under Catbells: Greenside, Patterdale: Rosthwaite, Borrowdale: Loweswater: Buttermere: Nether Wasdale: Broughton in Furness.

An up-to-date leaflet can be had from the National Park Authority: 017687 72803. Reservations: Keswick Tourist Information
Youth Hostels are everywhere. The small or remote ones, which are the nicest, are closed for a day or two each week (eg Ennerdale Tilberthwaite, Ennerdale Black Sail, Honister, Skiddaw House, Legburnthwaite Thirlmere). General enquiries 01727 845047

3   Tourist Information

Keswick: 017687 72645
Grasmere: 015394 35245
Ambleside: 015394 32582
Windermere: 015394 44444

Tourist Information (continued)
Patterdale: 017684 82414
Pooley Bridge: 017684 86530
Coniston: 015394 41533
Kirkby Stephen (Chapter 1) 017683 71199
Whitehaven (Chapter 1) 01946 695678

WEATHER 01768 775757

4   Ethics and Environmentalism

From the point of view of an ice-age, size nine Vibram soles are a pretty minor geological agency: "call that erosion? Go on with you, dig me an Eskdale!"

Still, hillwalkers do damage hills. Hillwalkers' cars do damage valleys. Preaching doesn't usually work - but anyway, here are the steps that I myself take to reduce the damage caused by the steps I take.

FOOTPATHS: Where a path is established, whether trodden or built, walk on the path or elsewhere altogether. Don't walk on the verge alongside.

Where a path is eroded pebbles and bare rock, step on the rock. As well as being good for the path, it's good brain-foot education for the scrambling higher up.

A steep slope with intact vegetation can take quite a bit of traffic - provided that traffic is spread out. Concentrate it, perhaps by building some cairns, and a line of earth footprints forms. Regrettably, the line is always straight up the slope: it'd be better as zig-zags. Once the earth footprints join together the water gets in, and the rains of one Winter will form an eroded hole from the top of the slope to the bottom. So on such slopes, I go zig-zag and keep right away from any forming footprints.

Pitched path costs around £1 per inch. If you join the National Trust, you pay for about a metre of path.

SCREE: Scree-running is fun. But once a couple of hundred people have run down a scree, it's finished; and there's a scar that'll take a century to weather over. So I no longer run screes. Fortunately, steep snow is just as much fun, and a lot less painful to fall over on. Also you don't have to take it out of your boots at the bottom.

LITTER: We all despise a Womble, but there's no disgrace in taking away a little bit of someone else's litter.

CAIRNS: Cairns are less intrusive than trig points, and trig points are less intrusive than piles of empty cans. Still, 90% of cairns are pointless items of human self-assertion. Useful cairns are on summits, or at the top of tricky descents like Lord's Rake. Useful cairns mark paths that are safe ways off in mist. It can safely be assumed that every useful cairn in Lakeland has already been built.

Unhelpful cairns are on knolls that aren't summits but could be taken for summits in mist; and on parallel paths beside the main path. Try following cairns from Mickledore to Scafell

Pikes. Cairns everywhere is exactly as useful as cairns nowhere.

If demolishing an unnecessary cairn, do not simply kick it down. Disperse the stones carefully around the landscape, striving for a natural effect.

CARS: Arrive in a car, and you're an alien metal monster right up to the moment you step onto the hill. Arrive by train, and your holiday starts on the platform at Euston. Use a B&B, and leave more of your money in Cumbria than the £2.40 in the pay-and-display. Use local buses, and make local busses more plentiful and cheaper for local people. At least some of my readers will be articulate, middle-class folk with word-processors; bus companies pay more attention than, perhaps, they should, to the needs and desires of such people.

There is a usable bus network in Lakeland. It takes twice as long as the car, and costs twice as much. Use it anyway, and encourage it to improve. Getting rid of the car is the single simplest step towards saving Lakeland from Lakeland-lovers.

Half-Daywalk — Wallowbarrow Gorge

We take small Sunday walks from car parks with our parents, and then we leave parents behind and head up to the summits. Vigorous in youth we stride the daylong ridges, valley to valley with small tent or bivvy bag, smelly and (if male) unshaven. And then one day we settle down; and suddenly we're once again looking for that short walk. That walk for a husband who hates hills, for a wife who wants woods, and for a couple of toddlers who like nothing so much as falling in the river and driving home in Daddy's big fleece and nothing underneath.

Here is that walk. Three miles, but long for its length. It starts at Seathwaite in Dunnerdale.

Go through a gate with footpath sign opposite Seathwaite's small church, and turn right, alongside the Tarn Beck, to a wooden footbridge. Due to a bend, the bridge appears to cross from the far bank to the near one rather than from near to far.

A tree-root path leads back left, to the high and wonderful footbridge over the Duddon. It's a high stone arch. Turn right, upstream, through the Wallowbarrow Gorge.

Here the river runs through a deep wooded ravine, with crags above, and big boulders fallen from those crags underfoot. You'll move slowly over the jumbled boulders, when you aren't stopped altogether enjoying the view. Be tactful, and let your companions think of the clever 'gorge-ous' pun on their own.

The path climbs, to look down through trees onto the river, and out through trees to Coniston Old Man. You can see the valley road opposite, work out the river's former course down the other side of Pen hillock, and deliver a little talk on glaciation and meltwater channels.

The river rises to rejoin the path. A little wooden footbridge crosses the Grassguards Gill, and now on the right are the stepping stones. The stones are large, and widely-spaced: the wire hawser to hang onto is not as much help as you might suppose. If the river is high or the toddlers don't fancy the stepping stones, simply turn back and enjoy the gorge again backwards.

Otherwise, cross the stones and go up to the road above. Turn right, back to the starting point: look out for a riverside path marked "no fires or camping" for the final quarter-mile.

INDEX